# BEYOND GOOD INTENTIONS

TURNING POINT Christian Worldview Series
Marvin Olasky, General Editor

---

# BEYOND GOOD INTENTIONS

## A Biblical View of Politics

## Doug Bandow

CROSSWAY BOOKS • WHEATON, ILLINOIS
A DIVISION OF GOOD NEWS PUBLISHERS

For my parents, Don and Donna Bandow

## *TABLE OF*

# CONTENTS

# ACKNOWLEDGMENTS

*T*his book was conceived by Marvin Olasky, who generously approached me about writing it. His thoughtful suggestions have not only helped shape the final product–though, alas, the responsibility for any mistakes remains mine–but also forced me to rethink some long-held assumptions about God's law and specific issues. P.J. Hill, who has devoted much effort to helping Christians understand economics, also reviewed the manuscript and made many helpful comments. My thanks, too, go to the Fieldstead Institute and Crossway Books for publishing the Turning Point Christian Worldview Series.

Ed Crane of the Cato Institute deserves praise for his critical support for my work over the years. We differ sharply in our view of matters spiritual; I speak for myself, not the Institute or any of its other staff members, when I write about the living reality of Christ. But Ed has generously tolerated my eccentricities, helped sharpen my political analysis, and provided me with a forum for my ideas.

Heartfelt appreciation is also due Jean Golub, for her patience when I was preoccupied and her encouragement when I was discouraged. In Proverbs Solomon asked, "a faithful man who can find?" (20:6). I have found a faithful lady.

Finally, much credit for this book must go to my parents, Don and Donna Bandow, who both rewarded my intellectual curiosity and, more importantly, reflected God's selfless love in their own lives. They, along with my sister and brother-in-law, Shelly and Birkley Wical, have provided me with a family life that abounds with love and support. My father also spent hours reviewing my manuscript, highlighting sloppy grammar and thinking.

# *INTRODUCTION*

*A*s Christians, we have an obligation to care for those around us. We are to reflect God's love as we interact with the world, to be the salt of the earth. And that seasoning role extends to the realm of politics and government.

Indeed, the state is a divinely ordained institution, "God's servant to do you good," wrote Paul (Romans 13:4). Believers obviously have a critical role in ensuring that government fulfills its proper duties.

But doing good deeds, both in and out of government–in effect, implementing the liberal Protestant "social gospel"–is not the same as living the gospel of Christ. Works are important; James wrote that without them our faith is dead. But Paul reminded the Colossian church that its members were to set their "minds on things above, not on earthly things" (Colossians 3:2). Faith in the living Christ, the Son of God, is necessary to be a Christian, at least in a Biblical rather than a cultural sense. The Jewish people, for example, heard God's message, but it "was of no value to them because those who heard did not combine it with faith" (Hebrews 4:2). Indeed, the Jewish nation failed because it "pursued a law of righteousness ... not by faith but as if it were by works." We can obtain righteousness, explained Paul, only "by faith" (Romans 9:31, 32, 30).

Indeed, Christians should have no illusions that the state can build an earthly utopia, rescuing man from his fallen condition. For it is Christ, not government, that saves: "I give them [my sheep] eternal life and they shall never perish; no one can snatch them out of my hand," he told the crowds (John 10:28). And how does one gain eternal life? jesus explained, "whoever hears my words and believes him who sent me has eternal life and will not be condemned; he has crossed over from death to life" (John 5:24). In short, a believer's most important responsibilities are spiritual: "our citizenship is in heaven," wrote Paul (Philippians 3:20).

The fact that our worldly civic responsibilities are secondary does not, however, mean that they are unimportant. One need only look at the horrors unleashed by atheist totalitarian states—Hitler's Germany, Stalin's Soviet Union, Mao's China, Pol Pot's Kampuchea, Mengistu's Ethiopia, to name just a few—to see the importance of Judeo-Christian values undergirding the political system. Even in our own nation we are seeing a serious deterioration in moral standards: families are breaking down, 1.5 million abortions are performed annually, the political system increasingly promotes envy rather than justice, and so on.

Believers can play a critical role by acting as the polity's conscience, calling it to account for violations of God's Law. We should not be disinterested in more mundane policy disputes, whether foreign treaties or budget matters; indeed, some of us make a living analyzing and writing about just such issues. But a Christian's most important duty is to uphold broad Scriptural standards, not to devise detailed legislative programs. For the Bible provides Christians with a general perspective rather than a specific agenda. God's message is uniquely one of justice and righteousness, not the minimum wage, federal job training programs, aid to the contras, and unilateral nuclear disarmament. Scripture can help lead us to policy positions on a number of issues, such as abortion, but God has anointed no political philosophy as His own.

Moreover, good intentions are not enough. Christians not only must have pure and loving hearts that reach out to their neighbors, but also the wisdom to develop policies that actually achieve their desired ends. "Suppose a brother or sister is without clothes and daily food," wrote James. "If one of you says to him, 'Go, I wish you well; keep warm and well fed,' but does nothing about his physical needs, what good is it?" (James 2:15, 16). In the same way, believers who declare their support for worthy ends but then back ineffective—or even counterproductive—means do little more than salve their own consciences.

This sort of ill-considered activism does more than

embarrass an individual cleric or denomination; it trivializes the transcendent message of the gospel. Observes Charles Colson, former Nixon aide turned Christian worker: "One of the greatest" pitfalls of religious political activism "is the tendency Christians have to believe that because the Bible is 'on their side' they can speak with authority on every issue. Many church bureaucracies have succumbed to this temptation in recent decades, spewing out position papers on everything from public toilet facilities to nuclear war. The New Right has engaged in such excesses with its scorecards covering the gamut of issues from trade legislation to the Panama Canal. When Christians use the broad brush, they become simply another political interest group, pontificating on matters about which they are often woefully uninformed."[1]

Even where believers understand the Bible correctly, they too often pass over the question of whether Biblical values are to be enforced by the civil authorities. We are to help the needy, but Scripture does not direct us to seize the resources of nonbelievers to redistribute to the poor. Mosaic Israel executed adulterers, but we have passed from the original covenant between God and the nation state of Israel to the New Covenant between God and the Body of Christ. The moral standards advanced by Christian political activists remain unchanged, but their implications for policy in a secular state dominated by unbelievers may be very different than they were several thousand years ago.

Not that most Christians on both the right and left do not genuinely believe they are doing the Lord's work. And in some ways they clearly are. The Moral Majority, for instance, rightly takes a stand over declining moral standards; the evangelical left correctly challenges a consumerist society in which a dependent underclass wallows in poverty and hopelessness. The Catholic bishops properly bring to the foreign policy debate a concern for justice. But implementing such Biblical principles requires us to apply reason within revelation, to look at impact as well as intent. As a result, on many issues there simply is no single "Christian" position. And believers should stop acting as if there is.

What I hope to do in this book is sketch out a Biblical view of politics that eclipses any particular secular ideology. I begin with an overview of the relationship of religion and politics, and then move on to summarize some of the major problems faced by our nation, as well as the inability of any existing human philosophy to rescue us.

The core of a Christian's perspective on public policy must be his understanding of God's purpose for government, which I discuss next. In understanding the state's role, however, it is important to remember that God's transcendent goal is spiritual; politics is not everything, an issue I cover in the succeeding chapter, followed by a review of the different theological positions on church/state relations over the years. Then come the application chapters–a general review of principles Christians should use to evaluate proposed policies, followed by two chapters reviewing specific issues–and a concluding wrap-up.

The object of this book is not to conjure up the one, true Biblical legislative agenda which all Christians should rally around. Nor do I intend to suggest that believers who disagree with me are any less spiritual or devout than I am. To the contrary, I am impressed with–indeed, profoundly challenged by–many of my brothers and sisters in Christ who possess far different ideological perspectives but who have dedicated their lives to doing God's work and have sacrificed far more than I have. Instead, I hope to challenge believers to, first, recognize that there are no easy solutions to many of today's problems, and, second, to use their God-given wisdom to thoughtfully work through the difficult issues that face all of us.

"In this world you will have trouble," Christ counseled us. And that warning applies to our participation in politics no less than any other human activity. But Christians, no matter what their philosophical differences, know that there is an answer: "take heart! I have overcome the world," said Jesus (John 16:33). In the end we must look to Christ, not government, not human wisdom, not anything or anyone else, for the fulfillment of God's Kingdom.

# ONE

# A Christian
# Political Perspective

Religion and politics have been intertwined throughout recorded history. Whether the belief be paganism, Judaism, Christianity, Islam, or atheism, the faithful have often looked to the state for support and sustenance. Even in today's increasingly secular world, many of the worst cases of regional conflict and sectarian strife–Iran/Iraq, Israel and its Arab neighbors, Lebanon, Northern Ireland–involve nationalistic struggles for religious supremacy.

It is perhaps not surprising that conflicting views of God are regularly used to justify the often bitter competition between different races, cultures, and nations. But as often as not, it is schisms within a particular sect that have triggered the worst state-sponsored violence. Time and again an established order under attack has turned to the civil authorities to maintain theological orthodoxy–a la the Inquisition.

Unfortunately, Christianity, no less than any other religion, has often allied itself with the governments of its day. At such times the transcendent gospel, a message of God's eternal love for man, inevitably suffered, ending up submerged in the world's values. Religion merely became another tool for those with political power to satisfy their own selfish desires, whether wealth, position, status, sensuality, or power. The closer the relationship of church and state, the more spiritually irrelevant and institutionally fractured the Body of Christ seemed to become.

Of course, Christ said that He came to bring disunion to the earth: "From now on there will be five in one family divided against each other, three against two and two against three" (Luke 12:52). But there is nothing in Jesus' ministry to suggest that He intended the church to use coercion either to foment or crush theological dissension. Instead, Christ's principal call was, and remains, for man to give up the things of the world, following God above all else. The pain that fulfillment of this demand causes the average individual is no less searing than the most bitter political or ethnic conflict; however, Christian discipleship is something that can be achieved only through a personal transformation inaugurated by the Holy Spirit, not by any act of government.

Nevertheless, Jesus enjoined His followers to be "the salt of the earth" (Matthew 5:13). If we are to live in the world we must interact with–and influence–public institutions.

And it is good that Christians do so. For, writes theologian Richard John Neuhaus, "the naked public square is a dangerous place."[1] There are any number of ideologies and philosophies competing for ascendancy in society. If religious-based values are not dominant, some other beliefs will be. At best the result will be relatively benign democratic rule. If Christian principles are excluded entirely, however, the worst secular ideologies are likely to rule. Obvious examples include Hitler's Germany, Stalin's Soviet Union, and Mao's China, where the godless "public square" succumbed to the most brutal forms of inhumanity possible. Despite the obvious disimilarities between democratic humanism and totalitarian atheism, in both cases the state has taken over the role of God and the Body of Christ, providing the transcendent justification for life, to serve the general polity, and the material means to survive, government transfer payments.

Nor is there any substitute for God's transcendent morality. The Nazis went to extraordinary lengths to preserve a veneer of legality. "The law is a friendly fellow, amenable to our wishes, plastic in the hands of the powerful," writes Neuhaus.[2] No human philosophy or ethical system can provide an overarching framework to guide individual relations. For by what standards can one group of men declare their values to be superior to those of someone else? Communism and fascism are powerful, successful ideologies; they are evil not because they conflict with the democratic ideal, but because they transgress God's Law, which is better reflected by republican forms of government.[3]

Indifference to politics is not an option for Christians for another, more practical reason: the state is simply too pervasive to ignore. Virtually every aspect of life is regulated by some level of government, and religion is no exception. Congregations cannot build churches without permission from local zoning authorities; many states strictly regulate private education and home schooling. Municipalities often forbid Christians from favoring fellow believers in their hiring and other business decisions. Washington, D.C., has even required Georgetown University, a Catholic institution, to fund gay groups. Federal welfare programs have increasingly supplanted private philanthropy and left Christians financially less able to fulfill their charitable duty. Indeed, forced government exactions–taxes as well as mandatory military service–create potential conflicts with a number of basic Scriptural tenets, raising some of the most important issues of Christian discipleship.

Equally important, public institutions have come to govern an ever larger share of Americans' interpersonal relations. Responsibility for medical assistance, care of the elderly, resolution of personal disputes, assistance to the needy, community services, and even many commercial transactions have increasingly shifted from private hands to one or more government agencies. Whereas Christian values once permeated American society through the involvement of individuals and organized religion in all areas of life, many once-private activities have been effectively nationalized and, as a result, are becoming increasingly secularized. For many people the state has become the church, even God: government employs them, houses them, feeds them, regulates them, and even gives them purpose and a reason for being.

Thus, for believers to ignore the rapidly expanding public sector would be to emasculate the Christian message, terminating God's transcendence wherever the state entered. Nor is the issue simply evangelism. If we Christians care about those around us–and Jesus' message is that we must love our neighbors if we are to follow Him–we must concern ourselves with institutions that have such an important impact on people's lives. It is not enough that we act righteously; are the institutions that operate in our name also acting justly?

What role, then, should Christians play in politics, particularly in the American democratic system? Is there a uniquely Christian view of public policy?

Many believers have certainly thought so over time.

Indeed, religion has provided a distinctive backdrop for government, beginning with the nation's founding. If America was not precisely a Christian republic, its people were religious and brought their faith into the public sphere.

However, the fact that politics and religion were not seen as incompatible does not mean that believers agreed on the public perspective that Christians were expected to have. Indeed, throughout America's history laity and clerics alike have often found themselves on different sides of important issues, including some that go to the core of Christian theology and democratic philosophy.

For example, the issue of slavery not only divided America before the Civil War; it also rent asunder the major denominations. Christians in both North and South firmly believed that God was on their side: "In churches across the land, hands hammered on pulpits, and impassioned preachers roared for purification of God's favored nation. In the North, this fiery call seared the South for its sinful ways. In the South, it scathed the wayward North."[4]

The Baptist, Methodist, and Presbyterian denominations split apart. Congregationalists did not formally divide only because of the church's atomized structure. Other major sects, such as Catholics, Lutherans, and Episcopalians, survived as entities though their members showed the same regional division. Indeed, this religious rupture contributed to the violent breakup of the federal union. For as such national institutions as political parties and churches divided along geographic lines, Americans found increasingly little in common with citizens in other sections of the country.

Once war broke out, "the churches promptly went to battle on opposing sides, exactly like feudal bishops," writes historian Paul Johnson.[5] Clerics in North and South alike proclaimed the justice of their cause and exhorted the populace to battle. Said Granville Moddy, a northern Methodist: "We are charged with having brought about the present contest. I believe it is true we did bring it about, and I glory in it, for it is a wreath of glory around our brow."[6] The national government's ultimate victory was analyzed in similar theological terms—with southern and northern churches naturally reaching conflicting conclusions.

Peace helped heal denominational wounds, but clerics and parishioners again ended up on different sides of another regional split a century later: civil rights. A number of northern churches led the fight to end Jim Crow laws and pervasive discrimination against blacks; many southern religious leaders, including former Moral Majority head Jerry Falwell, defended segregation (a position he later repudiated). Believers in North and South worshiped the same God and read the same Bible, but their perspectives on perhaps the most important issue of the day at points decades apart were equally irreconcilable.

Nor do different churches show any greater unity on issues today. The most dramatic political phenomenon of the last decade or so is probably the entry of evangelicals into the political process. In recent years most theologically conservative Christians had eschewed politics, but a combination of factors—the leftward shift in the mainline churches, the perceived assault by the courts on religious values, and the rise of the televangelists, among others—started bringing more of them to the polls. Then the candidacy of Jimmy Carter, a self-proclaimed "born-again" Christian, helped catalyze organized evangelical political involvement. In fact, George Gallup proclaimed 1976 to be "The Year of the Evangelical." For the first time in many years the U.S. government was headed by an avowed believer.

However, Carter's religious convictions had no obvious impact on his administration: Carter as president proved to be indistinguishable from other liberal Democrats. Though religiously motivated votes helped elect him—indeed, probably provided more than his narrow margin of victory—Carter carefully avoided allowing the appearance of any religious overtones in his policies. In fact, Carter seemed to go out of his way to meet the concerns of left-wing interest groups that might fear his theological views.

So his religious constituency turned against him. Evangelicals who voted heavily for Carter in 1976 supported Ronald Reagan in 1980. The conservative Republican played to Christian activists with his high-profile support for school prayer and opposition to abortion. Falwell, for one, said he would mobilize voters for Reagan "even if he has the devil running with him."[7] In practice Reagan achieved little of substance on the social issues that were most important to his religious constituency, but the Reagan administration cloaked itself in religious rhetoric. As a result, evangelicals overwhelmingly backed Reagan in 1984.

The rush of theological conservatives into the arms of the political right was not matched by the mainline Protestant churches. The laity of most denominations is largely middle-of-the-road, like nonreligious Americans, a majority of these church members voted for Reagan, though without the enthusiasm found in evangelical ranks.

More significant, however, was the gulf between the leaderships of the different churches. Falwell, a Southern Baptist, celebrated the Republican renaissance; evangelist Tim LaHaye formed the American Coalition for Traditional Values to encourage conservative Christian activism since, in his view, "the only way to have a genuine spiritual revival is to have legislative reform."[8] The attitude of leaders of the more liberal Protestant denominations that had long advocated the "social gospel" and the welfare state was quite different. United Methodist Bishop Nichols told his fellow bishops in November 1980 that the Reagan victory might have resulted from "the weakness of the 'saints.'" He was hopeful for the future, "if the people of faith will be strengthened by defeat and address themselves to the new agenda which is upon us."[9]

The division between religious right and left has grown increasingly bitter during the Reagan years. Budget policy, welfare spending, the arms buildup, Central America and U.S. support for the Contras—passionate believers intensely disagree over the implications of the gospel for these issue areas. Both sides have accused the other of using God, ignoring Scripture, and failing to acknowledge the only true Christian position. In 1981, for instance, the National Council of Churches denounced the Reagan administration for veritable apostasy: in Reagan's "vision of America the fittest survive and prosper, and there is little room for public purpose since it interferes with private gain. Compassion is a weakness in the competitive struggle of each against all." The Council, naturally, proposed an "alternative vision" based on "religious faith and biblical images of divine intent."[10] Conservative evangelical criticism of President Carter and later Democratic Presidential aspirants was equally sharp.

Nor is the split simply evangelical versus mainstream. The Catholic hierarchy is largely united in its opposition to abortion, but has divided into a large liberal faction and a smaller conservative wing over matters like the economy and Central America. Denominations such as Churches of Christ and United Methodists have found themselves increasingly riven by disputes on a range of issues between a liberal leadership and a more centrist laity.

Even evangelicals are not truly united. A 1984 Free Congress Foundation poll found them to be more conservative than average, but still in favor of the Equal Rights Amendment and divided over increased military spending. There is an influential group of theonomists, or "Christian reconstructionists," some of whom would use the government to enforce Biblical principles. The televangelists represent a conservative middle that is hawkish on defense but is most interested in social issues. A vigorous, if numerically small, number of leftist believers, represented by individuals like Ron Sider and Jim Wallis and such organizations as Evangelicals for Social Action and *Sojourners* magazine, are receiving increasing attention. And black Pentecostals are more likely to support a leftish Jesse Jackson than a conservative Pat Robertson for President, even though they might prefer the latter for their pastor.

The tension between different religious perspectives on politics is even greater internationally for the Catholic church. Liberation theology–the marrying of Marxism, minus its doctrinal atheism, and Christianity–has become popular in recent years. This anomalous mixture has great appeal in many Latin American countries; Franciscan friar Leonardo Boff returned from a visit to the Soviet Union in 1986, declaring that "socialism provides better conditions for a Christian to be authentic."[11] But Boff's position is scorned by the Vatican, presided over by a Pope who grew up in Communist-ruled Poland. However, even he, at times, speaks as if he believes the U.S.S.R. and U.S. are morally equivalent.

So who speaks for God?

The issue was brought into dramatic focus in this country with Pat Robertson's failed presidential bid. Robertson, the former head of the Christian Broadcast Network and son of a U.S. Senator, based his campaign on uniting the nation's forty-eight million born-again Christians. Though Carter was an avowed evangelical and Reagan articulated Christian values, Robertson was perceived as a political preacher rather than a religious politician. He attempted to broaden his electoral appeal by leaving "The 700 Club" TV show, but his support remained largely confined to evangelical churches. Born-again activists could deliver a straw poll, county meeting, or even an occasional statewide caucus to Robertson, but nothing more. In fact, most Christians did not even vote for him: George Bush carried the born-again constituency in the South. And far more evangelical leaders supported the unsuccessful candidacies of Senator Robert Dole (R-Kansas) and Representative Jack Kemp (R-New York) than Robertson, even though Kemp had stated that his religious views would not interfere with his politics–"I'm in Caesar's world and I don't plan to make that a part of my campaign."[12]

Evidently most American evangelicals decided that Robertson, despite being a preacher, did not best represent God in the public realm. His campaign did have one signal success: bringing a number of previously apolitical Christians into the political process. But the vision of partisan religious politics, with block voting by the large Christian mainstream, turned out to be an embarrassing illusion.[13] (Jesse Jackson mobilized the black churches and parts of the religious left with greater success. However, his appeal was ideological rather than theological; Jackson has always been a politician before he was a preacher, and he has never proclaimed himself to be spiritually reborn.)

In fact, the influence of the religious right has probably been ebbing since 1984, when the relation of religion to politics became an election issue. The Republican Party showcased the conservative/Christian alliance at its national convention. In his prayer opening the convention, evangelist James Robison thanked God "for the leadership of President Reagan."[14] In turn, President Reagan declared that "without God democracy will not and cannot long endure."[15] Democratic presidential nominee Walter Mondale denounced the mixing of policy and theology, while his running mate, Geraldine Ferraro, charged that Reagan was not "a good Christian" because of his budget cuts. New York Governor Mario Cuomo squabbled publicly with the Catholic Church over the role of faith and policy.

In the end, what should have been the religious right's greatest victory seemed to be its ultimate undoing. By appearing to turn Christianity, and its message of a transcendent God, into a political football, these religious activists discredited their own efforts. Moreover, the more hard-line religious conservatives ensured conflict with equally genuine believers with different political perspectives because they developed not a general Biblical critique of policy but rather a specific policy agenda; as a result, the issue became their personal predilections rather than godly principles such as justice, peace, and concern for the poor. "Never had the church itself been so dangerously polarized," writes Charles Colson.[16]

Moreover, the perception–in most cases neither fair nor accurate–that religious activists were intent on spreading the gospel by force, rather like the ancient Christian emperors who commanded the heathen to accept baptism or die, spawned an explosion of sentiment against the political preachers and their friends in government. People for the American Way capitalized on the religious right's miscues, gaining prominence by criticizing conservative clerical politics. Secular Jewish leaders reacted particularly strongly against Republican overtures to fundamentalists. And even parts of the general public began to see Jerry Falwell, with his Moral Majority, and other well-known religious activists as a threat to their privacy and freedom.

The truly limited nature of the religious right's power became obvious when the Democrats regained control of the Senate in 1986. The poor public acceptance of the movement was highlighted when Falwell changed the name of the Moral Majority to the Liberty Federation. And even as Robertson was gearing up for his presidential bid in 1987, Falwell announced that he was "getting back to basics," abandoning the Federation and politics in favor of his ministry.[17] Robertson's dramatic failure after finishing second in the Iowa caucuses merely confirmed that Christians disagree on the candidates, the issues, and even the proper role of faith in politics. Though believers will undoubtedly continue to be involved not only in elections but also in specific legislative struggles–the Methodists first came to Washington in 1916 to support the temperance movement and virtually every other denomination and church is now represented in the nation's capital–their high-profile role at the right hand of Presidents now seems over, at least temporarily.

Nevertheless, the defeat of high-profile religious partisans like Robertson should not cause Christians to retreat from political confrontation, turning control of the public square over to whatever transitory majority that happens to achieve political ascendency. Believers have a Biblical responsibility to apply their beliefs in their civic as well as private lives. An important aspect of that duty is simply responding to attacks from an increasingly hostile secular state.

The relationship between religion and politics has been an issue since the founding of the republic. But a system that originally welcomed Biblical standards in political discourse while denying the ecclesiastical establishment access to government power has increasingly applied Thomas Jefferson's famous "wall of separation" metaphor to religious values as well as church institutions. Religious symbols in public places have increasingly come under attack.[18] Prayer in school, still a leading evangelical issue today, was banned by the Supreme Court in 1962. State schools may not display copies of the Ten Commandments or conduct Bible reading. Government aid for private schools has also been strictly circumscribed—so sensitive has the High Court been to any perceived public support for religion that it has voided legislation allowing tax credits for private school tuition, since many of them are church-related. The role of the Senate chaplain, the engraving of "In God We Trust" on coins, and the saying of prayers at state university graduation ceremonies have all been challenged, though so far unsuccessfully. A case involving Zion, Illinois' use of the cross in its city seal is now pending in federal court.

And though in 1984 the Supreme Court upheld the right of Pawtucket, Rhode Island, to include a creche in its regular Christmas decoration—on the grounds that the display was "devoid of any inherent meaning" and served a "legitimate public purpose"[19]—come Christmas the cases involving local creches, either sponsored by government or placed on public property by private groups, seem ubiquitous. In December 1987, for instance, the local chapter of American Atheists threatened a lawsuit over San Diego's annual display of a nativity scene in a downtown park. "You have compromised the Constitution of our nation," chapter director Stephen Thorne wrote the city.[20] Similar disputes arose in Warren, Michigan, which also exhibited a Star of David. Indeed, public displays of the menorah for Hanukkah in Chicago and Columbus, Ohio, generated similar controversies at the same time.

This move to eliminate not only government subsidies of religion, but also to expunge any public mention of spiritual matters, has become particularly evident in the state school system. Far more important than the Supreme Court's ban on official prayer is the decision of many local administrators to forbid students and teachers to gather, before classes or during breaks, to pray or study the Bible. Though in 1981 the Supreme Court ruled that a public university which allowed other student groups to meet on campus had to extend the same right to religious organizations, that ruling has not yet been extended to elementary or secondary schools.

As a result, we see cases like the Harper Elementary School in Evansville, Indiana, whose principal barred Christian workers from meeting together before classes. Other teachers and aides gathered and talked about politics and sports, but religion was verboten. A member of the school board expressed his fear that children might see the teachers with a Bible and that school officials would have to ensure that the workers didn't leave behind any religious materials. "We don't want the children exposed to them," he said.[21] In this case at least, a public education meant insulation from any mention of a subject of enormous concern to tens of millions of Americans.

The unwillingness of many school administrators, even those not hostile to religion, to risk getting involved in what has become a controversial issue has carried over into the private sector, particularly textbook publishers. A major federal study conducted by Paul Vitz, a professor of psychology at New York University, reviewed some sixty social studies texts used by nearly nine of every ten elementary school students nationwide. He found a "total absence of any primary religious text about typical contemporary American religious life."[22] The books also ignored important religious events abroad like the Protestant Reformation–and Jesus' ministry and death.

Even the People for the American Way and Americans United for the Separation of Church and State condemned the failure of U.S. history classes to mention the transcendent spiritual faith which has motivated groups from the early Pilgrims to the modern religious right. Subsequently Doubleday announced that it planned to reintroduce religion into its textbooks, but that decision will take years to affect what children actually read and are taught.

Moreover, supposed government indifference or neutrality toward religion has increasingly given way to hostility. The state has begun imposing worldly values on the church, threatening its ability to live up to its Biblical responsibilities. For instance, though the church, in representing the Body of Christ, has many unique corporate responsibilities, govern-

ment now uses antidiscrimination laws to try to eliminate the
church's distinctive character. Religious organizations are
often unable to set doctrinal standards for employment: the
Dayton Christian School, charged with providing a Bible-based
education for children, was barred from relying on religion in
its hiring decisions. A case is now before the federal courts
involving the Mormon Church's right to hire only Mormons
in its nonprofit activities. New York City cut off municipal
funds to any organization that refused to hire homosexuals;
the Catholic church chose to forego its city contracts to provide welfare services rather than to violate the Church's teachings.

And in 1988 Catholic Georgetown University found itself
compelled to grant a gay students' organization the same privileges, including funding, as other campus clubs. The nation's
capital passed an ordinance banning discrimination on the
basis of "sexual orientation" in 1977, and sued Georgetown for
refusing to recognize and subsidize gay student groups. A 5-2
majority on the D.C. Court of Appeals ruled that the university did not have to "officially recognize" the groups, but that it
nevertheless had to give them the same "tangible benefits,"
such as school funding. The District's "overriding interest" in
the "eradication of sexual orientation discrimination," said the
judges, outweighed "any burden" placed on Georgetown's religious rights.[23] In March 1988 the school decided not to appeal,
settling the case instead; under D.C. law Georgetown was
liable for the plaintiffs' $600,000 to $900,000 in legal fees. In
this case fundamental church doctrine, which goes to the core
of the church's raison d'etre–upholding Christian values and
promoting moral purity–was sacrificed to satisfy a city ordinance that responded to a vocal pressure group.

The implications of this principle for the Christian
church, if adopted elsewhere, are ominous indeed. For if religious institutions can be forced to sanction conduct that runs
counter to Biblical teaching, why can't the church itself be
forced to accept such conduct?

On October 4, 1983, the leadership of the Collinsville
Church of Christ, located in the Oklahoma town of the same
name, announced to the congregation "the withdrawing of fellowship from our sister in Christ, Marian Guinn." Guinn, who
was divorced, had acknowledged forming an intimate relationship with a local businessman and politician. She resisted counseling and refused to end the association. The church's elders,

relying on Matthew 18:15-17, where Jesus detailed the procedure for church discipline, made their public pronouncement.

Guinn then sued the church for violating her privacy and causing her emotional distress. In 1984 a Tulsa jury awarded her $390,000. Though the state was not technically a party in the case, it was the government that eviscerated the right of the Church of Christ to set conditions for membership. State tort law allowed someone who had been baptized into the Body of Christ and who understood the local church's standards to then claim unfair injury when those rules were enforced; a state judge, charged with upholding the Constitution, failed to protect the right of believers to hold a fellow parishioner accountable for her behavior.

Defending the church from such government intrusions is an important enough reason for Christians to be politically active. But believers have a responsibility to do more than just fight a rearguard action against state interference, like those in the Guinn and Georgetown cases, or to demand genuinely neutral access to public facilities, whether meeting at the Harper Elementary School or using accurate textbooks in public schools across America. Believers must promote a political vision which transcends specific ideologies or policies.

The goal should not be a detailed legislative agenda for the next Congress or President. Nor should it be an endless series of policy pronouncements on the issues of the day. For there is no simple, single Christian position on controversies like comparable worth, Central America, nuclear weapons, income redistribution, and the like. Debate over issues like these may be informed by Christian principles, but few can be decided by direct reference to Bible verses. Even where Scripture endorses a specific policy, whether the Jubilee Year or the stoning of adulterers, Christians must engage in honest Biblical exegesis before attempting to apply those passages today. In any case, we must use reason within revelation, especially where the Bible is silent. Issues like the Panama Canal Treaty are questions of prudence, not theology. In short, Christians should seek to develop an overall Biblical philosophy of government that can unite all believers, whether on the right or left, rather than a religious litmus-test that will only divide them.

Nor should believers' political objective be to directly seize control of the secular state, for simply electing Christians to positions of influence will alone solve nothing. Tim LaHaye, chairman of the American Coalition for Traditional Values, said in 1985 that "if every Bible-believing church in America would trust God to use them to raise up one person to run for public office in the next ten years ... we would have more Christians in office than there are offices to hold."[24] There is no evidence, however, that spiritual purity correlates with either a particular political ideology or managerial competence. Luther once observed that he would prefer to be governed by a competent Turk rather than an incompetent Christian, and his point remains valid today. Thomas Jefferson may have been a deist, but he probably made a better President than would have many of his Christian contemporaries.

Moreover, additional Christians in government, despite their shared spiritual perspective, would be scarely more united than believers generally: Just as the Body of Christ has splintered over virtually every contemporary issue, so too would Christian politicians divide. Republican Senators Mark Hatfield and William Armstrong are both reputed to be devout evangelical Christians, yet their voting records diverge dramatically. In fact, LaHaye and his fellow advocates of more believing politicians are not nonpartisan: they implicitly assume that all the new Christian candidates would be conservative, which makes their agenda more ideological than religious. It may be valid nevertheless, but it seems to represent more worldly political principles than a genuinely Christian public perspective.

Another political dead end for believers is the effort to turn the United States into a self-avowed Christian republic. It is true that God will reward a nation that follows him: "Blessed is the nation whose God is the Lord" (Psalm 33:12). But God requires heartfelt obedience, not formalistic obeisance.

Nevertheless, some Christians believe that the nation need only return to its historical religious roots. In fact, some of the early colonists believed in the total Christian society. And many of the leading founders of the U.S. were Christians who incorporated Biblical principles into the new system of government. By the time the Constitution was ratified, however, no significant political leader nor segment of the public thought they were recreating Israel of old on the new continent.

For precisely this reason other religious activists have been agitating since 1863 to amend the Constitution to make

Christianity the nation's official religion. But this is a secular nation, one peopled by a majority that does not recognize the Lordship of Jesus Christ. No high-sounding phrase added to the nation's governing law can change that. Unless Christians want to secede to start their own country, something that goes directly against Christ's injunction for His followers to be the salt of the earth, our responsibility is to find the best way to reflect Christian values in a political system that must rule believer and nonbeliever alike.

What, then, should be our perspective on politics and public policy? To promote basic Christian principles both in overall civic life and, more specifically, in government.

First, Christians need to fulfill our Biblical responsibilities, within the church and to the community around us. We should have and live with a passion for helping the poor, promoting justice, and otherwise demonstrating the love of God. In this way we will indirectly sow Christ's message thoughout society, including in public institutions.

Indeed, the more Christian values permeate the polity, the fewer the number of issues requiring resolution in the political process. The expansive state has increasingly replaced God as the Creator and Sustainer of life in the view of many. Members of the Body of Christ, individually and through the church, can combat this modern form of idolatry not only by preaching the gospel, but also by fulfilling our duty "to do good to all people" (Galatians 6:10). In that way cooperation will have replaced confrontation as a way of meeting human needs–and God, not government, will receive the glory.

In fact, if the church expects to credibly lecture the state and society-at-large, it must provide a principled example to follow. The Catholic bishops' pronouncements on the economy are suspect because of their lack of Biblical support and economic sophistication, as well as their reliance on government coercion, issues that will be dealt with in Chapter 9. However, an equally serious problem is the failure of that Church to implement its own principles of economic justice. Admits retired Bishop William McManus, "Rarely, however, have the U.S. bishops as a group spotlighted their own performances as the chief administrators of a 40-million-member organization with thousands of institutions and programs to manage."[25]

Further, Christians need to live and otherwise promote

the sort of moral values that properly undergird any society and government. Indeed, the existing democratic, capitalist system can function well only so long as its participants follow a basic moral code that is best represented by what has been termed the Judeo-Christian ethic. Wrote John Adams, "Our Constitution was made only for a moral and religious people. It is wholly inadequate for the government of any other."[26]

Today, however, we seem to have lost that fundamental social consensus. Our welfare system is failing to halt–indeed, is probably promoting–the disintegration of inner-city communities, where basic Christian values such as self-reliance, chastity, and honesty are disappearing. The legal system is rewarding injustice and undermining other social institutions as it encourages people to eschew personal responsibility as they look for someone, anyone else to compensate them for their mistakes or imagined wrongs. The market economy is faltering as businesses twist the law to void contracts and lobby government for special favors. And our political system of representative government is degenerating into a spoils system for the influential. The problem in these cases is not so much incorrect policy as inadequate moral standards. Christians must help supply the transcendental framework for society that incorporates these important values.

Second, Christians need to frame the debate on policy issues in Biblical terms. This does not require believers to cite Scripture when lobbying agnostic or atheistic legislators; instead, it implies an emphasis on basic Biblical priciples that provide a unique perspective for analyzing candidates and issues. If Christians "are not serving Christ in politics according to the norm of biblical justice, they are serving some false god that will lead to injustice," writes James Skillen, executive director of the Association for Public Justice.[27]

Articulating Biblical values will not necessarily yield particular policy conclusions. In the fall of 1987 the National Conference of Catholic Bishops released a statement asserting–correctly–that "the religious communities are inevitably drawn more deeply into the public life of the nation" today "because the moral content of public choices is so central."[28] However, the bishops went on to present their specific legislative agenda encompassing the minimum wage, welfare reform, a nuclear test ban treaty, and so on.

The bishops, by introducing a broad Christian political

vision, will help shape today's political debate in a manner that should yield policies more congruent with the Christian worldview. But their laundry list of proposals detracts from the moral content of their message: whether a nuclear test ban would really help maintain the peace and a higher minimum wage would actually assist the poor are empirical rather than Scriptural questions. Religious leaders are best at providing spiritual guidance and worst at developing practical public policies.

Among the Biblical principles with political implications at stake–all of which will be analyzed in greater detail in Chapter 4–are a commitment to justice, a belief in the sacredness of life, an emphasis on personal and communal responsibility for the less fortunate, a respect for individual autonomy, a bias against the expansive godlike state, a desire to protect the family unit, and an obligation to promote peace. Together these form the real "seamless garment" that represents Biblical or Christian justice.

In fact, though of late many American churches have grown ever more partisan in their support for particular policies and pieces of legislation, there was a time when they articulated, rhetorically at least, an overall Christian philosophy. In 1952, for instance, the Methodist General Conference reaffirmed its emphasis on social activism: "We firmly believe that it is not only our duty to bring Christ to the individual but also to bring the society within which we live more nearly in conformity with the teachings of Christ. We believe that the free democratic way of life ruled by Christian principles can bring to mankind a society in which liberty is preserved, justice established, and brotherhood achieved."[29] Perhaps the greatest tragedy of the liberal Protestant denominations is that they have largely abandoned Christ as they have attempted to promote the "social gospel."

Of course, general values often suggest particular policies, but Christians should be extraordinarily careful before claiming that God's Word requires a specific course of action. For the Bible is long on principles by which men are to live their lives, but very short on rules men are supposed to force other men to abide by.

Where Christians believe a course of action to be Scripturally based, they should be uncompromising in their support for it. There will be resistance from some non-Christians, of course. The ACLU and Planned Parenthood, for

instance, challenged the amendment drafted by Representative
Henry Hyde (R-Illinois) to end federal funding for abortions on
the grounds that it violated the First Amendment "by imposing a peculiarly religious view of when a human life begins."[30]
The plaintiffs followed Hyde to Mass and searched his con-
stituents' mail for religious references. The Supreme Court
rightly rejected the argument, for a Christian's theologically
based moral framework is as valid in public discourse as are
the secular humanist views held by an atheist.

At the same time, however, Christians must never lose
track of their most fundamental task: spreading the Good
News of Jesus Christ. Government cannot transform men's
hearts, and politics will never be pure as long as its participants are sinners. For the church, at least, trying to make the
world a slightly better place will never be more important than
saving men's souls. The Body of Christ can achieve more by
emphasizing the importance of sexual purity than by campaigning in favor of anti-sodomy laws, for instance.

High-profile ministers must be particularly vigilant not
to let political involvement tar the eternal Christian message.
"We should resist being taken in by inflated and romantic
views of politics," writes Neuhaus, for "it is in the interest of
politicians and the hordes of people who make their living by
talking about what politicians do to disguise the stark and
simple truth that they are engaged in getting and keeping
power."[31] Unfortunately, political activists on both left and
right are only too happy to use clerics to achieve their wordly,
and often anti-Christian, goals.

In fact, some of the religious right's strongest conservative allies have privately expressed opposition to its moral
agenda. They view the alliance as one of convenience, allowing them to manipulate religious issues and the passions they
arouse for maximum political advantage. In such cases the
Body of Christ becomes just another interest group engaging in
partisan politics and begging for one or another special government favor. And it is the gospel that suffers: many people associate Jerry Falwell, for example, not with God's Good News or
Falwell's genuine good works, but with social repression and
political opportunism.

Religion and politics do go together. However, their partnership should emphasize transcendent principles rather than
specific policies. And the relationship between these two king-

doms, as Augustine referred to them, should never be a comfortable one. The state is ordained of God, but it is a temporary, worldly institution run by sinful man. In fact, the twentieth century has demonstrated again and again that the power of government to do evil is far greater than its potential to do good. The promise of the Kingdom of Heaven is quite different, and Christian political activists must never forget that God, not the state, will ultimately bring about His Kingdom.

# The Failure of the Bipartisan Welfare State

*I*n December 1987 the United States Congress was at its most natural–and its worst. Before leaving town for the holidays, Congress voted to shut down two conservative newspapers, endorsed the right of legislators to fly their girlfriends on federal planes, rewarded a Senator's campaign supporter with an $8 million grant to the contributor's favorite charity, and distributed rancid slabs of pork to universities, developers, municipalities, and other favored interests across the country. The federal government had yet again degenerated into a form of civic pornography that our democracy seems incapable of controlling.

Indeed, both the administration and Congress became increasingly incapable or unwilling to act responsibly. Throughout 1987 President Reagan was mired in a scandal that demonstrated his ignorance of controversial intelligence work and his aides' disdain for the constitutional process; he raised new questions about his grasp of foreign policy as he ignored seventy years of bloody history in lavishly welcoming Soviet leader Mikhail Gorbachev to Washington.

The President's domestic agenda was virtually lifeless. Despite his rhetoric about bringing people "to their feet with our closing act,"[1] he largely attempted to get along with his critics. As successive aides went on trial for various offenses, the stench of corruption floated above an administration that had arrived to revolutionize Washington. And President Reagan, despite his reputation for being the "great communicator," provided virtually no leadership on the many political and moral challenges facing America.

Yet Congress' behavior was even more venal. Its leadership was tainted by conflicts of interest, vote-buying, and personal immorality. Both House and Senate, in Democratic hands, were riven by rabid partisanship. And legislators rarely took their minds off the next election, refusing to make any hard decisions. Capitol Hill's failure was perhaps most grievous on the budget: legislators spent most of 1987 ignoring statutory deadlines, flouting their own rules, and refusing to approve individual appropriations bills. In December of that year Congress finally wrapped up $603 billion worth of programs in a single bill–after playing a political game of chicken with the President that threatened to shut down the government–and went home.

The process, a repeat from 1986, does grave violence to the constitutional scheme. By combining outlays for most federal programs into one mammoth Continuing Resolution instead of the thirteen traditional separate bills, Congress emasculates the President's veto power. To block even the smallest expenditure the President has to be willing to kill the entire measure. Few individual issues are worth that price.

Even worse, reliance on the Continuing Resolution allows Congress to evade public scrutiny for its actions. The 1987 appropriations bill ran 1,200 pages; a companion measure, the Omnibus Budget Reconciliation Act, ran another 1,000. Influential legislators, particularly those chosen to sit on the conference committee that reconciles House and Senate versions, are able to hide obscure but costly amendments from the public, press, and even their colleagues. As a result, leading congressmen routinely repay campaign favors and settle political scores without being accountable to anyone. For even if their handiwork is discovered, no President is likely to veto the entire bill to block it.

This perversion of representative democracy represents the great corruption of the American republic, a process that political scientist Jerry Herbert summarizes as lost "in luxury, dependence, and ignorance."[2] That is, the system is suffering from the public's pursuit of self-interest to the exclusion of the common good, willingness to trade their freedom for material wealth, and lack of interest in public affairs.

Consider the December 1987 legislation, which was a masterpiece by even Capitol Hill's own unenviable standards, filled with pork and poison for friends and enemies of influential legislators. There were, for instance, the mundane highway boondoggles–$90,000 for a left-hand turn lane to a street in San Diego, $14.2 million in highway improvements for the Washington, D.C. suburbs, and a $28 million highway bypass project in New Mexico. Dams and other transportation projects also rated generous federal attention, including $1.345 million to rehabilitate three private rail lines in New York and $13 million to reinforce a private South Carolina dam. The federal sweepstakes also made a winner of South Dakota's senior Senator, Larry Pressler, who pushed through a $350,000 grant to clean up Mount Rushmore.

Congress ordered nearly $7 million in outlays by the Economic Development Administration on projects that did not meet even the agency's lax standards, but which were in the districts of influential members. A Kellog, Idaho, Bavarian-style ski resort rated $6.4 million in public money, and Congress approved a $2.6 million grant to the Fisheries Promotional Fund. Rural electrical cooperatives, which have benefitted from some $53.1 billion in federal subsidies between 1973 and 1987, pushed through an amendment allowing them to refinance $2 billion in federally guaranteed loans without a prepayment penalty, saving them an estimated $400 million to $500 million.

Money also flowed for special interest research projects: $60,000 to the Belgian Endive Research Center, $50,000 on New Mexico wildflowers, $260,000 to the Center for Cranberry and Blueberry Research, $285,000 to Penn State University to study milk consumption, $350,000 to create a cornstarch-based biodegradable plastic, $435,000 on sugar cane, $500,000 on sugar beets and sunflowers, $2.7 million to the Polymer Institute at the University of Southern Mississippi, and $25 million to the University of Florida.

Moreover, Congress moved to expand farm subsidies, which cost $49 billion during in 1986 and 1987 alone. The legislators approved an expenditure of $10 million to buy sunflower oil from sunflower growers–and store it at taxpayer expense. Even worse, Congress enriched the already wealthy by lifting the $250,000 limit on loans to beekeepers. This agricultural program benefits between 2,000 and 2,500 honey producers and has cost up to $100 million a year; Congress' action was expected to funnel another $6 million to just 15 large producers.

Some of Congress' grants were even more narrowly

focused, benefiting just one friend and political supporter. In a highly reported case, Senator Daniel Inouye (D-Hawaii), while serving in the Conference Committee, inserted into the compromise bill a $8 million grant to Ozar Hatorah, a Jewish charity, to build schools in France for North African Sephardic Jews, some of whom have lived in France for years. Zev Wilson, a member of the organization's board of directors, was a friend of Inouye and had contributed $1,000 to the Senator's last campaign. Under intense public pressure Inouye, who was concerned about possible damage to his candidacy for Majority Leader in 1989, asked Congress to rescind the appropriation.

Less well reported but even more scandalous was House Speaker Jim Wright placing in the Continuing Resolution a $25 million airport for Fort Worth that had been previously rejected by a House committee. The airport would go in the midst of nearly 17,000 acres of land owned by H. Ross Perot, Jr., who planned on creating an industrial development park. The expected profit for Perot, who suggested the airport and calls Wright "a personal friend of mine," is in excess of $300 million.

America's finest also worked overtime that Christmas to protect their own perks. Representative Charles Wilson (D-Texas) pushed through two amendments to cut the budget of an agency that refused to ferry his girlfriend around Pakistan. Representative Tom Bevill (D-Alabama), chairman of the House Appropriations Energy and Water Development Subcommittee, took the opposite tack: he included a provision in the Continuing Resolution preventing the Army Corps of Engineers from selling its three executive jets, criticized by Army auditors but used by Bevill and other congressmen.

Finally, Congress attacked more than the taxpayers' wallet in December 1987. It threatened the underpinnings of a free, democratic republic–a robust press. Senator Edward Kennedy (D-Massachusetts) has long been a target of Rupert Murdoch and his *Boston Herald*. The Federal Communications Commission prohibits "cross-ownership" of a TV station and newspaper in the same market, but it had temporarily waived the rules for Murdoch, who owned both the *Herald* and the *New York Post*, along with TV stations in both cities. Kennedy enlisted Senator Ernest Hollings (D-South Carolina) to add language, which neither chamber of Congress had previously approved, prohibiting any change in FCC rules or any extension of existing waivers–a provision that affected only Murdoch. Murdoch's only alternatives were a fire sale or a shutdown.[3] By mid-1988 he had sold off the *Post*, essentially for its real estate value, and was preparing to sell his Boston TV station, in order to keep the *Herald*.

In short, Congress proved that Americans now suffer under not only an imperial presidency but also a dictatorial Congress, one that legislates in secret, bullies the media, enriches its friends, and punishes its adversaries. Yet despite polls that find significant public dissatisfaction with Congress, voters are unwilling to hold their representatives accountable. Reelection to the House has become almost automatic; in the 1986 election 98 percent of congressmen were reelected.

The problem is not a partisan one. If Republican Presidents of late have been caught lying and overreaching their authority, there is probably no President who more ruthlessly and selfishly used and abused his power than Lyndon Johnson, a man who grew rich in public office and who engaged in more than his share of vote-stealing. It is the Democratic congressional majority that is responsible for the bulk of Capitol Hill's misbehavior,; but when given the opportunity Republicans, whatever their rhetoric about fiscal responsibility, are equally eager to use federal funds to buy votes. And few politicians of either party have proved willing to take public responsibility for their own mistakes.

Unfortunately, positive change seems unlikely in the near future. The 1988 presidential race proved to be one of the most dismal on record. Two Democratic contenders, Senator Joseph Biden (D-Delaware) and former Colorado Senator Gary Hart, were forced out of the race after exhibiting serious character flaws; Hart later reentered the race, proclaiming that he would not be the first adulterer to serve in the White House.

Of the other Democrats, Senator Paul Simon (D-Illinois) represented the unvarnished left-utopianism that proved so disastrous during the Carter presidency, while Senator Albert Gore (D-Tennessee) tried to wrap up his pro forma liberalism in a more moderate package. Representative Richard Gephardt (D-Missouri) reversed his once moderate stance to espouse a strident economic populist platform, one infused with more demagoguery than common sense. Baptist minister and black activist Jesse Jackson outflanked the Democratic field on the left with a variety of radical and often uninformed views. Questions about his character remained largely unasked as his rivals refused to seriously engage him in debate. Massachusetts Governor Michael Dukakis advocated a compassionless, technocratic liberalism; the "Massachusetts miracle" upon which he staked his campaign was built on policies, such as tax cuts, that Dukakis had opposed. Only former Arizona Governor Bruce Babbitt seemed to recognize that the traditional Democratic policy of tax and tax, spend and spend had nearly wrecked the country, and his courage came more in talking about sensitive issues than in proposing sensible solutions.

On the Republican side Robert Dole, the Senate Minority Leader, assiduously tried to recast his 1976 hatchetman image, only to return to form in a quarrel with the nearly invisible George Bush about their respective class origins and records in public office; neither evinced a willingness to anger any interest group, large or small. Alexander Haig acknowledged one of the major reasons he was in the race was to deny Bush the nomination. New York Representative Jack Kemp, once a conservative heart-throb, advocated painless, "feel-good" economic policies and demagogued against his opponents on the Social Security issue just as Democrats have traditionally done to Republicans. Former Delaware Governor Pete duPont gained respect but few votes with his issue-oriented campaign.

Finally, Pat Robertson tried to build a mainstream campaign but was dogged by controversy over issues such as his handling of the Freedom Council, doctoring of his biography, and conduct during the Korean War. Some of his more curious opinions, such as the possibility that the computer microchips in credit cards being the Mark of the Beast referred to in Revelation, once freely advanced in print and on TV, also gained him unwanted attention. In the wake of his second-place showing in Iowa came a string of "funny facts" on subjects such as missiles in Cuba, contributing to his political collapse in the South.

In short, two centuries after the Constitution was approved and the new nation formed, the American republic has seen the quality of its political discourse fall to abysmal lows. Its public officials, with disappointingly few exceptions, are ignorant, myopic, and self-serving; while in 1787 a group of relatively young men developed a framework of government intended to last for centuries, most politicians today don't look beyond the next election.

And the state of the body politic seems equally poor. In colonial and revolutionary America issues were hotly debated and a sense of community good was understood. Today's electorate is largely apathetic and unread. The activists are balkanized into different interest groups that single-mindedly pursue their own financial gain at public expense. The overriding question that many voters now pose to candidates at all levels seems to be not what is right?, but what benefits me?

Indeed, the 1980s have witnessed the failure of both interest group liberalism and the conservative counterrevolution. Neither has provided the answer to persistent problems of economic instability, poverty, family breakup, international conflict, and spiritual impoverishment.

The roots of America's crisis in government lie in man's sinful nature, of course. But if politics cannot provide an earthly utopia, the right kind of government could help promote a social order that was more rather than less godly. In fact, the original constitutional scheme did a reasonable job of containing the worst effects of human failings; unfortunately, that legal structure suffered severe blows in early upheavals such as the Civil War and essentially collapsed during the 1930s and the Great Depression. For while the New Deal, Roosevelt's multifaceted program of federal spending and regulation, did little to rejuvenate the economy–in fact, the Depression actually deepened in 1938 and ended only when the U.S. shifted into full production during World War II–it did dramatically transform the relationship between the individual and the state.

And the resulting damage has, in some cases, only recently become evident. Over the last five decades government has become an immoral god, turning envy into policy, stripping individuals and communities of their traditional social responsibilities, destroying economic opportunities for the disadvantaged, engaging in amoral foreign intervention, and fostering a general spiritual decline.

## THE POLITICS OF ENVY

We see, for instance, the institutionalization of envy. Interest groups, or "factions," naturally existed from the very beginning of the republic. But the framers of the Constitution sought to use specific restrictions on government power, the federal design with autonomous states, and the separation of federal power between three different branches to limit the influence of such selfish pressure groups. If businessmen and farmers occasionally won special privileges from government, the instances were exceptions rather than the rule. These largely anomalous cases apparently were not seen as an example to be followed by the general population.

However, the New Deal turned a trickle of transfers into a flood. Businessmen organized themselves into government-supported cartels. Retirees–whatever their personal financial status–began receiving Social Security. "Public service" jobs, particularly through the Works Progress Administration, became thought of as a right. And farmers, big and small, lobbied for programs that entitled them to subsidies irrespective of the demand for their crops or their personal wealth.

Indeed, perhaps no program better illustrates the transfer society run amok than farm subsidies. From the 1940s through 1970, agricultural outlays were a constant, if not overwhelming cost, topping $5 billion only twice. However, during the 1970s costs began to escalate, spinning out of control the following decade as Congress engaged in a bidding war for rural votes. Direct payments to farmers, which do not include federal research, cheap home loans, subsidized electricity, and other similar benefits, ran $26 billion in 1986 and $23 billion in 1987.

The subsidy system disproportionately benefits the rich: only 17 cents of every federal dollar goes to those in the greatest financial trouble. The perverse melange of deficiency payments, nonrecourse loans, set-asides, and the like encouraged farmers to go deeper into debt but discouraged exports; the mid-1980s then witnessed a painful shake-out in the farm sector, which only further increased pressure to expand government subsidies. For example, Congress in 1985 created a $1.1 billion program to pay dairy farmers, who had received an average of $2 billion a year in subsidies, to go out of business; 144 producers received more than $1 million each. Said one, "It's almost like one of those lottery tickets."[5]

This ethic that government exists for the purpose of everyone living off of everyone else now pervades society. During the 1970s federal college loans were made available to even upper-income families; screams of anguish greeted the Reagan administration's attempts to trim the benefits. Charities and community groups began to expect generous federal funding for their activities. Developers and other wealthy business interests gained access to a plethora of government handouts through programs like Urban Development Action Grants, Community Development Block Grants, the Small Business Administration, and the Economic Development Administration. And Social Security, one-third of whose recipients have incomes above $30,000, became inviolable. In fact, by the mid-1980s 18 percent of all American households received at least one means-tested welfare benefit; 28 percent collected Social Security or railroad retirement checks from the government. Uncle Sam directly employed five million people and indirectly paid the salaries of an untold number of others through vast purchases of everything from tanks to consulting services.

There are obviously economic consequences to the institutionalization of greed and envy. Higher tax rates discourage productive activity; the opportunity to use government to seize wealth rather than to produce it channels individuals into activities designed to redistribute income rather than to create it. Indeed, more and more resources are consumed in legal and political fights for control rather than in economic activities which generate real social benefits. Total congressional campaign spending alone has jumped from $77.3 million in 1972 to $450 million in 1986, a sixfold increase.

A more subtle, but perhaps ultimately more important, result of the onset of the transfer society has been to weaken some of the fundamental precepts which once undergirded our diverse nation. One unifying principle had always been a respect for the property of others; another was believing in one's own primary responsibility to care for oneself and one's family. Further, there was the common understanding, at least when the nation was founded, that government was to act only to promote the "general welfare."

Now, however, these ideals are increasingly trampled underfoot by the mobs seeking special favors from the state. Millionaire honey producers think nothing of shaking down lower-income taxpayers for more loans, comfortable retirees demand their checks even if it means their children might never collect Social Security, and families expect their poorer neighbors to help them pay for their homes, care for their children, and send their kids to college. Government action has increasingly degenerated into petty squabbles over how much to give to which voting bloc.

## DECLINING INDIVIDUAL RESPONSIBILITY

People are also turning away from their personal responsibilities to one another. The basic, unmet human needs in the U.S. remain vast, despite this nation's wealth and power. Not only is the government's focus increasingly on welfare for the well-to-do–in 1986 just $55 billion, or 5.6 percent of the budget, was directed specifically towards the poor–but the private sector views helping the disadvantaged as a steadily decreasing priority. People give, but don't sacrifice; they send checks, but don't get personally involved.

Yet America was built on a very traditional notion of individual and communal responsibility for oneself and one's neighbors. People were in the first instance accountable for their own lives, and responsibility for social problems then moved outward concentrically from the individual to family, church, and community as others were considered to be "their brother's keeper." If this important value slowly eroded as America grew, the nationalization of problems during the New Deal greatly accelerated the process.

In 1921, for instance, a deep recession saw between three million and five million people out of work; businessmen and labor leaders met at a national Unemployment Conference to, in then-Secretary of Commerce Herbert Hoover's words, "mobilize local and private groups to act with a national purpose."[6] Within two weeks 209 local committees had been formed and organizations were housing the unemployed, raising funds for relief efforts, and creating employment bureaus. Similarly, when the Mississippi River flooded in 1927, there was an enormous, concerted relief effort–but it was largely voluntary. A nationwide radio appeal raised $17 million, and 150 "towns of tents" were established for those left homeless. Governments, particularly local ones, were involved, but their efforts were considered to be supplemental, a backup to organized private assistance.

Today this spirit survives in some areas. In 1985 a tornado struck Northwestern Pennsylvania, destroying the towns of Atlantic and Albion. Atlantic and its surrounding farms were rebuilt within two months, largely through the efforts of the local Amish community. However, Albion residents viewed disaster relief more as a federal responsibility. And they waited for government payments and insurance reimbursements before beginning the rebuilding process. In short, "an expanding public sector may have conditioned us to wait for government to solve problems, rather than to take spontaneous civic action," concluded the President's Council on Private Sector Initiatives in 1986.[7] Indeed, some churches will lobby for a new government program before they will offer any assistance themselves.

There are now national unemployment insurance and job-training projects, disaster loans, and federal money to rebuild roads and bridges. Some human suffering is obviously alleviated by such programs, but the price has been high. Government relief programs can be costly and ineffective: the Comprehensive Employment and Training Act, or CETA, spent more than $60 billion before being abandoned by Congress. It was treated as a political pork barrel by municipalities, funding patronage machines controlled by local politicos rather than helping the disadvantaged; just 14 percent of its trainees got unsubsidized private sector jobs. Among CETA's expenditures were $640,000 for education about homosexual lifestyles and $30,000 to build an artificial rock for rock climbers. The program underwrote attendance at a nude sculpture class, dance classes, a homosexual play, and training for a college track meet.[8]

Moreover, big-spending public works projects actually destroy jobs, diverting private resources to less productive, politically inspired projects. For instance, the 1983 Emergency Jobs Bill was supposed to create 600,000 jobs within ninety days of its enactment: the General Accounting Office audited the program and found that it took months before any meaningful number of jobs were created and money went to such well-to-do communities as Hyannis, Massachusetts. In the end just 35,000 jobs, at a cost of $88,571 each, were created. That $3.1 billion invested privately would have yielded far more, permanent positions.

The reflexive turn to government has also diluted the sense of individual responsibility that provides an important motivation for all of life's endeavors. Unemployment insurance, for instance, causes some joblessness by allowing people to pass up work that they would otherwise feel obligated to take.

More fundamentally, these sorts of government programs have loosened communal ties. A community and its various constituent parts–such as family, church, business association, and labor union–can provide a flexible, personalized form of support tailored to meet individual needs. Such efforts require direct involvement in the lives of those being helped. And that has two important advantages: building mutually supporting relationships that can benefit both parties, and accountability to someone who both cares about the needy person and understands his needs and abilities. In contrast, today's welfare system has provided aid without human involvement, leading to long-term dependence on an unfeeling public dole.

Further, the steady advance of the sterile bureaucratic state has actually hindered the fulfillment of the private philanthropic spirit that still exists in many Americans. Voluntarism "long has been a defining characteristic of the United States," observed the President's Council on Private Sector Initiatives, "but as we approach the final decade of the 20th century, that defining characteristic finds itself hedged about with restrictions and barriers."[9] For instance, the Meals on Wheels program began as a private effort to feed needy seniors; its success sparked federal interest in the project. Unfortunately, however, the government effectively took over the program, stifling the personal charitable impulses that gave rise to the program in the first place.[10]

And today, strict restaurant regulations prevent eateries and charities in Los Angeles from using surplus food to feed the homeless. While the finest restaurants in a dozen cities, including New York, Chicago, and Atlanta, donate extra food to local soup kitchens and churches, Los Angeles county officials require, among other things, that leftovers be labeled. The regulations, for the alleged benefit of consumers, are prohibitively expensive to meet. Complains Los Angeles restaurateur Ken Frank, "I wish we could do more. There's a need out there. But it's illegal."[11] And this is not an isolated example.

## ECONOMIC OPPORTUNITY

We are also facing the closing off of economic opportunity for many Americans, especially the poor. As an immigrant nation, the U.S. was built by allowing its people to make the most of their freedom. If poorer families at times suffered enormous hardships, they were usually able to leave a better legacy for their children. And the standard of living of the American working class grew at a staggering rate compared to that in Europe and elsewhere.

However, the emergence of the envious state has closed many of the traditional avenues of economic advancement for the disadvantaged. Influential interest groups now routinely lobby to keep potential competitors off of the economic ladder of opportunity. And government is all too often their willing ally.

For instance, many states tightly restrict access to different occupations, effectively preventing poor people from going into business for themselves. While some states control entry into only a handful of specialized professions, such as medicine and law, others have created elaborate educational and testing requirements for TV repairmen, beauticians, librarians, guide dog trainers, tile layers, well diggers, and a host of other occupations. The right to ply more than 1,000 trades is restricted by government. Even worse, the states have usually delegated to current practitioners, who have an incentive to exclude potential competitors, the right to set standards and judge applicants. The regulations are always justified as protecting consumers, but they often do little more than raise the cost of entering the profession. Concludes Tulane University professor S. David Young: "Occupational regulation has served to limit consumer choice, raise consumer costs, increase practitioner income, limit practitioner mobility, deprive the poor of adequate services, and restrict job opportunities for minorities–all without a demonstrated improvement in quality or safety of the licensed activities."[12]

One example often cited by black economist Walter Williams is taxicabs. In Washington, D.C., entry costs are low; anyone can hack after paying a small permit fee and passing a simple test. However, in New York City a medallion, or the right to drive a cab, costs upwards of $125,000. Not surprisingly, immigrants and minorities are more likely to drive a taxi in Washington than in New York–legally, at least. For the great demand for taxi service in New York's ghettos, which are largely ignored by the licensed cabs, has created a large fleet of illicit "gypsy" taxis. (In fact, there are more unofficial operators than medallion drivers, leading to constant calls for stricter city enforcement to put the underground cabs out of business.)

A similarly restrictive regulatory regime for truckers resulted from pressure by the Teamsters Union and the American Trucking Association. For decades the Interstate

Commerce Commission controlled every aspect of that industry. Some of the regulations, such as requiring trucks to travel empty on return trips, were ludicrous, but they helped enforce the cartel that protected existing firms. The public lost an estimated $15 billion annually through waste and higher prices. And minorities, who have had their entry into the nation's economic life hindered by a legacy of Jim Crow laws, poor education, and racism, suffered, both as consumers and as potential truckers, the most from this unfair system.

For example, in 1979, before the trucking industry was substantially deregulated, St. Louis businessmen Timothy Person sought to fulfill his dream of nearly three decades by becoming the first black cross-country mover. The petition by his family-run Allstates Transworld Van Lines, whose revenues reached $200,000 in a good year, for an ICC national operator's permit was successfully opposed by such industry behemoths as United Van Lines and Allied Van Lines. They complained that he would "adversely" affect their market. His response: "Our forefathers didn't write that we would have free enterprise only so long as a handful of people are guaranteed profits."[13]

Other examples where government has become a tool of economic oppression abound. Labor unions steadfastly support the minimum wage because it sets a wage floor for their members; people without enough education or skills to earn the minimum go without work as a result. Minority youth are placed at particular risk. A 1977 Joint Economic Committee study concluded that "with increases in the Federal minimum wage the teenage unemployment rate relative to adult unemployment usually rises."[14] A similar protectionist measure is the Davis-Bacon Act, which requires that federally funded construction projects must pay the "prevailing wage," usually defined as union scale. The law was passed in 1931 as an express attempt to protect northern construction workers from competition from lower-wage southern blacks; it has the same effect today. Inner-city rehabilitation projects that receive government support, for instance, cannot afford to employ local ghetto youths. And trade protectionism has been used to enrich shareholders, corporate executives, and well-paid industrial workers at the expense of consumers, particularly poor ones.

Today the ethic that government is a tool to be used to hamper or eliminate one's competition pervades the entire economic system. Businesses and unions, professionals and laborers, and most everyone else seems to search continuously for ways to gain these sorts of privileges, as well as traditional pork barrel expenditures, from government.

## FOREIGN INJUSTICE

The U.S. has increasingly subsidized injustice overseas. George Washington, in his much-heralded farewell address, warned the nation against "entangling alliances." In the late-nineteenth century America, despite having broken free from the yoke of a colonial power, initiated its own imperialistic crusade against Spain. This unilateral intervention led to the very "entangling alliances" that Washington had warned of. In World War I, for example, the U.S. joined with democratic Great Britain and France and autocratic Russia in the latest round of centuries of European wars over commerce, territory, and influence. Though Woodrow Wilson pushed for American involvement as part of his grandiose hopes to play peacemaker, the U.S. ended up abetting the selfish imperial designs of Britain and France, laying the groundwork for an even more terrible war three decades later.[15]

World War II yielded a global order in which the United States produced roughly half of the earth's goods and took on the role of international policeman, committed to containing the Soviets around the world. In the early post-war years American power was virtually unrivaled, but as colonies gained independence U.S. influence shrank. Nevertheless, politicians of right and left desperately tried to sustain Pax Americana, irrespective of the cost. They relied on overseas troop deployments, as in Europe, Korea, and Japan; involvement in regional conflicts, such as Korea; intervention in wars that mixed external aggression with internal civil war, such as Vietnam; covert action to overthrow hostile regimes, as in Iran and Chile; and overt support for authoritarian but pro-Western leaders, as in the Philippines, Zaire, Korea, Iran, and Nicaragua, to name but a few.

This active internationalist policy is subject to a number of practical criticisms, including the fact that America's prosperous and populous allies spend substantially less on their defense than does the U.S. But a deeper, moral flaw is consistent American support for tyrannical regimes that routinely violate the most important principles this nation supposedly stands for.

Since the end of World War II the U.S. has provided close to $400 billion in grants and loans to foreign nations. While some of that money has supported democratic states, much of American aid has propped up venal autocrats who oppressed their own people. Right-wing favorites who have since been deposed by their own people include Iran's Shah Pahlavi, the Philippines' Ferdinand Marcos, and Nicaragua's Anastasio Somoza; in fact, the U.S. created the National Guard that kept the Somoza dynasty in power for decades.[16] Other American-aided clients, like Mobuto Sese Seko of Zaire and Augusto Pinochet of Chile, are still hanging on. Foreign assistance has also flowed regularly to dictatorships on the left. The Nicaraguan Sandinistas received $105 million before American policy changed; Mozambique, Angola, Hungary, Romania, and Tanzania are a few of the other Marxist states that have profited from American generosity.

Allying this nation with thuggish foreign regimes may be justified when absolutely necessary to achieve what are believed to be higher goals–U.S. cooperation with Stalin's Soviet Union to defeat Hitler's Germany in World War II may be an example–but such objectives should be morally compelling. And in those cases policymakers should recognize the conflict and carefully balance the competing interests. Today, in contrast, the U.S. promiscuously attempts to buy common political influence around the world with what are thinly disguised bribes: in return for underwriting brutal political repression and statist economic policies, the State Department ensures that the American ambassador can get in to see local officials. Such access may be convenient, but it does not justify the harm U.S. aid often does to Third World peoples.

Moreover, allowing run-of-the-mill power politics to override basic moral values involving human freedom and dignity has had a corrosive impact on our own system. First, officials who regularly disregard such principles in their international dealings are less likely to treat them seriously in domestic politics. Second, unsavory policies often cannot be conducted except through reprehensible means: government in secret, restrictions on liberty, and the like have flowed naturally from a foreign policy that has lost its moral bearings. In short, U.S. foreign policy generally fails to promote the sort of just international order that would be consistent with Biblical principles.

## MORAL VALUES

Perhaps most fundamental of all, we are seeing a breakdown in moral standards. That America faces a serious deterioration in the moral and spiritual values which underly the republic has become a conservative cliche'. But that doesn't make the crisis any less real. The United States was formed only because the people shared a common ethical outlook, based generally on Judeo-Christian precepts. Individuals were responsible for their own lives; the community was expected to take an active role in preempting and solving social problems. Society was built upon a family structure that took very seriously the respective responsibilities of its members. Values such as honesty and responsibility helped make capitalism work well; a general belief in chastity and monogamy promoted a stable, sustainable social structure. People hoped to advance economically, particularly to help their children live a better life, but they realized that there were other important values–involving their families, communities, and God–upon which their lives had to be based.

While the government's potential positive influence over basic morality is limited, the public sector has increasingly aided and abetted the destruction of these values. For instance, the political process has become a system of legalized theft, with personal gain rather than public interest becoming the standard for government action. Many political leaders provide examples that should not be followed, exhibiting the worst rather than the best ethical principles.

The state has also too often discouraged rather than encouraged individual and communal efforts to help those who are less fortunate. A faceless welfare system has created incentives for family breakup and teen pregnancy. The notion of basic values has disappeared from classrooms across America. If envy has become the highest political value for many, greed has naturally become the chief motivation in their private lifes.

The result is that the nation is suffering from an ethical crisis. Commentators have endlessly jeered at the celebrated instances of avarice on Wall Street, exemplified by Ivan Boesky and the insider trading scandal. But the values of Wall Street are largely the values of Main Street. The stakes may be higher, but the principles are the same.

For the lack of honesty transcends misappropriating private information for gain, like Boesky did. The same attitude motivates the stockroom employee to pilfer from his company and a customer to shoplift–practices that are uncomfortably common. Businessmen who turn to the courts or Congress to escape contracts that they voluntarily signed are as venal as any insider trader.

This moral deterioration is also reflected by the continuing decline in community support for the disadvantaged. Americans give an average of two percent of their income to charity. Two cents out of every dollar earned in an enormously wealthy society in the face of enormous unmet needs of homelessness, poverty, sickness, and hunger. The potential comparisons are endless: philanthropic support compared to spending on dog food, football tickets, or movie rentals. Though individual Americans still respond vigorously to well-publicized cases of individual need, the concerted communal response is disappointing.

Finally, there is the issue of sexual morality. Pornography is available in department stores; manufacturers of jeans, perfume, and underwear advertise sensuality to sell their products. Television provides a constant stream of programs that implicitly endorse promiscuity, adultery, and homosexuality. A Louis Harris & Associates study of the 1987-88 TV season estimates that 65,000 sexual references are broadcast during prime time every year.

Yet these disturbing phenomena merely reflect the deeper sickness of society. One out of five fourteen-year-olds has had sex; nearly half of all sixteen-year-olds are sexually active. This breakdown in traditional mores has been particularly pervasive in inner-city black communities, where more than half of all babies are born out of wedlock. A Johns Hopkins University study found that the average age when sexually active inner-city Baltimore youth first had sex was fourteen for girls and twelve for boys. Children are having children, locking themselves into poverty; one generation after another of single-parent households is forced to subsist on welfare; and there are few responsible fathers to act as male role models for young men who grow up in a culture virtually devoid of morals. Poverty, crime, hopelessness, and despair result.

And white, middle-class society, if not collapsing in quite such dramatic fashion, is also paying a price for its lack of godly values. Pregnancies among white teens have increased by 800 percent since 1940. There are half as many divorces as marriages every year; nearly one-fifth of families with children are headed by a single female. Even those families that escape official separation are being pulled apart by the related forces of careerism and materialism. Parents make their jobs into an idol, placing them before God, their spouses, and their kids; teenagers, with no transcendent values to guide their lives, look for satisfaction in drugs, sex, and possessions.

And the values of America's young elite appear to continue to grow more worldly. The 1987 survey by the American Council on Eucation and the Higher Education Research Institute at UCLA found that a record high three-fourths of college freshmen believed that it is either "essential" or "very important" to be "very well off financially." Only 39 percent felt the same way about developing "a philosophy of life." Interest in helping others in need and promoting racial understanding also continued to slide.

Recognition of the seriousness of the deterioration of American morals has led to increased calls from across the political spectrum for teaching values in school, using sex education classes to encourage students to say "no," and creating ethics courses at business schools. However, such measures are at best attempts to use a Band-Aid to stop a hemorrhage: abstract education cannot obscure the reality of an immoral world. In any case, there is no unanimity on what values should be promoted, nor any transcendent basis, other than religion, upon which to develop new ethical codes. Legislators may demand new laws, but they have yet to provide any real answers.

## IS THERE ANY HOPE?

In surveying the seemingly endless and endemic problems faced by our nation, it would be easy for a Christian to give up, retreating from the world into personal and church activities. But it is precisely in such an atmosphere that the influence of believers is most needed.

Moreover, there are positive trends that could be exploited by Christians committed to applying Biblical principles to politics. Indeed, despite all of its problems, the American system remains remarkably resilient. Economically, the nation continues to advance, despite budget and trade deficits, a stock market crash, and a collapsing dollar. December 1987 marked the sixty-first straight month in which jobs were created–for a total of fifteen million since 1983. In early 1988 unemployment fell to 5.4 percent, the lowest rate in a decade.

Moreover, America, despite its frequent support for repressive foreign regimes, remains a beacon of freedom for millions of political refugees and economically disadvantaged around the world. Debates over issues such as support for the Nicaraguan contras have increasingly taken on a distinctly moral tone by both sides. And if direct U.S. influence abroad is waning, democracy and civil liberties continue to advance. For instance, the human rights group Freedom House estimated that in 1987 the proportion of the world's population that is free finally passed the proportion that was not–for the first time since the group developed its rating system in 1973.

As for moral rectitude, the public has demonstrated some stirrings of its long-buried conscience. The scandals on Wall Street generated attention on the question of ethics, even if they did not provide any answers. Charitable giving is increasing, however slowly. And the proportion of the population that believes premarital sex is wrong is increasing, rising from 39 percent in 1985 to 46 percent in 1987.

Leaders of the black community have begun to focus on self-help measures, including moral education involving teens. A pilot school program designed to teach young people to say no to sex has had surprisingly positive results: the number of kids believing that premarital sex was OK fell from 64 percent to 35 percent. Further, community pressure has led a number of stores, like the Seven-Elevens owned by the Southland Corporation, to stop selling soft-core magazines like *Penthouse* and *Playboy*. And a survey by the Hartford Seminary's Center for Social and Religious Research found that an increasing proportion of so-called baby-boomers are regularly attending worship services.

But these nascent trends, these ever-so-slight movements toward a better America, need to be nurtured. However, Christians should not expect traditional politicians and ideologies to do the job. Not only is government's influence over personal morality quite limited, but incumbent officeholders have little incentive to reform the very system that has so benefited them. Congress is primarily interested in buying votes for the next election. The 1988 presidential candidates were almost as sensitive to the slightest murmuring by the smallest interest group; envy rather than moral leadership was the leading campaign theme for most of the contenders. And it is still considered improper in polite establishment circles to discuss the relationship of traditional morality to problems like AIDS.

Unless they are prepared to abdicate their role as the salt of the earth, Christians cannot use the failures of the current system, of both liberal statism and conservative welfarism, as an excuse to stand aloof from the political process. Instead, they must develop a uniquely Christian perspective, one that focuses on principles rather than specific issues, a new paradigm for analyzing problems and developing solutions.

# THREE

# The Need For
# a New Political Paradigm

We live in a fallen world. And this nation, whether especially blessed of God or not, is no exception. Even a society as affluent as America's suffers from pockets of grinding poverty and hunger. Yet the majority of people seem more interested in purchasing the latest electronic gadget than in assisting those in need. Compassion has become chic, but only so long as it involves a rock concert or someone else's money and time.

The pervasive social diseases of envy and greed have generated a destructive epidemic of crime–from common street muggings to white-collar scams to political corruption. Indeed, the nation's capital combines all three in prodigious proportions. Murders were at a record high in 1987, a majority of them tied to the thriving drug trade; in the same year residents of fashionable Georgetown lined up to loot a malfunctioning automatic teller machine, many of them later boasting of their success to local reporters. And Washington, D.C., is the home of 20,000 registered lobbyists, 3,700 associations, and 3,300 political action committees, most of which are dedicated to using Congress to increase their own wealth or that of their clients, at the expense of the public.

War rages in foreign lands, in many cases fueled by U.S. as well as Soviet arms and money. In an attempt to meet the demands of international politics and finance, this nation often enriches the foreign elites who crush the poorest of the poor. Even the leader of the most oppressive of foreign regimes, Mikhail Gorbachev of the Soviet Union, is feted in Washington when doing so is believed to enhance a President's falling political popularity.

Personal morals are now treated by most people as quaintly antique. A presidential candidate can, with no apparent shame or remorse other than over the damage done to his campaign, engage in flagrant adultery. As male homosexuals die daily from AIDS, gay activists insist that morality be left out of the discussion: they indignantly demand increased federal funding of medical research, as if the public has a responsibility to find a way to make promiscuity safe again. At the same time, compassion often seems in short supply when Americans come face-to-face with the victims of AIDS in work or school. And so it goes.

In such a world, what is the answer?

At base, there is no human solution. Man is not perfectible through human means. No new ideology, lifestyle, program, or technology can reverse the flaws that directly grow out of his sin nature. Wrote the Apostle Paul to the Roman church: "I know that nothing good lives in me, that is, in my sinful nature. For I have the desire to do what is good, but I cannot carry it out. For what I do is not the good I want to do; no, the evil I do not want to do–this I keep on doing. Now if I do what I do not want to do, it is no longer I who do it, but it is sin living in me that does it" (Romans 7: 18-20).

Left to ourselves, then, we would have no hope. But when Paul asks "Who will rescue me from this body of death?," he has the answer–"Thanks be to God–through Jesus Christ our Lord!" (Romans 7: 24, 25). Because of Jesus' redemptive role, "there is now no condemnation for those who are in Christ Jesus because through Christ Jesus the law of the Spirit of life" sets us "free from the law of sin and death" (Romans 8:1-2). In short, Christian faith, not political activism or anything else, is the way to salvation: The Lordship of Jesus Christ over every person is the one grand solution to the earth's ills.

But we don't live in a world in which everyone is a believer. Nor are we likely to do so anytime soon. There are, of course, those who believe that the end times are upon us and that Jesus will soon establish His direct, 1,000 year reign. But eschatological theories cannot save Christians from struggling with the complexities of life today. Jesus said that we would not know the time of history's fulfillment, and His followers have spent nearly 2,000 years awaiting His return. We must act on the assumption that the United States and the other 160-odd nations around the world will exist next month and next year.

In a such a world believers have an obligation, first, to spread the gospel."Go and make disciples of all nations, baptizing them in the name of the Father and of the Son and of the Holy Spirit, and teaching them to obey everything I have commanded you," Christ told the eleven before leaving them for the last time (Matthew 28:19, 20). The most important, most fundamental message of the Bible–under both the Old and New Covenants–is that people need to build a right relationship with God. All else, including doing "good" works, pales incomparison.

Nevertheless, Christians have a clear civic obligation. "Submit yourselves for the Lord's sake to every authority instituted among men," wrote the Apostle Peter, "for it is God's will that by doing good you should silence the ignorant talk of foolish men" (1 Peter 2:13, 15). Peter went further, directing believers to "honor the king," while Paul instructed the members of the Roman church to "give everyone what you owe him," including taxes, revenue, respect,and honor (1 Peter 2:17; Rom. 13:7).

Submission implies active involvement to bring Christian principles to bear on the institution being obeyed. Christ's disciples are, of course, directed to be the "salt of the earth," and nowhere is the state exempted from that principle. Moreover, it is obvious that Peter and Paul both envisioned a government operating in a way consonant with God's purposes. Peter exhorted Christians to do good in submitting to authority, while Paul stated that the ruler "is God's servant to do you good" (Romans 13:4).

Yet history has made painfully apparent the fact that man's governing institutions have almost always strayed from God's path, often in hideous ways. This was true even of ancient Israel. The high priest Aaron constructed the golden calf, King Saul disobeyed God on numerous occasions, losing his throne as a result, and King Solomon eventually worshiped Baal and other false gods. Governments that made no pretense of following God have departed even further from His principles. "The kings of the earth take their stand and the rulers-gather together against the Lord and against his Anointed One," wrote King David (Psalm 2:2). In fact, if this century has taught mankind anything, it is the failure of government "as an agency of benevolence," writes historian Paul Johnson:

The state had proved itself an insatiable spender, an unrivalled waster. Indeed, in the twentieth century it had also proved itself the great killer of all time. By the 1980s, state action had been responsible for the violent or unnatural deaths of over 100 million people, more perhaps than it had hitherto succeeded in destroying during the whole of human history up to 1900. Its inhuman malevolence had more than kept pace with its growing size and expanding means.[1]

Thus, simply given government's potential for doing evil–primarily because of the opportunity that a powerful coercive institution presents to sinful men who are adept at seizing control of human organizations–Christians must get involved in politics. One aspect of their role is obvious: opposing what couldbe termed the satanic state under a Hitler, Stalin, or a Mao which persecutes the church, murders its people, and wages war on its neighbors. Yet there is nothing uniquely Christian in such a perspective. The gospel message provides a transcendent basis for preserving individual dignity and freedom, but all "enlightened" humanistic philosophies, however shaky their moral foundations, reject the satanic state as well.

The Christian's task is not so clear in the democratic United States. Where the church itself is under attack, whether due to local zoning regulations or state tort law or federal tax regulations, believers should rise to its defense. But being the "salt of the earth" requires Christians to evidence a broader perspective, a commitment to infuse government, as well as other human institutions, with Biblical principles and not just to prevent the state from discriminating against the church. How can one transmit those values to publicinstitutions?

At one level Christians who serve in government can exhibit "the fruit of the Spirit," which, explained Paul to the Galatian church, "is love, joy, peace, patience, kindness, goodness, faithfulness, gentleness and self-control" (Galatians 5: 22, 23). If the average citizen might not fully appreciate a joyful civil servant, he certainly would like to see the average clerk at the Department of Motor Vehicles exhibit patience. However, this sort of private infusion of Christian values into government agencies does not affect their public purpose. It may be good that the policeman who arrests someone for smoking marijuana exhibit restraint and that the Small Business Administration official arranging a federal loan show faithfulness, but the larger question is whether they should be doing what they are doing. That is, are their underlying public roles justified? It is here that the construction of a Christian political vision becomes more difficult.

Indeed, it is fair to ask if a Biblical political view is really necessary. There are, after all, a number of dynamic visions of social change now competing in the political marketplace, all of which claim to possess the answer to the world's problems. And many of them have sought to at least accommodate, if not subsume, religious concerns.

There is, for instance, the Communist alternative. No other human philosophy has had so great an impact on so many people in so short a time. But communism is no option for a Christian. Liberation theology, which borrows from Marxist thought and class analysis, nevertheless has distinctive theological roots and will be discussed in Chapter 6. As an unalloyed political philosophy, communism is incompatible with Christianity for three basic reasons.

First, Marx was an atheist, and Communist governments from the Soviet Union to China to Romania have done their best to destroy the church and suppress belief. If some of those nations now seem prepared to make an accommodation with religion, it is only because their systems are failing and Christianity has refused to die. In fact, Cuba's Fidel Castro has gone to extraordinary lengths in recent years to relate his philosophy to that of Christianity, but he wants to take religion on his terms: a revolutionary subsidiary of communism, a theological adjunct that buttresses rather than challenges a philosophy that is unshakably both secular and materialist. Christ, rather than Castro, as Lord has no place in such a system.[2]

Indeed, the explicit materialistic roots of communism place it more directly in conflict with Christianity's spiritual basis than does capitalism, despite the latter's reputation for greedy consumerism. Capitalism may give freer rein to worldly desires, but it does not impose that goal upon those committed to spiritual concerns. In contrast, communism attempts to forcibly set material satisfaction, for the collective if not the individual, as the highest human good. The latter system does not eliminate man's desire to own things—communism may fail to satisfy those demands, but they remain as powerful as ever in men who remain as sinful as ever. The conspicuous consumption of the nomenklatura, or ruling class, in Communist societies demonstrates the universality of consumerism.

For instance, Alexandra Costa was the wife of a Soviet diplomat in the U.S. when she defected. She later said that it was not for material goods that she chose to live in America: she never had to wear Russian-made clothes or do without Western conveniences. And under glasnost, Soviet publications are beginning to explore the existence of consumer privilege in the supposedly classless society. In January 1986 the Soviet cultural newspaper *Sovetskaya Kultura* published an article that acknowledged: "Opportunies for the timely development of one's abilities are still dependent to a large extent on one's geographical location and on the social and economic standing of one's parents."[3]

Second, communism has inevitably given rise to the Gulag-state. Individuals who are precious in God's eyes are considered to be mere cogs in a system that exists solely to glorify the collective. Whether Marx and Engels intended the horrors that their philosophy unleashed is irrelevant. For the consequences have flowed naturally from an ideology, especially with its Leninist gloss, that places no value on individual existence and no restraints on collective action. A system devoted to materialism and vesting near-absolute power in the few over-the-many can only lead to disaster, given man's sinful nature.

That mass murder and repression are not aberrant examples of communism is evident from the uniform experience from lands that have either embraced or been forced to accept it. By sheer numbers, at least, Stalin and Mao rank as the two greatest killers of all time; Kampuchea's Pol Pot wins the grisly contest in terms of percentage of population murdered. What were successively believed to be the new utopias–the future that worked, so to speak–the Soviet Union, China, Cambodia, Vietnam, Cuba, and now Nicaragua–have been successively exposed as havens for human villainy.

Third, the system is simply a failure. Though die-hard adherents of Marxist thought remain, they are concentrated more in Western universities than in the nations that officially exalt his name. Comparisons between the U.S. and the U.S.S.R. may seem trite, but there is no problem, whether poverty, consumerism, or imperialism, that would solved by moving toward communism. Under Glasnost the Soviet media are now full of stories about a system in which life expectancy is falling, homelessness is rife, the average one-earner family with a child is below the Soviet poverty line, four out of every five retirees are poor, and soon. "Destitution is a perennial feature of our life," stated the magazine Ogonek in July 1986.[4]

Not surprisingly, then, virtually every Communist nation, with the notable exception of Cuba, is moving away from Marxist doctrine. China, Vietnam, Poland, Hungary, and even the Soviet Union have begun to open up their economies; the latter three nations have even begun to experiment with political reforms. As an ideology of hope, communism is dead.

Another overarching political philosophy, one which is closely linked to communism despite their theoretical opposition to each other, is fascism. This ideology once captivated the nations of Germany, Italy, and, to some extent, Spain, and gained the respectful attention of such Western democrats as Winston Churchill. Today the purest form of fascism is primarily a fringe force, discredited by Adolf Hitler's Holocaust and global war. Nevertheless, variants survive in a number of nations, emphasizing nationalism, racism, economic populism, and xenophobia.

If such a collection of views would appear to hold no attraction for the average believer today, there are a number of clerics and avowed Christians who have tried and still try to reconcile neo-fascist ideology with Christian theology. "At first glance," writes historian Robert Ericksen, one would think "that pastors might be too sensitive to spiritual values to give [Hitler] support. But such was not the case."[5] Orthodox Lutheran theologian Paul Althaus, for instance, looked to National Socialism to wipe away the moral decay evident under the Weimar Republic. "We may express our thanks to God and ourjoyful preparedness when we see a state which after a time of depletion and paralysis has broken through to a new knowledge of sovereign authority, of service for the life of the Volk," he wrote; "we Christians know ourselves bound by God's will to the promotion of National Socialism."[6]

Though many German evangelicals, who took Biblical principles and Christian discipleship more seriously than the mainline denominations, opposed Nazism, their stance was not unanimous, and it weakened over time. An evangelical bishop for Hassau-Hessen, Dr. Dietrich, even circulated a letter endorsing Hitler's June 1934 purge, which killed religious opposition figures as well aspolitical opponents. Only the so-called Confessing Church publicly rejected Nazi doctrines.

And there are now far-right groups in America, such as the Christian Identity movement, that have constructed a racist strain of Christianity to justify their white-supremacy theories. It is hard to imagine how they could be genuine Christians, that is, followers of the Christ whose ministry is detailed in the Gospels, but they cite the same Bible. Similarly skewed are South African churches which support apartheid–the Nederduitse Hervormde Kerk, for instance, explicitly bars nonwhite members and has become the unofficial spiritual guardian for the ultra-right Conservative Party. (In contrast, the Dutch Reformed Church, long an establishment apologist for apartheid, has moved toward true Biblical Christianity, declaring racial segregation to be wrong and backing open church membership.) Lastly, there is a variety of right-wing movements, like that of Le Pen in France, which are more generally nationalistic and xenophobic than racist.

That totalitarian fascism is inconsistent with Christianity should be obvious from the German experience. Like communism, Nazism was fundamentally atheistic: Hitler tolerated the churches only because most clerics either supported him or groveled before him. He eventually advanced a Nazified theology that bore little relation to the Christianity of the Bible, and he vowed to solve the "religion problem" after the war. As the notorious Nazi "people's court" judge Roland Freisler told Count Moltke, a Catholic member of the July 1944 conspirators against Hitler, "Christianity and we Nazis have onething in common and one only: we claim the whole man."[7]

Beyond this inherent conflict is the fact that fascism, like communism, submerges the individual to the collective, sets the material and nationalistic betterment of the mass as the highest value, and places no constraints on the power of the state. The natural results were racial slaughter and imperialistic war.

The modern, more limited variants of fascism–the ultra-right groups in the U.S. and South Africa, for instance–are advocating a philosophy that may be less expansive and vile than traditional fascism, but which is no less inconsistent with Biblical values. Their theology is not part of the Bible; the Christian Identity movement, which is an amalgam of several different white-power groups, holds that American whites are part of the lost tribes of Israel and that blacks are "pre-

Adamic" peoples. Indeed, the tension between Christianity and white racism is too great for some. There is, for instance, a Church of the Creator, a new white supremicist organization that describes itself as the "first and only Racial Religion." The Church of the Creator has developed what it terms The White Man's Bible which "exposes the Judeo-Christian hoax."[8]

Even if the segregationist white South African churches do not depart from traditional Biblical doctrines, they have nevertheless entirely missed the pointof the gospel message. Christ came to bring the Good News to all men–a category that surely includes blacks. And when Paul enumerated the fruit of the Spirit, he did not limit their application to whites (or coloreds, who fall in the middle of apartheid's racial hierarchy). While not theologically based, the sort of conservative, anti-immigrant nationalism that is demonstrating some electoral success in nations like France suffers from a similar flaw: it degrades the dignity of individuals, valued by God, because of their skin color or nationality. These movements do not advocate the overarching, statist philosophies that once consumed Germany and Italy, but they offer no option for Christians.

Dramatically opposed to the statist philosophies of communism and fascism is modern libertarianism, an outgrowth of the classical liberal philosophy that helped sweep aside the traditional and monarchical systems from Europe.[9] However much libertarianism differs from the other two ideologies in their specifics, it also offers a comprehensive vision or worldview.

The libertarian philosophy is coherent even if there is some disagreementover the particulars. The movement includes anarchists and "mini-staters"; views on foreign policy range from isolationist to mildly interventionist. Both abortion and capital punishment generate heated division and debate. Nevertheless, the fundamentals remain undisputed: individuals have a virtually absolute right to control their own lives, the collective good is primarily advanced by giving free rein to personal initiative, and the state is to be as small and unobtrusive as possible.

Though some individual libertarian activists have tended to treat their ideology as a whole-life philosophy, classical liberalism differs sharply from communism and fascism by its failure to claim the souls of men. The issue is primarily man's relationship to the state, not to God or one's fellowman. The government most certainly does not take the place of God. In this way libertarianism avoids one of the most significant potential conflicts with Christianity.

Moreover, by its "fruit," classical liberalism is consistent with Biblical values in a way that the totalitarian systems are not. Modern Western societies have had their share of abuses, ranging from European colonialism to the World War II camps for Japanese-Americans, but they were neither the logical nor inevitable result of that philosophic tradition, as were Hitler's death camps a consequence of Nazism. Indeed, these sorts of violations of basic human rights were actually inconsistent with the West's classical liberal heritage.

In fact, in its devotion to individual rights, classical liberalism broadly mirrors the high value in which God holds every person. People are created, called to serve, and judged by God as individuals; libertarianism, in contrast to communism and fascism, also treats people as separate persons with independent value. Similarly, the concern of classical liberal philosophers with the danger of overweening state power matches biblical warnings about royal misbehavior. While libertarians usually do not explicitly talk of sin, they advocate a political system designed to limit the harm that can be caused by evil, fallen men.

Yet classical liberalism does not itself reflect a Christian political view. Some strains of libertarian thought trend toward anarchism, which recognizes no legitimate role for government.[10] As will be discussed in chapter 4, however, the state is ordained of God to regulate relations between sinful man. In this way pure anarchism conflicts with Biblical principles.

However, theScripturally mandated functions of government–largely to promote justice and protect individuals from domestic and foreign aggression–are very limited. Thus, the "small government" libertarianism that now permeates the intellectual arena is fully consistent with Christianity.

Classical liberalism also lacks a sense of concern over communal responsibilities and moral values, even though a laissez-faire state requires a set of shared principles, such as honesty and charity, to operate smoothly.[11] Libertarianism does not actually oppose such values, nor is the state necessarily able to promote them, but there is a value-free sterility to classical liberalism that makes it insufficient to act as a Christian worldview.[12]

Finally, classical liberalism has arisen out of the eighteenth-century Enlightenment; its philosophical roots lie in what is a fundamentally humanist school of thought. Says leading free market economist Milton Friedman, "We take freedom of the individual or perhaps the family as our ultimate goal in judging social arrangements."[13] This sort of freedom is an important value for believers, but it is not the highest Biblical principle. That does not mean that the libertarian ideology results in anti-Christian policies, of course, but, writes Brian Griffiths, dean of the City University Business School in London, "from a Christian point of view it is important to recognise that all the major intellectual defences of capitalism as an economic system have been conducted within the context of a thoroughly secular philosophy."[14] Christians need to base their political vision first in God and His purpose, not nature and natural law.

This century has seen the rise of welfare state liberalism, an ideological mutation of classical liberalism, which dominates today's system despite the presidency of Ronald Reagan. This philosophy, like libertarianism, does not claim the whole man, nor has it caused the large-scale human holocausts thatmake fascism and communism inimical to Christians.

Nevertheless, modern liberalism is exhausted, a movement that offers few solutions for the many serious problems that face the nation today. It, like classical liberalism, is a fundamentally humanist philosophy, one which is based on the presumed goodness of individuals. Though it pays more attention than libertarianism to a citizen's communal responsibilities to his neighbors,welfare state liberalism has virtually discarded the notion of individual duty in favor of coercive public action. Modern liberalism also often emphasizes collective blame in matters such as crime, which in its extreme conflicts with the Scriptural standards of individual responsibility.

Liberalism has played an important role in raising the issue of compassion and care for the neediest in society, but, as was discussed in Chapter Two, it has created a governmental system which is wasteful, often ineffective, and frequently counterproductive. Indeed, a transfer system intended to help the poor has been twisted into an entitlement system for the the politically well-connected. In this way welfare state liberalism has often allowed interest groups to use humane, even godly, rhetoric as a cover for oppressing the poor and disadvantaged.

Further, today's liberalism has no moral component, no answer to social decline and the decay in basic values. The issue is not so much whether there is a political solution to the problem of personal ethics–a Christian who looks to the state to foster a moral revival has lost sight of God's role–but whether one recognizes the issue and reviews the relationship between public decisions and private values. In contrast, many of the most vocal liberal interest groups are dedicated to pre-venting morality from even being discussed in the public arena. Consider the secularization of the schools, for instance, where religion has been essentially eliminated from textbooks, and the way gay-rights activists and many Democratic politi-cians have treated the AIDS epidemic, literally shouting down anyone who mentions the relationship between moral behav-ior and the likelihood of infection.

This does not mean that a Christian cannot hold liberal views–liberalism has become the ideology of choice of the heirarchies of the major Protestant denominations, of course–just as there is nothing to prevent him from sharing libertarian beliefs. But he must be more than a liberal.

Traditional conservatism faces a weariness similar to that of liberalism. In theory it does not conflict with Christianity; indeed, conservatives probably cite, even venerate tradition and Judeo-Christian values more than anyone else. Yet in prac-tice the movement suffers from many of the infirmities of lib-eralism.[14] Most notably, its political leadership, if not its intel-lectuals, are as committed to the transfer society and the politics of envy as is the left. For there are no greater defenders of pork barrel politics than senior Republican legislators.

Moreover, the traditional conservative movement has shown some hard edges that should concern any Christian. There has, for example, often been a sense of disinterest in fun-damental issues of justice such as racial discrimination, civil liberties, and poverty. Conservatives may, in fact, have been more right than liberals on the specifics of many of these issues, but conservative involvement in such politic debates has often not even been generally informed by a true Biblical vision. Moreover, in the international sphere the right has been more willing than the left to ignore moral concerns and human rights in the pursuit of power politics. Whether the practice of Realpolitik can be made consistent with Christian ethics is a difficult issue, since some compromise seems necessary in a violent and unprincipled global system in which a nation's survival may be at stake. But a Biblical worldview certainly requires that moral issues be raised and balanced against whatever other interests may be at stake.

Moreover, despite the traditional conservative emphasis on values, many of the leading proponents of Judeo-Christian moral standards have fallen short in a very public way. The Reagan administration, for instance, has spawned a legion of influence-peddlers, seeking to turn brief periods of public service into private riches. Of course, Washington has long hosted lobbyists on both the right and left, but the newest wave of "public affairs consultants," as First Family Friend turned lobbyist Michael Deaver once termed himself, have exhibited greater crassness and hypocrisy.

Indeed, Deaver, one of Reagan's most intimate aides, was convicted of perjury for lying to a congressional committee over his lobbying activities. But Deaver's moral failings exceeded his legal culpability: he picked up some $4 million in fees in his first year, including $250,000 to make one phone call to the Secretary of Transportation to try to protect TWA's management from a takeover bid. Before he was ruined from bad publicity, the London PR firm Saatchi and Saatchi reportedly offered him $18 million for his business, roughly a million dollars for every year he had known Reagan. Deaver's conviction did not stop him from cashing in with a book that portrayed him as a vainglorious aide far more interested in the trappings of power than in policy. Yet never once did President Reagan criticize the behavior of Deaver or other past appointees who exemplified the worst of the moral laxity routinely condemned by conservatives.

As the Reagan administration entered its final year the conservative coalition that he had helped bring to power began to unravel. Though Reagan's limited-government, socially-conservative philosophy was broad enough to tie together libertarians primarily committed to a free market, New Right activists with a greater focus on social issues, and traditionalists who were dedicated to international containment and anti-communism, these strands were badly frayed as his term in office neared its end.

This fracturing of the conservative coalition has spawned

conservatism." His program is not explicitly Biblically based, many of his specific policy proposals are flawed, and he places undue confidence in government action to restore values in a population that has lost them; but his work represents an important attempt to refine a traditional political philosophy to account for "cultural" values, that is, the fundamental principles that individuals live by. Indeed, it is not Weyrich's specific legislative agenda but his mode of analysis, with its emphasis on values, that is most important. For this new conservative thinking highlights the importance of compassion and humane treatment of labor, along with the problem of Yuppie values; though it advocates a larger government role than approved by traditional conservatives, it nevertheless does not seek to have the state swallow the individual, as do fascism and communism.

Perhaps most important of all, Weyrich, a Catholic, understands the importance of Biblical values in the development and maintenance of a just and prosperous society. His recent manifesto states: "There is a necessary, unbreakable, and causal relationship between traditional Western, Judeo-Christian values, definitions of right and wrong, ways of thinking and ways of living–the parameters of Western culture–and the secular success of Western societies: their prosperity, their liberties, and the opportunities they offer their citizens to lead fulfilling, rewarding lives. If the former are abandoned, the latter will be lost."[15] Cultural conservatism does not represent a Christian view, but it has introduced a value-laden analysis into the political debate. And that critique can help direct Christians in developing their own unique public perspective.

Another ideological grouping which has coexisted with both liberalism and conservatism is populism. This philosophy, however it is defined, offers little in the way of Biblical values. For though the specific program offered by populists varies greatly depending upon whether they happen to be southern farmers, midwestern small businessman, or blue-collar workers, the movement generally sees government as a means of redressing various popular resentments–economic, social, and racial. In practice, issues such as justice and compassion are usually submerged beneath an enraged demand for "getting mine."

Populism could be framed in a way that would make it consistent with a Christian worldview–the confrontation with perceived sources of oppression, for instance, is a consistent Biblical theme. But in practice, populism has proved to be a philosophy susceptible to demagoguery and unconcerned with justice for disfavored groups. As a result, believers should look elsewhere for Biblical principles.

There are other political philosophies as well, but they tend to fall within the interstices of those already mentioned. The New Left, democratic socialism, and Tory conservatism, for instance, all incorporate their own unique package of issues, but none provides a uniquely Christian perspective on public policy. They may or may not be consistent with Biblical values, but a Christian needs to move beyond all of them in developing his own worldview.

We live in a fallen world, and there is no answer other than personal redemption through Jesus Christ. All human institutions, including government, have been corrupted by man's fall. However, Christians cannot stand aloof from politics: quite simply, the stakes are too great. Christians are to be the salt of the earth, a light on the hill, and nowhere is a believer's influence more important than in moderating the behavior of the coercive institution that has increasingly been used for evil purposes.

A genuine Christian perspective is not reflected by any major existing ideology. Some philosophies, such as communism and fascism, are almost completely inconsistent with Biblical values: they claim the allegiance of the whole person and encourage sinful men to commit the most barbaric crimes against God and man. Other ideologies, such as classical liberalism, which helped give birth to the American republic, and the welfare state liberal/conservative amalgam which represents America's governing consensus today, are variously consistent with Christian ethics–which involves a unique way of looking at man's relationship to God and society rather than a detailed policy agenda. But these philosophies are an inadequate base for a Christian's involvement in politics, resting as they do upon secular premises and ignoring Scriptural principles.

Therefore, there is a need for a new Biblical political paradigm. The effort to develop one is not new, of course, for over the years there have been almost as many religious views of politics as there have been Christian sects. But centuries of often tedious debate have made the task no less urgent today. And the place to start is with a Christian's source of authority, the Bible.

# Biblical Principles:
# The Role of Government

*T*he political realm is part of the creation and as such is subject to God's rule."The earth is the Lord's, and everything in it, the world, and all who live in it," wrote David (Psalm 24:1; see also Psalm 97:9 and Psalm 99:2). Kings are to serve him "with fear" (Psalm 2:11) Ultimately all earthly princes will recognize God's authority, for God "breaks the spirit of rulers; he is feared by the kings of the earth" (Psalm 76:12). Indeed, "all the kings of the earth will revere" God's glory (Psalm 102:15)

Similarly, Paul instructed the church in Colosse that Christ "is the image of the invisible God, the firstborn over all creation. For by him all things were created: things in heaven and on earth, visible and invisible, whether thrones or powers or rulers or authorities" (Colossians 1:15-16). Citing the Psalms, Paul wrote that Christ "has put everything under his feet" (1 Corinthians 15:27; see also Hebrews 2:8). And to the Philippian Church Paul explained that "God exalted him /Christ/ to the highest place and gave him the name that is above every name, that at the name of Jesus every knee should bow, in heaven and on earth and under the earth" (Philippians 2:9-10).

As an institution, government is ordained by God and is to be based on his principles. Wrote the prophet Isaiah, "For to us a child is born, to us a son is given, and the government will be on his shoulders" (Isaiah 9:6). In fact, Jesus announced that "all things have been committed to me by my Father" (Matthew 11:27). And Christ told Pilate, "You would have no power over me if it were not given to you from above" (John 19:11).

However, the Kingdom of Heaven–manifested now through God's incomplete rule over men's hearts–has not yet been fully realized. Thus, the civil authorities are often serving other, false gods: "None of the rulers of this age understood it [God's wisdom], for if they had, they would not have crucified the Lord of glory," explained Paul (1 Corinthians 2:8). Which makes it especially important for Christians to be active in civic affairs, applying reason within God's revelation.

This does not mean that believers should treat the state as either a redemptive or an eternal institution. "No man can redeem the life of another," wrote the Psalmist (49:7). God has retained final authority over mankind: the Lord "will judge the world in righteousness and the peoples with equity." (Psalm 98:9) Indeed, the author of Hebrews observed that Christ's sacrifice was necessary because the Levitical priesthood and the law it enforced were incapable of bringing perfection. The solution was not an enhanced role for the state, but Jesus' permanent priesthood (Hebrews 7:11-28).

Moreover, worldly rulers and their kingdoms are no less subject than other people to God's judgment: "the end will come, when he [Christ] hands over the kingdom to God the Father after he has destroyed all dominion, authority and power," wrote Paul to the Corinthian church (15:24). Similarly, the prophet Isaiah warned "In that day the Lord will punish the powers in the heavens above and the kings on the earth below" (Isaiah 24:21).

Nevertheless, despite its imperfections, and the fact that it, like every other human institution, is under God's judgment, the state remains a tool of God. That being the case, Christians have several responsibilities toward it. The first is to pray for public officials. In his letter to Timothy, Paul enjoins that "requests, prayers, intercession and thanksgiving be made for everyone–for kings and all those in authority, that we may live peaceful and quiet lives in all godliness and holiness" (1 Timothy 2:1, 2). Similarly, through the prophet Jeremiah God directed the Jews who had been exiled to Babylon to "seek the peace and prosperity of the city to which I have carried you into exile. Pray to the Lord for it" (Jeremiah 29:7).

The second responsibility of believers toward the state is obedience. When confronted by the Pharisees over the issue of paying taxes to Rome, Christ Himself instructed His listeners to "give to Caesar what is Caesar's" (Matthew 22:21). Though He proclaimed His and the disciples' exemption from the temple tax, Jesus paid it anyway, "so that we may not offend them" (Matthew 17:27). Peter told believers to "Submit yourselves for the Lord's sake to every authority instituted among men" (1 Peter 2:13). Paul expounded upon the same theme in his letter to the Roman church. To rulers to whom taxes, revenue, respect, and honor are owed, Christians are to give them. And since the authorities have been established by God, "he who rebels against the authority is rebelling against what God has instituted, and those who do so will bring judgment on themselves" (Romans 13:2).[2]

This duty is not absolute, of course. Believers must place their commitment to God before the dictates of the state. Paul instructed Timothy that believers were to pray for civil leaders, not to them. When the members of the Sanhedrin ordered Peter and John to stop preaching Christ's resurrection, they refused: "Judge for yourselves whether it is right in God's sight to obey you rather than God" (Acts 4:19, 20). Brought before the Sanhedrin again the apostles stated, "We must obey God rather than men" (Acts 5:29). Similarly, Shadrach, Meshach, and Abednego all refused to worship King Nebuchadnezzar's golden idol, and Daniel persisted in praying to God despite Darius' decree forbidding the worship of any god other than him (Daniel 3, 6).

Moreover, godly disobedience is justified in instances other than the worship of false gods. The purpose for which government was instituted is to do good. When Paul wrote the Roman church direct obedience to authority, he said that "rulers hold no terror for those who do right, but for those who do wrong" (Romans 13:3). Similarly, Paul told Titus to "Remind the people to be subject to rulers and authorities, to be obedient, to be ready to do whatever is good" (Titus 3:1). If the state breaches its duty to do right–if it exceeds its divine mandate–believers have a responsiblity to disobey. In fact, Paul stated that submission to authority was a matter of conscience as well as fear of punishment (Romans 13:5). More generally, Peter wrote of the need for Christians to "turn from evil and do good" and to keep "a clear conscience" (1 Peter 3:11, 16). These principles require Christians to assess whether the state is acting correctly and within biblical parameters.[3]

An example of a government acting improperly, thereby

requiring disobedience, was when the Egyptian Pharaoh instructed the Jewish midwives to kill male newborns. The midwives refused, instead lying to the nation's ruler; God rewarded them for having "feared" him (Exodus 1:15-21). In deed, the entire Jewish exodus from Egypt was in effect a repudiation of established civil authority. Another instance of godly disobedience occurred when Rahab the prostitute hid the Israelite spies in her home and lied to the King of Jericho to protect them. After Jericho fell the Israelites spared her and her family's lives (Joshua 2, 3:23-25).

The exact contours of the Biblical duty to defy public authority are unclear and need not be resolved here.[4] However, the Christian's general duty to obey public authority combined with the state's godly role naturally gives believers a third responsibility: to use Scriptural principles to shape public policy.

Indeed, by doing so Christians will be fulfilling Jesus' injunction that they act as "the salt of the earth" and "the light of the world" (Matthew 5:13, 14). Christians, he said, are to "let your light shine before men, that they may see your good deeds and praise your Father in heaven" (Matthew 5:16). This command applies no less to one's role in civic life than any other human endeavor.

The Bible neither encourages nor discourages Christians from holding public office.[5] What does the Bible say about government? The state is a divinely ordained institution that is to regulate relations within a secular society, not inaugurate the kingdom of heaven. For, as discussed earlier, God has reserved that task to himself. There are biblical principles that need to be applied to government, but the civil authorities will disappear when God's Kingdom is fulfilled.[6]

Though the dominant message of the Gospel as well as the law and the prophets is man's relationship to God, there is no shortage of lessons regarding how man should interact with man, including through the public institution known as government. Among the most important principle is that state's power should be limited. Civil authority is also to respect the right of believers to worship God; protect citizens from violence, theft, and fraud; and promote justice and righteousness. Government may also have some duty to help the needy, though the best reading of Scripture suggests that such a role is not mandatory. All of these rules appear to remain generally applicable today; any state, even one that does not acknowledge God's sovereignty, is theoretically capable of administering them, though in practice most governments fall far short of the scriptural ideal.

Another set of biblical principles involves more intangible aspects of social responsibility. The civil-religious authorities of ancient Israel enforced a variety of godly moral norms, ranging from bans on adultery and sorcery to restrictions on selling property and charging interest on loans. These rules provide a godly standard, but one which civil government no longer appears to be entrusted by God to enforce.

Finally, there are a variety of standards set forth both in Christ's teachings and the letters of the apostles that explicitly govern individual lives. Most of these–such as love–were meant to have little direct impact on public policy, operating instead to affect the manner in which believers act in government and the political arena.

These different Scriptural guidelines will be covered in turn: limited state power, respect for the believer's right to worship God, regulation of violent and fraudulent conduct, justice and righteousness, help for the needy, moral and social responsibility, and godly virtues.

## LIMITED STATE POWER

The first commandment given to Moses was that "You shall have no other gods before me" (Exodus 20:3). Though the "other gods" during the time of ancient Israel included Baal and similar supposed deities, some secular rulers, notably the later Roman emperors, also claimed to be gods. In fact, in at least two instances the Lord punished kings for making or tolerating such preposterous claims. Through the prophet Ezekiel, God told the ruler of Tyre that he would "bring foreigners against you" because "in the pride of your heart you say, 'I am a god'." (Ezekiel 28:7, 2). And Herod was struck down after he allowed the people to acclaim him to be divine (Acts 12:22-23).

Moreover, in a broader sense the all-powerful state acted as a secular god. From the Pharaoh who held the Jews in captivity and ordered the murder of their newborn sons to the totalitarians of fascism and communism to the cradle-to-grave welfare state, civil authorities have continually attempted to usurp God's role. It is God, not the state, who is to give life

meaning, set moral standards, and direct human activity. Yet
people yesterday and today look to politics and public action
as the answer to life's problems, big and small; salvation has
become a secular issue. In short, "statism is a rejection of
God," writes R.J. Rushdoony.[7]

Indeed, the revelation to John gives a picture of the idolatrous, all-powerful government–"the beast" as it is referred to.
Writes John: "I saw a beast coming out of the sea. He had ten
horns and seven heads, with ten crowns on his horns, and on
each head a blasphemous name.... The dragon [Satan] gave the
beast its power and his throne and great authority.... Men worshiped the dragon because he had given authority to the beast,
and they also worshiped the beast" (Revelation 13:1-4).

John's vision is thought by some theologians to apply to
Rome, with the ten horns referring to the Seleucid kings who
succeeded Alexander the Great. However, writes Dean Robert
Mounce of Western Kentucky University, "The beast is more
than the Roman Empire. John's vision grew out of the details
of his own historical situation, but its complete fulfillment
awaits the final denouement of human history. The beast has
always been, and will be in a final intensified manisfestation,
the deification of secular authority."[8]

The Bible suggests that a strong government is bad not
only because it may demand to be treated like God, but also
because it will treat its citizens unjustly, infringing their freedom
and eventually enslaving them. The inescapable problem is that
man is a fallen creature, all too willing to do wrong. For example, God declared that His people "are skilled in doing evil"
(Jeremiah 4:22). And James explained that fights and quarrels
"come from your desires that battlewithin you" (James 4:1).

In fact, giving unconstrained power to sinful men will
inevitably lead to disaster–and the more expansive the
authority, the greater the potential for abuse. Warned the
author of Ecclesiastes: "If you see the poor oppressed in a district, and justice and rights denied, do not be surprised at such
things.... The increase from the land is taken by all; the king
himself profits from the fields" (Ecclesiastes 5:8, 9). The fundamental problem is the misuse of political power. "Again I
looked and saw all the oppression that was taking place under
the sun: I saw the tears of the oppressed–and they have no
comforter; power was on the side of their oppressors–and they
have no comforter" (Ecclesiastes 4:1).

The problem is exacerbated if the civil rulers lack the knowledge of God. Explained Paul, God's and man's judgment differ: "We do, however, speak a message of wisdom among the mature, but not the wisdom of this age or of the rulers of this age, who are coming to nothing. No, we speak of God's secret wisdom.... None of the rulers of this age understood it, for if they had, they would not have crucified the Lord of glory" (1 Corinthians 2:6-8). Jesus, when He told His disciples that they were to be servants, observed that "those who are regarded as rulers of the Gentiles lord it over them and their high officials exercise authority over them" (Mark 10:42).

Not surprisingly, then, God told the Israelites that they should limit the power of their king. First, though the Lord would choose their ruler, they were to "appoint" him (Deuteronomy 17:15. See also 2 Kings 23:30; 1 Samuel 10:21). The king was not to acquire too many horses or gold and silver, for instance, or "consider himself to be better than his brothers" (Deuteronomy 17:14-20). In fact, the Lord counseled His people about the dangers posed by expansive civil government. When the Israelites demanded that God give them a king, He cautioned, through the prophet Samuel, that:

> This is what the king who will reign over you will do: He will take your sons and make them serve with his chariots and horses.... He will take your daughters to be perfumers and cooks and bakers. He will take the best of your fields and vineyards and olive groves and give them to his attendants. He will take a tenth of your grain and of your vintage and give it to his officials and attendants. Your menservants and maidservants and the best of your cattle and donkeys he will take for his own use. He will take a tenth of your flocks, and you yourselves will become his slaves. (1 Samuel 8:11-17)

And God emphasized that the Israelites' decision to surrender their individual freedom and autonomy should not be taken lightly, for it would be irreversible. After they had become the king's slaves, God said, "you will cry out for relief from the king you have chosen, and the Lord will not answer you in that day" (1 Samuel 8:18). Samuel's prophecy came to pass, of course. During the reign of Solomon, Israelite laborers

were drafted to build his palace. Israel was split apart because
Solomon's son, King Rehoboam, promised to intensify the burdens his father had placed on the people. King Ahab seized the
vineyard of Naboth, who was killed through the trickery of
Queen Jezebel; King Jehoiakim later taxed the land and confiscated gold and silver to pay foreign tribute. Jewish governors
under the Persians "placed a heavy burden on the people,"
seizing silver, food, and wine, and "also lorded it over the people" (Nehemiah 5:15). And so it went.

God's warning demonstrates His concern for individual
liberty. There are, of course, different Scriptural meanings of
"freedom." When Paul wrote that "where the Spirit of the
Lord is, there is freedom," he was speaking of a spiritual liberty from the bondage of sin. In this case freedom is not synony-
mous with license. While a person's right to act is in one sense
greatly restricted under this concept–one must walk, according
to Christ, on the narrow rather than the wide road-it results in
the most complete fulfillment of God's purpose for creating
man. That is, only by recognizing Christ's Lordship and thereby binding ourselves to follow God's Law can we be spiritually
free. Since spiritual liberty in this sense lies at the heart of the
gospel message, government has no authority over it.

There is also another sense of liberty that permeates the
Bible: the ability of people to receive what they sinfully
demand. God allowed Adam and Eve to make their fatal decision to eat the fruit of the tree of the knowledge of good and
evil. In fact, God gave Adam and Eve virtually unrestricted
rights within his realm, telling them, "You are free to eat from
any tree in the garden" except the tree of the knowledge of
good and evil (Genesis 2:16, 17). God led an ungrateful nation
out of captivity in Egypt; he gave the Israelites the Promised
Land despite their grumbling and his foreknowledge that they
would almost continually disobey him. God warned His people against having a king, but gave them what they asked for.

Similarly, Jesus permitted people to reject Him. Christ
grieved as the rich young ruler, for instance, walked away, but
would not override the man's personal will. The consequences
for those who fail to follow Jesus are, of course, catastrophic:
"only he who does the will of my Father who is in heaven"
will enter the kingdom, Jesus said (Matthew 7:21). But God
never tells us to try to force others to love and obey Him, even
were such a thing possible. To the extent that government

attempts to wield Christ's "winnowing fork," whether through heresy trials or other means, it is encroaching on the most fundamental of God's prerogatives.

Finally, the Bible recognizes the more traditional forms of political and economic liberty. The prophet Jeremiah spoke to the nation of Israel about freedom in the context of both personal slavery and national independence (Jeremiah 34:14, 17). The Exodus embodied these values as well. Moreover, the beast in John's vision exercises enormous economic power: "no one could buy or sell unless he had the mark" (Revelation 13:17). And God's warning to the people about the consequences of having a king revolved around public control over their lives, families, and property. Indeed, it is noteworthy that the reach of the state today in the U.S. far exceeds that spoken of by Samuel. Government at all levels takes 36.8 percent of the nation's production, regulates virtually every form of human endeavor, seizes property almost at will, and until 1973 regularly drafted hundreds of thousands of men into the military.

Rushdoony makes the intriguing observation that political and economic freedom–particularly independence from the paternal welfare state–has a spiritual dimension, since it forces men to walk by faith. "Ultimately," he writes, "our faith must be in Christ or in Caesar, and it is better by far to walk by faith in Christ than to walk by sight under Caesar."[9] Certainly the wider the latitude of action allowed an individual the greater the variety of situations in which he must exercise moral judgment and seek to advance biblical principles; freedom also enhances his opportunity to enjoy God's creation.

## RESPECT FOR THE BELIEVER'S RIGHT TO WORSHIP GOD

Inherent in the concept of a government ordained by God to do good is allowing men to serve Him. Indeed, Jesus taught that the greatest commandment was to "Love the Lord your God with all your heart and with all your soul and with all your mind" (Matthew 22:37). Obviously a government based on godly principles must not hinder people in fulfilling this command–to give "to God what is God's," as Jesus explained to the Pharisees (Luke 20:25). Peter and John rejected the demand of the Sanhedrin, an ecclesiastical body which exercised considerable civil power, that they cease teaching in Jesus' name: "We must obey God rather than men" (Acts 5:29). And John's characterization of the state as "the beast" probably reflected the persecution of Christians under Nero and other Roman emperors.

The government's duty is not simply negative, to not penalize believers or supplant the role of the church in social matters. For Paul instructed Timothy to pray for those in authority "that we may live peaceful and quiet lives in all godliness and holiness" (1 Timothy 2:2). This implies preserving an environment in which people can serve God. The state should strive to maintain a peaceful society in both domestic and foreign matters; public policy, whatever its specifics, should be based on, and be perceived to be based on, principles of justice and righteousness rather than expedience and venality. In short, the government need not directly advance religion as much as maintain a public atmosphere of civility and tolerance in which Christian values can flourish.

## REGULATION OF VIOLENT OR FRAUDULENT INTERPERSONAL CONDUCT

Perhaps the state's most important role is to protect citizens from the sinful conduct of their neighbors. The Bible indicates that government is to act to preserve order–people's ability to live "peaceful and quiet lives," in Paul's words–in a sinful world. The state is to be a godly agent to not only allow men to follow God but also to contain the harm that would occur in the absence of any contraints on evil behavior. "Do you want to be free from fear of the one in authority?" asked Paul. "Then do what is right and he will commend you. For he is God's servant to do you good. But if you do wrong, be afraid, for he does not bear the sword for nothing. He is God's servant, an agent of wrath to bring punishment on the wrongdoer" (Romans 13:3, 4).

One goal of the state is just retribution: "It is mine to avenge; I will repay," God said through Moses, and that pledge is reiterated by Paul (Deuteronomy 32:35; Romans 12:19). God instructed the Israelites "to take life for life, eye for eye, tooth for tooth, hand for hand, foot for foot, burn for burn, wound for wound, bruise for bruise" (Exodus 21:23, 24).

Deterrence–encouraging even evil men to respect the law–is another objective of government. Paul wrote that fear of punishment is one reason for compliance with the authorities (Romans 3:5). As Calvin explained it, in this way government was "to cause those who, unless constrained, feel no concern for justice and rectitude, when they hear its terrible sanctions, to be at least restrained by a fear of its penalties."[10]

This role for the civil authorities arises naturally out of God's creation. Life itself is a gift of God: "the Lord God formed man from the dust of the ground and breathed into his nostrils the breath of life, and man became a living being" (Genesis 2:7) And that God-created life is to be protected. The sixth commandment is short and simple: "you shall not murder" (Exodus 20:13).[11]

In providing standards to guide the ancient state of Israel, God set forth death as the punishment for murder, but distinguished between intentional and accidental killings and set rules of evidence (Numbers 35:16-34). Kidnapping and rape were also capital offenses. (Deut. 24:7; 22:25) Lesser forms of punishment were provided for a "malicious" witness who gave false testimony (Deuteronomy 19:15-21). Other unspecified crimes were penalized by flogging (Deuteronomy 25:2, 3).

For similar reasons the civil authorities also preserved private property from dispossession through either force or fraud. God created land and its fruits and proclaimed them to be good (Genesis 1:10-12). The Mosaic code protected property ownership; the eighth commandment, for instance, specified that "You shall not steal" (Exodus 20:15). The Lord declared through the prophet Isaiah that "I hate robbery and iniquity" (Isaiah 61:8). Theft of oxen or sheep required a repayment four- or fivefold (Exodus 22:1).

The law also forbade an Israelite from shifting property markers. "Do not move an ancient boundary stone or encroach on the fields of the fatherless, for their Defender is strong; he will take up their case against you" (Proverbs 23:10; Deuteronomy 19:14; Deuteronomy 27:17). The Israelite assembly was also warned not to lie, deceive one another, or to "defraud your neighbor or rob him" (Leviticus 19:11, 13).

Businessmen were not to defraud their customers through the use of dishonest scales or standards (Leviticus 19:35, 36; Deuteronomy 25:13-16; Proverbs 20:10, 23; Hosea 12:7). The workmen's wages were not to be held back overnight (Leviticus 19:13). Through the prophet Malachi, God denounced those "who defraud laborers of their wages," a complaint echoed centuries later by James (Malachi 3:5; James 5:4). Moreover, the Lord provided for explicit penalties for a neighbor who deceived or cheated someone who left goods in his care (Leviticus 6:1-7). And the Psalmist observed that "the wicked borrow and do not repay" (Psalm 37:21).

Of course, individuals are but stewards of God's creation: "The earth is the Lord's, and everything in it, the world, and all who live in it" (Psalm 24:1). But God largely placed those resources into private rather than public hands and lauded the man who "leaves an inheritance for his children's children" (Proverbs 13:22). Where the property was acquired justly, the civil authorities apparently had an obligation to protect their possession. (See, for example, Deuteronomy 17:8, which refers to "lawsuits" in the courts.)

In fact, private economic transactions fill both the Old and New Testaments.[12] There is little in the New Testament about the government's role in guaranteeing private property ownership, but that right appears to have been respected. And to be effective, ownership must have been enforceable in civil courts.

This principle of protecting people's lives and property also applies to defense against other peoples or nations. God directed the Israelites to take possession of the Promised Land by conquest; war was a function performed by the collective body. Later Old Testament kings frequently sought God's guidance through His prophets before going to war. Such a procedure is obviously impossible today, without prophets or a godly civil leadership. The Bible takes their place for believers, but it provides few standards pertaining uniquely to the conduct of foreign policy. Even less is said on such issues in the New Testament. In His Sermon on the Mount Jesus said that we are to be "peacemakers" (Matthew 5:9). And James wrote that "Peacemakers who sow in peace raise a harvest of righteousness" (3:18). More generally, a country's actions in the international arena should be consistent with other broad Biblical values, such as preserving justice and righteousness.

## JUSTICE AND RIGHTEOUSNESS

"You are not a God who takes pleasure in evil," wrote David: "with you the wicked cannot dwell" (Psalm 5:4). In a later Psalm David explained that "the Lord is righteous, he loves justice" (Psalm 11:11). This theme is repeated in Isaiah 61:8 and Jeremiah 9:24. Not surprisingly, then, individual Christians have a clear responsibility to promote justice and righteousness.[13] "Who may dwell in your sanctuary?" asked David. One "whose walk is blameless and who does what is righteous." Among the many characteristics of personal righteousness are speaking the truth, doing one's neighbors no wrong, keeping one's oath, not charging usury, and not accepting a bribe (Psalm 15). Job was righteous, for he assisted the poor, fatherless, blind, lame, needy, and victims of the wicked (Job 29:12-17).

The New Testament also speaks of the importance of both justice and righteousness. The Gospels state that Jesus came to fulfill Isaiah's prophecy that the Messiah would come and "proclaim justice" and lead "justice to victory" (Matthew 12:18, 20). Christ complained that the Pharisees ignored "the most important matters of the law" including justice (Matthew 23:23). Paul preached in Athens that God "will judge the world with justice" (Acts 17:31). And Christ, wrote Paul, came as man's redeemer to demonstrate God's justice (Romans 3:25).

God's righteousness is an equally persistent theme throughout the Gospels and the epistles. "For in the gospel a righteousness from God is revealed, a righteousness that is by faith from first to last" (Romans 1:17). And "in keeping with his promise we are looking forward to a new heaven and a new earth, the home of righteousness" (2 Peter 3:13; see also Galatians 5:5; Romans 14:17, 18). Christians have an obligation, in the words of Paul, to "pursue righteousness" (1 Timothy 6:11; see also Matthew 6:33, 5:6; 1 Peter 2:24).

Civil rulers, too, are to be just and righteous. Solomon requested God to "Endow the king with your justice, O God, the royal son with your righteousness" (Psalm 71:1). (The Psalm appears to apply simultaneously to earthly rulers and the Messiah.) God spoke to the royal house of Judah and ordered it to "Administer justice every morning; rescue from the hand of his oppressor the one who has been robbed" (Jeremiah 12:12).

However, corporate duty differs from the personal responsibility. Individuals must respond virtuously to the needs and rights of their neighbors; government must regulate, coercively yet fairly, relations between both righteous and unrighteous men. In short, the contrast is personal virtue versus public impartiality.[14]

Several themes about the state's role occur throughout

Scripture. Government is to act as a neutral arbiter, vindicating the rights of the weak. It is not to become a tool of the powerful to rob and oppress. For instance, Solomon set forth several tasks for the godly ruler/Messiah: "He will judge your people in righteousness, your afflicted ones with justice.... He will defend the afflicted among the people and save the children of the needy; he will crush the oppressor" (Psalm 72:2-4).

Moreover, through Jeremiah the Lord spoke to the King of Judah: "Do what is just and right. Rescue from the hand of his oppressor the one who has been robbed. Do no wrong or violence to the alien, the fatherless or the widow, and do not shed innocent blood in this place" (Jeremiah 22:1-3). God went on to speak to King Shallum, declaring, "Woe to him who builds his palace by unrighteousness, his upper rooms by injustice, making his countrymen work for nothing, not paying them for their labor," and, "your eyes and your heart are set only on dishonest gain, on shedding innocent blood and on oppression and extortion." In contrast, the king's father "did what was right and just, so all went well with him. He defended the cause of the poor and needy" (Jeremiah 22:13, 17, 15, 16).

The prophet Micah denounced "you rulers of the house of Israel, who despise justice and distort all that is right; who build Zion with bloodshed, and Jerusalem with wickedness. Her leaders judge for a bribe, her priests teach for a price, and her prophets tell fortunes for money" (Micah 3:9-11). Amos provided a similar list of public offenses: despising those who tell the truth, trampling the poor, oppressing the righteous, taking bribes, and depriving the poor of justice in court (Amos 5:10-12).

The New Testament deals far less with the government's role in promoting justice and righteousness. Jesus warned his listeners that the Pharisees "devour widows' houses" (Mark 12:40). And after meeting Christ, Zacchaeus the tax collector agreed to repay anyone he had cheated (Luke 19:8). Moreover, John the Baptist instructed tax collectors and soldiers not to take more than they were legally authorized to (Luke 3:12-14).

Of particular note is the fact that the Bible makes no distinction between the protection of the rights of the godly and ungodly. Even within the covenant nation of Israel God directed his people not to "oppress an alien; you yourselves know how it feels to be aliens, because you were aliens in Egypt" (Exodus 23:9). Similarly, through the prophet Malachi God said that he would "testify against" those "who deprive aliens of justice" (Malachi 3:5; see also Zechariah 7:9; Deuteronomy 24:14,17; Deuteronomy 27:19).

Rich and poor are to be dealt with impartially as well. The treatment of the needy is of special concern to God, presumably because they are the least able to protect their own interests, especially in the face of a government that usually favors the powerful: "the righteous care about justice for the poor" (Proverbs 29:7; see also Proverbs 29:14). However, God commanded, "do not pervert justice; do not show partiality to the poor or favoritism to the great, but judge your neighbor fairly" (Leviticus 19:15). And, instructed Moses, "do not show partiality in judging; hear both small and great alike" (Deuteronomy 1:17).

Christian justice, then, protects all men in their enjoyment of God's blessings. Civil government is to prevent oppression irrespective the victim's identity. In this way the Biblical concepts of justice and righteousness focus on process and are therefore very different from the modern notion of "social justice," which demands equality of economic and cultural outcomes.[15] The prophet Amos instructed the people to "maintain justice in the courts" (Amos 5:15). Similarly, the Israelites were told, "Do not exploit the poor because they are poor and do not crush the needy in court" (Proverbs 22:22). Isaiah attacked those "who acquit the guilty for a bribe, but deny justice to the innocent" (Isaiah 5:23; see also Deuteronomy 16:19-20). And Solomon asked for "a discerning heart to govern your people and to distinguish between right and wrong" (1 Kings 3:9).

Moreover, God directed the Israelites not to "deny justice to your poor people in their lawsuits. Have nothing to do with a false charge and do not put an innocent or honest person to death" (Exodus 23:6). Jesus' parable about the unjust judge, though used to illustrate God's willingness to hear His people, suggested a similar meaning of justice. The widow went to the magistrate and pleaded, "Grant me justice against my adversary" (Luke 18:3). She appeared to be asking for a fair hearing of a legal complaint, not some form of economic redistribution.

Similarly, the other godly admonitions to governments, cited earlier, center around oppression, violence, robbery, extortion, and conscription. In sum, the Lord ordained government to establish a just order in which individuals are protected from the arbitrary exercise of power. In this way Biblical justice focuses on individual, not class, distinctions. Argues Rushdoony, "The requirements of justice are the requirements of the second table of the law, that man's life, home, property, and reputation be respected in word and deed." He rightly attacks class-based "social justice" as meaning "the denial of justice because social justice is anti-personal. It is not the property of the individual, nor his life, home, and reputation which counts but the demands of a class as embodied in the state."[16]

Of course, some Christians argue that individualized oppression may occur without the use of violence–that a business with a large share of the market can "oppress" consumers, for instance. Such an interpretation is not necessarily inconsistent with Scripture. For one could read broadly admonitions like Zechariah's: "Do not oppress the widow or the fatherless, the alien or the poor" (Zechariah 7:6). Yet while the law of ancient Israel did maintain a certain economic balance among Hebrews, most notably in terms of debt and land ownership, such issues do not appear to have been treated as matters of Biblical "justice." Indeed, the Year of Jubilee, which provided for the redemption of land that had been sold, was predicated on man's relationship to God, not to his countrymen: "The land must not be sold permanently, because the land is mine and you are but aliens and my tenants" (Leviticus 25:23).[17]

Moreover, Jesus' parable of the vineyard owner who paid all of his workers the same irrespective of when they started working suggests that seemingly "unfair" economic outcomes which may result from a "fair" process–in this case, free bargaining between laborer and owner–are not unjust (Matthew 20:1-16). This meaning is not certain, however, since the story's primary purpose was to make a theological point about the Kingdom of Heaven.

Finally, the Bible routinely links oppression and the use of force and fraud. The prophet Micah complained of evil men who "covet fields and seize them, and houses, and take them. They defraud a man of his home, a fellowman of his inheritance"; Israel's "rich men are violent," he added (Micah 2:2, 6:12). King David wrote of the man who "trusted in his great wealth and grew strong by destroying others" (Psalm 52:7). Ezekiel combined oppression of the poor and needy with robbery and failure to return a property pledged to back a loan

(Ezekiel 18:12). James criticized the exploitative rich who have "failed to pay the workmen" and "condemned and murdered innocent men" (James 5:4, 6). Jeremiah attacked "wicked men" who "have become rich and powerful" and whose "evil deeds have no limit" (Jeremiah 5:26-28). None of these passages involve voluntary exchange, even between people with "unequal" bargaining power, a nebulous concept upon which it is virtually impossible to legislate sensibly.[18]

Indeed, the form of economic oppression that would appear to come closest to the Biblical meaning would be the use of government by influential interest groups to restrict competition, enhance their own market position, and extort subsidies. In this case power as it is commonly understood is on the side of the oppressor, as the author of Ecclesiastes warned (4:1). Similarly, the prophet Isaiah proclaimed: "Woe to those who make unjust laws, to those who issue oppressive decrees, to deprive the poor of their rights and rob my oppressed people of justice, making widows their prey and robbing the fatherless" (Isaiah 10:1-2).[19]

Interestingly, Augustine apparently interpreted godly justice in a similar way, for he believed that the only thing that distinguished a state that taxed from a band of highwaymen that stole was justice:

> Justice being taken away, then, what are kingdoms but great robberies? But what are robberies themselves, but little kingdoms? The band itself is made up of men; it is ruled by the authority of a prince, it is knit together by the pact of the confederacy; the booty is divided by the law agreed on. If, by the admittance of abandoned men, this evil increases to such a degree that it holds places, fixes abodes, takes possession of cities, and subdues peoples, it assumes the more plainly the name of a kingdom, because the reality is now manifestly conferred on it, not by the removal of covetousness, but by the addition of impunity.[20]

Scripture also appears to sharply distinguish justice from morality. The latter issue is obviously important and is dealt with extensively in the Bible, but it is a separate matter. Christians, writes Stephen Monsma, a state senator and university professor, "are called to hold certain private, personal standards of morality that have little to do with political justice. Government is to pursue justice–not morality apart from justice. To the extent that justice and morality overlap, one can say that the justice-promoting activities of government also promote morality, but it is the pursuit of justice that is the controlling factor, not the pursuit of morality apart from justice."[21]

## HELP FOR THE NEEDY

The plight of the poor is a persistent concern of God's. Through the prophet Isaiah the Lord declared that "The poor and needy search for water, but there is none; their tongues are parched with thirst. But I the Lord will answer them" (Isaiah 41:17). And poverty will never disappear as an issue. Wrote Moses: "There will always be poor people in the land. Therefore I command you to be openhanded toward your brothers and toward the poor and needy in your land" (Deuteronomy 15:11). Similarly, Jesus stated that "The poor you will always have with you" (Mark 14:7).

Every individual has a responsibility to help care for the hungry and needy. "If there is a poor man among your brothers in any of the towns of the land that the Lord your God is giving you, do not be hardhearted or tightfisted toward your poor brother," instructed the Lord (Deuteronomy 15:7; see also Leviticus 25:35). Similarly, David wrote, "the righteous give generously" (Psalm 37:21).

Personal accountability for helping the poor is also evident throughout the New Testament. For instance, John instructed his listeners to share their clothes and food with those who had none (Luke 3:11). Christ told the parable of the Good Samaritan, who cared for the victim he found along the road, to illustrate what He meant when He taught that we were to love our neighbors (Luke 10:30-35). Jesus also told His listeners to "sell your possessions and give to the poor" (Luke 12:33).

The Apostle John asked: "If anyone has material possessions and sees his brother in need but has no pity on him, how can the love of God be in him?" (1 John 3:17). Moreover, James, in an epistle warning Christians of the danger of following Mammon, wrote, "Religion that God our Father accepts as pure and faultless is this: to look after orphans and widows in their distress" (James 1:27). Paul even urged the idle to work so "that he may have something to share with those in need" (Ephesians 4:28).

The Old Testament set forth a number of ways in which the Israelites were to help the poor.[22] Similar concern for organizing relief efforts was evident in the first-century church. For instance, Paul wrote Timothy that families had first responsibility to care for the elderly: "If anyone does not provide for his relatives, and especially for his immediate family, he has denied the faith and is worse than an unbeliever" (1 Timothy 5:8). If no family members were available, then the church was to support widows who devoted themselves "to all kinds of good deeds" (1 Timothy 5:10). And the Jerusalem church provided a daily distribution of food (Acts 6:1).

Indeed, God spoke broadly to "my people" through the prophet Isaiah, declaring that their fasting was not acceptable: "Is not this the kind of fasting I have chosen: to loose the chains of injustice and untie the cords of the yoke, to set the oppressed free and break every yoke? Is it not to share your food with the hungry and to provide the poor wanderer with shelter–when you see the naked, to clothe him, and not to turn away from your own flesh and blood ... then your righteousness will go before you ... if you spend yourselves on behalf of the hungry and satisfy the needs of the oppressed, then your light will rise in the darkness" (Isaiah 58:6-10).

In contrast, the role of the civil authorities in carrying out charitable duties is less certain.[23] Old Testament law apparently did not provide for official enforcement of practices such as gleaning. For instance, Ruth asked Boaz for permission to harvest grain from his field (Ruth 2:7). And it appears that God, not the civil authorities, judged those who did not fulfill their responsibility to help their fellowman. "He who gives to the poor will lack nothing, but he who closes his eyes to them receives many curses" (Proverbs 28:27). God warned that he would strike anyone who took advantage of a widow or an orphan (Exodus 22:22). Those who do not help the needy "will be found guilty of sin," while those who "give generously" will be blessed (Deuteronomy 15:9, 10). Moreover, the Lord declared Himself to be the defender of "the fatherless and the oppressed" (Psalm 10:18; see also Psalms 68:5; 70:5; 72:12-14; and 82:3, 4).

Christ's mission built on these promises. Jesus came to

fulfill the law and said that "Anyone who breaks one of the least of these commandments and teaches others to do the same will be called least in the kingdom of heaven, but whoever practices and teaches these commands will be called great in the kingdom of heaven" (Matthew 5:19). Similarly, Paul told the church in Galatia that "A man reaps what he sows" (Galatians 6:7).

Is the state required to help provide for the needy? There is nothing to bar government from creating a welfare program–at least a system that does not have other, anti-biblical consequences, such as fostering family breakup. And today's confusing melange of programs performs poorly on this score, as will be detailed in Chapter Eight.

Many Christians, of course, are committed to an activist government role in alleviating poverty, but only one Scripture in any way suggests that public support is mandatory. And that interpretation is dubious because the passage appears to be directed more toward the Messiah than earthly kings. Pleaded Solomon, "Endow the king with your justice, O God, the royal son with your righteousness.... He will defend the afflicted among the people and save the children of the needy" (Psalm 72:1-4).

It is true that God will judge a nation that forgets the disadvantaged (Psalm 9: 18, 19; see also Isaiah 3:14-15). One of the reasons given for the destruction of Sodom was its lack of concern for the poor (Ezekiel 16:49). In fact, the Lord "humbles those who dwell on high, he lays the lofty city low; he levels it to the ground and casts it down to the dust. Feet trample it down–the feet of the oppressed, the footsteps of the poor" (Isaiah 26:5, 6). Arguably the people of such a city could, through their civil authorities, compel the stingy to give in hopes of preventing their own destruction, but Scripture does not suggest that they do so. Instead, voluntary, individual support for the poor remains the preferred means of fulfilling God's mandate.

Moreover, it is of note that Paul would not order members of the Corinthian church to contribute toward the relief fund he was gathering for the Jerusalem Christian community: "I am not commanding you, but I want to test the sincerity of your love by comparing it with the earnestness of others" (2 Corinthians 8:8). Indeed, after warning that those who sow sparingly will reap sparingly, Paul stated that "Each man should give what he has decided in his heart to give, not reluctantly or under compulsion, for God loves a cheerful giver" (2 Corinthians 9:7). If Paul was not willing to command believers in a church that he had founded to help their less fortunate Christian brethren, would he have advocated that the civil authorities tax unbelievers for the same purpose?

In studying the Biblical duty toward the needy, we must remember that the Bible holds people personally responsible e to try to avoid poverty. For instance, Paul directed members of the church in Thessalonica "to keep away from every brother who is idle," for they were "to settle down and earn the bread they eat" (2 Thessalonians 3:6, 12). A person's individual responsibility for his material state pervades Proverbs (10:4; 20:4; 21:25; 24:30; 26:14-15).

In fact, God indicates that those who follow him may be rewarded financially. "Blessed is the man who fears the Lord," wrote the Psalmist. "Wealth and riches are in his house, and his righteousness endures forever" (Psalm 112:1, 3; see also Proverbs 10:22). Major Biblical figures like Abraham grew wealthy and Christ frequented the homes of important community figures without commenting adversely on their material success.

People may also be poor through no fault of their own; Job's temporary poverty, for instance, had a unique spiritual dimension. Uncontrollable circumstances may also be the cause. Widows, orphans, and the handicapped are obviously particularly vulnerable. And it is to these people, who are not responsible for their problems, that the Bible appears to limit assistance.[24] Moreover, most of the "poverty programs" mentioned in the Bible required either effort or a test of spiritual purity. Gleaning the fields, for instance, involved field work. Widows supported by the New Testament church had to be dedicated to God and their fellow believers and to perform good deeds.[25]

Finally, Christians seeking to understand their Biblical obligations to the poor must recognize the difference between material and spiritual poverty. For instance, in the Beatitudes Jesus focused on the "poor in spirit" and "those who hunger and thirst for righteousness" (Matthew 5:3, 6). Thus, if God intends the so-called "preferential option" for the poor that liberation theologians and others often speak of, it is for those who recognize their spiritual need for God, and not to those

who are simply lacking in the things of this world.[26] The two
may go together. Christ observed that "it is easier for a camel
to go through the eye of a needle than for a rich man to enter
the kingdom of God" (Mark 10:25). But one's spiritual state is
paramount.

This may also be the form of poverty referred to by Isaiah
when, speaking of the promised Messiah, he declared that "the
Lord has anointed me to preach good news to the poor. He has
sent me to bind up the brokenhearted, to proclaim freedom for
the captives and release for the prisoners ... to comfort all who
mourn, and provide for those who grieve in Zion" (Isaiah 61:1-
3). Similarly, the prophet observed that "Once more the humble will rejoice in the Lord; the needy will rejoice in the Holy
One of Israel" (Isaiah 29:19). These passages suggest spiritual
triumph, not government income redistribution programs.

## MORAL, SOCIAL, AND ECONOMIC RESPONSIBILITY

God established rules governing virtually every aspect of the
Israelites' lives. The moral purity of the body may have been
his most critical concern. For example, the death penalty was
prescribed for those who practiced sorcery, committed bestiali-
ty, and sacrificed to another god (Exodus 22:18-20; Deuteronmy
13:9; 17:5). Sons who cursed their parents were also to be executed (Exodus 21:17). The same penalty was prescribed for
those who broke the sabbath, blasphemed, and committed a
variety of sexual offenses, including adultery and homosexuality (Exodus 31:15,; Leviticus 24:14; 20:10-16; Deuteronomy
22:13-24). Other sexual practices were to result in the perpetra-
tors being "cut off from their people" (Leviticus 18:6-20, 29;
20:17-18). And a man who seduced a virgin had to pay a bride
price (Exodus 22:16).

The law set forth a number of other rules: stray animals
were to be returned, parapets were to built around roofs to stop
someone from falling off, and women and men were not to
wear clothing of the other sex. Standards were even set for the
Israelites' clothes (Deuteronomy 22:1-12).

God also regulated his covenant people's economic activities, enforcing a broad ethic of communal responsibility within the Jewish community. Millstones were not to be taken as
security (Deuteronomy 24:6). A pledged cloak was to be
returned by sunset–at least for a poor person–while a widow's
garment was not to be taken at all (Exodus 22:26; Deuteronomy

24:12; 24:17). No one was to charge usurious or excessive interest; apparently no interest was to be charged a fellow Israelite, at least a poor one (Exodus 18:17; Deuteronomy 23:19; Leviticus 25:35-36).[27] Every seven years the land was to be left untended and every 50 years, during the Year of Jubilee, land was to be redeemable by the original owner (Leviticus 25) Further, debts to fellow Israelites were to be cancelled every seven years (Deuteronomy 15).

Some of the social rules were enforced by God rather than the nation. For instance, sexual relations between a man and his aunt or sister-in-law would result in their being childless (Leviticus 20:20, 21). And punishment for breaking the economic rules was apparently left up to God. Nowhere does the Bible set forth a specific penalty for someone who, for instance, refused to discharge a debt. (In fact, we are not sure that the Israelites ever implemented the Year of Jubilee.) Instead, God offered both the carrot and the stick to encourage obedience. For instance, He promised that He would "richly bless" the people if they "fully obey" him (Deuteronomy 15:4, 5). He also told the Israelites that if they allowed the land to lie fallow in its seventh year, "I will send you such a blessing in the sixth year that the land will yield enough for three years" (Leviticus 25:21).

But for the person who did not return the pledged coat, God stated that "I will hear" the owner's cry (Exodus 22:27). And the Israelites were warned not to take advantage of each other in the context of the Year of Jubilee, "but fear your God" (Leviticus 25:17).

Are enforcement of these social and economic laws the proper province of civil government today? That is, does God require what are now secular authorities to implement these aspects of His Law?

The proper answer would appear to be no, for several reasons. The first is that some of the rules were to be applied only within the community of faith then represented by Israel. For instance, the cancellation of debts and restrictions on interest did not apply to foreigners (Deuteronomy 15:3; 23:20). The rules governing the release of slaves applied only to Jews (Deuteronomy 15:12; Jeremiah 34:8). Moreover, the communal economic practices of the early New Testament church involved only Christians (Acts 2:44-45, 4:32-35). There is no indication that they ever tried to expand their sharing outside of the Body of Christ.

Some of the other, more ceremonial decrees also may not have applied to non-Hebrews. Most of God's detailed moral laws were delivered to the twelve tribes through Moses before they entered the Promised Land. The rules' impact on the aliens who would eventually live in the Israelites' midst was not discussed in detail, though foreigners were explicitly excused from following Mosaic dietary restrictions (Deuteronomy 14:21). While most criminal sanctions, which protected the sanctity of life, presumably applied to Jew and non-Jew alike, even then there were differences: the kidnapper of an Israelite was to be executed, but no penalty was set if the victim was an alien (Deuteronomy 24:7). And we simply don't know whether penalties for breaking purely religious requirements, such as keeping the sabbath, also applied to aliens.

The second point is that these rules of "social responsibility" appear to be largely tied to the Israelites' status as the chosen people. In fact, the Psalmist Asaph wrote that God "decreed statutes for Jacob and established the law in Israel, which he commanded our forefathers to teach their children.... Then they would put their trust in God and would not forget his deeds but would keep his commands" (Psalm 78: 5-7). That is, God established the law to mold the nation of Israel as part of His overall plan of salvation.[28]

In fact, the Mosaic Scriptures devote far more attention to the Israelites' worship practices than to their civic responsibilities (Exodus 25-30, 35-40; Leviticus 1-9; and so on). Similarly, more complex rules were established to govern an individual's dedication of property to God than his commercial transactions with his neighbors (Leviticus 27).

Moreover, enforcement of many of the Old Testament standards required the active intervention of God. The people's obedience would be rewarded or punished by bountiful harvests or childlessness, for instance. Adultery could be proved through a supernatural test (Numbers 5:11-31). Both Moses and Aaron turned to God for direct guidance before they executed a sabbath-breaker (Numbers 15:32-36). In short, as a matter of principle the covenant Hebrew nation had a unique responsibility to maintain its purity and uniqueness; as a practical matter no civil state in today's predominantly secular world could show similar sensitivity to God's will.[29]

In fact, the move from the Old to the New Covenant apparently brought with it a shift from corporate to individual responsibility and judgment. God warned the Israelites that while compliance with His Law would result in good harvests and national success, disobedience would result in them being cursed, ravaged by disease, defeated in battle, and scattered throughout the earth (Leviticus 26:1-46; Deuteronomy 28:15-68). In contrast, Christ, who ministered to an Israel that was controlled by the pagan Roman Empire, placed the burden for fulfilling the law on the people individually, not as part of the Jewish nation. Those who did not maintain the law, He said, "will be called the least in the kingdom of heaven" (Matthew 5:19).

Third, most of the Old Testament rules dealt with matters of the heart as much as with conduct. Observed Paul, "a man is a Jew if he is one inwardly; and circumcision is circumcision of the heart, by the Spirit, not by the written code" (Romans 2:29). Meaningful enforcement of the law in such a case required God's direct involvement in the affairs of civil government, intervention that was possible only in a covenant nation like Israel. As the society became more diverse and the people less faithful, it quickly became impractical for government to enforce such standards.

It is true that godly people nevertheless had and still have an interest in promoting community compliance with God's standards. "Sodom and Gomorrah and the surrounding towns gave themselves up to sexual immorality and perversion," wrote Jude. "They serve as an example of those who suffer the punishment of eternal fire" (Jude 7). However, government could control only the improper conduct, not the inner spiritual corruption that so offended God. In fact, it was the lack of even ten righteous men, not the absence of a municipal vice squad, that caused God to destroy Sodom.[30] Wrote Peter on the fate of these two cities, God knows how "to hold the unrighteous for the day of judgment, while continuing their punishment. This is especially true of those who follow the corrupt desire of their sinful nature" (2 Peter 2:9).

R. J. Rushdoony separates Biblical law into matters of justice, which is concerned with maintaining "an orderly society in terms of God's order and for the continuing welfare of its members" and salvation, that is, promoting "the physical and spiritual health of man." He argues that "in replacing justice as a social goal with salvation by man-made laws, man is guilty of the great and central sin, of playing god. Salvation is the province and work of God, not man."[31]

In the original covenant state of Israel, God provided for both justice and salvation under the clerical/civil leadership of Moses. In this system, the corporate body had an important role in enforcing the religious law. However, the detailed legal regime failed. Explained Paul: "Israel, who pursued a law of righteousness, has not attained it. Why not? Because they pursued it not by faith but as if it were by works" (Romans 9:31, 32). God's New Covenant, inaugurated by Christ, transformed his relationship with humanity. As a result, the state no longer has a salvation role.

In fact, it appears that even in Old Testament times the civil authorities, once they were separated from the priesthood, abandoned enforcement of the law's detailed moral standards. The corruption of the government may very well have made it imperative for God to divest the state of responsibility for preserving the community's moral purity. For even nominally Jewish authorities often represented man rather than God. When kings like Solomon began sacrificing to Baal, for instance, they obviously could not be counted on to regulate peoples' worship practices. A Herod Antipas who married his brother's wife was unlikely to enforce God's standards of sexual propriety. Rule by Assyria, Babylon, Rome, and other pagan empires totally severed the connection between civil and ecclesiastical rule.

Even the Pharisees, who possessed both religious and civil power, could not be trusted to, say, enforce the keeping of the sabbath. Jesus constantly challenged their lack of genuine devotion to God. In short, once those in power failed to acknowledge the dominion of God, they lost their authority to enforce rules not directly related to the necessary ordering of a society filled with sinful, and irreligious, men.

Christ appeared to validate the civil authorities' retreat from enforcing moral norms that related primarily to one's relationship with God (in contrast to standards regulating one's conduct toward others, such as murder). When the Pharisees brought the adulterous woman to Jesus, they asked whether she should be executed in compliance with the law. He responded, "If any one of you is without sin, let him be the first to throw a stone at her," and, after they departed, sent her on her way with the admonition: "leave your life of sin" (John

8:1-11). His immediate point was not political, of course, but the result of his action was to deny the religious establishment's right to punish adultery. (Theoretically the Pharisees could not put her to death without the approval of the Roman authorities, but Jesus does not base his argument on that fact.)

Similarly, while Paul instructed the members of the Corinthian church not to associate with "anyone who calls himself a brother" but is immoral, he did not apply that rule to nonbelievers since "In that case you would have to leave this world." Anyway, he asked, "What business is it of mine to judge those outside the church?... God will judge those outside" (1 Corinthians 5:9-13).

Indeed, it would appear that God has transferred authority to enforce these sort of rules from the civil authorities to the church. Since there is no longer a geographic nation that corresponds to God's followers, the church is entrusted with promoting their spiritual health. As a result, the sanctions are different–excommunication instead of execution, for instance–but the ultimate objective is the same, to maintain the purity of the Body of Christ. Just as the Israelites, once they had conquered the Promised Land, did not go to war for the religious purpose of forcing their neighbors to comply with Mosaic law, the church today is not to try to judge nonbelievers. Their fate is to be left up to God.

If this were not the case, the task for civil government would have become impossible in practice once Christ emphasized compliance with the law in thought as well as in deed. "You have heard that it was said, 'Do not commit adultery.' But I tell you that anyone who looks at a woman lustfully has already committed adultery with her in his heart," said Jesus (Matthew 5:27, 28). While the civil authorities may be able to detect and punish adultery, no official, without divine wisdom, can judge lustful looks–or anger at one's brother, which Christ equated with murder (Matthew 5:21, 22).

Anyway, as Rushdoony points out, salvation is a responsibility of God, not the state. It is only Christ's blood that can "cleanse our consciences from acts that lead to death" (Hebrews 9:14). Similarly, wrote Paul to the Roman church, "The mind of sinful man is death, but the mind controlled by the Spirit is life and peace" (Romans 8:6). Indeed, "love is the fulfillment of the law," wrote Paul (Romans 13:10). Yet the state cannot command love. The government may control the impact of sin, such as murder, on others, but the civil authorities cannot make men moral and sinless by cleaning up their hearts, consciences, or minds.

## GODLY VIRTUES

Jesus and the apostles list in great detail the changes in attitude and behavior that individuals need to make to follow God. In the Sermon on the Mount, for instance, Christ said that the poor in spirit, meek, righteous, merciful, pure in heart, peacemakers, and persecuted would be blessed (Matthew 5:3-10). Paul wrote that "the fruit of the Spirit is love, joy, peace, patience, kindness, goodness, faithfulness, gentleness and self-control" (Galatians 5:22; see also Colossians 3:12 and 2 Peter 1:5-7).[32]

However, as important as these and similar characteristics are for Christians, there is nothing to indicate that government can either embody or enforce them. Paul, in particular, wrote on topics ranging from doctrinal heresy to church governance to eating meat sacrificed to idols, but he offered no instruction on civic involvement for Christians, other than to counsel obedience to authority.

Instead, people are to seek to attain godly virtues as they submit themselves to the lordship of Christ. "Be perfect, therefore, as your heavenly Father is perfect," Jesus told the multitude on the mount (Matthew 5:48; see also John 13:15; Ephesians 5:1,2). He taught His followers that they were to be different from their worldly neighbors: "whoever wants to become great among you must be your servant, and whoever wants to be first must be slave of all" (Mark 10: 42-44).

Jesus clearly placed responsibility for adopting Christian character on individual initiative, not the actions of government or any other outside agency: "If your hand or your foot causes you to sin, cut it off and throw it away" (Matthew 18:8). Peter wrote believers that they should "abstain from sinful desires, which war against your soul" (1 Peter 2:11). Later he admonished them to "make every effort to be found spotless, blameless and at peace with him" (2 Peter 3:14).

Some of the characteristics that Christians are supposed to exhibit nevertheless could have an impact on public policy. For instance, pacifists contend that loving one's enemies and turning one's cheek require the civil authorities to acquiesce in the face of foreign aggression. However, nowhere does Jesus apply His message in this manner.[33] He never implied that His mission was inconsistent with the traditional civil duties that God ordained government to perform; while Christ challenged the Pharisees over the private state of their hearts, He did not criticize their public role in punishing wrongdoers. Similarly, Paul acknowledged the avenging role of the civil authorities even as he preached the primacy of love (Romans 13:4).[34]

Thus, while love and the other fruits of the Spirit are expected to be exhibited by believers as they work–in or out of government–these values will not necessarily have any direct impact on the state's actions. For God has not revoked the authority of government to preserve order even where the impersonal yet fair administration of society-wide justice may appear to conflict with such personal Christian imperatives as mercy.

## THE STATE'S SCRIPTURAL ROLE

Government has a specific Biblical purpose, being ordained by God to regulate relations among men in a fallen world. The functions which Scripture mandates government to perform are few: preserving order, protecting life and property, and maintaining justice and righteousness. At the same time, however, the power of godly government must be limited, and no state can interfere with people's right to worship God. Though government may have a backup role in helping the needy, the primary responsibility for that task lies with individuals. In ancient Israel the Lord relied on the civil authorities to enforce religious law, but that grant of authority appears to have been limited to the covenant nation of Israel. Today, in contrast, the church is responsible for monitoring the spiritual health of believers and disciplining those who break God's commands. Christians in government are also responsible for exhibiting through their work a variety of virtues that suffuse Jesus' message–the fruit of the Spirit–but which have no direct application to substantive policies.

In between the polarities of what is required and what is prohibited lies a large area where our perspectives may be informed by Biblical standards, but where we must rely on prudential judgment to evaluate specific policy proposals. In this way our involvement in politics, like our interaction with people in so many other worldly endeavors, requires us to use the wisdom with which God has so graciously offered to endow us (James 1:5).

As a result, implementing a political vision based on Biblical principles is not as simple as listing them. If God's general purpose is clear, "an awkward consequence of the Christian view," writes Richard John Neuhaus, "is that we are frequently unsure what that intent is with respect to specifics at hand." But doubt is no excuse for a believer not to grapple with political issues; we must, in Neuhaus' words, "act in the courage of our uncertainties."[35]

# FIVE

# Biblical Principles: The Transcendence of the Spiritual

*C* hristian political involvement must be different from secular or humanist activism because the believer is dedicated to achieving a different ultimate objective, the Kingdom of God. And in focusing on that goal Christians, no matter how involved politically, should never lose sight of the fact that encouraging man's spiritual transformation remains their foremost duty. Indeed, argues Peter Leithart, "Christian reform is not basically political, though it has a political dimension."[1] For it is through the spiritual reordering of individual human beings, not a new public program, that God redeems us.

Indeed, the mere fact that government is ordained of God does not justify a church-state alliance, or clericocracy, to forcibly inaugurate God's Kingdom here and now.[2] Such an attempt is theologically flawed because it attempts to short-circuit God's planned eschatology. Not only is coercive Christianity Scripturally unsound, but it has resulted in untold injustice that contravenes everything represented by the gospel. Such a result should come as no surprise. As was developed in chapter 4, the state has a number of important Biblical duties, but they are civil rather than religious. Government is responsible for maintaining a just order for all men, while the church is accountable for the spiritual health of believers.

This is not to say that God is uninterested in secular institutions, but that they have no transcendent value. In contrast, "everything God does will endure forever; nothing can be added to it and nothing taken from it" (Ecclesiastes 3:14). Under both the New and Old Covenants God indicates that devotion to Him and a right heart are more important than earthly accomplishments. For instance, after the death of

Moses the Lord instructed Joshua: "Be careful to obey all the law my servant Moses gave you; do not turn from it to the right or to the left, that you may be successful wherever you go. Do not let this Book of the Law depart from your mouth; meditate on it day and night, so that you may be careful to do everything written in it" (Joshua 1:7, 8).

And Jesus' ministry was directed at effecting a dramatic transformation of men's hearts. He explicitly rejected the revolutionary course of the Zealots and withdrew when the crowds sought to crown Him king, confounding the popular expectation of a Messiah who would lead Israel to worldly liberation. Christ clearly subordinated political action to His spiritual mission when he stood before Pilate: "My kingdom is not of this world. If it were, my servants would fight to prevent my arrest by the Jews. But now my kingdom is from another place" (John 18:36).

Moreover, Jesus, though He challenged the ruling authorities for their ungodly behavior, provided no ideological program for His disciples. Instead, He focused on making individuals right with God. For instance, while Jesus demanded financial sacrifice on the part of His followers, He did not do so as part of an income redistribution program but to heal them spiritually. Christ told the rich young ruler, who triumphantly declared that he had kept all of the commandments, that "You still lack one thing. Sell everything you have and give it to the poor, and you will have treasure in heaven" (Luke 18:22). The young man walked away and Jesus lamented, "How hard it is for the rich to enter the kingdom of God"–not how higher taxes were needed to force the man to comply (Luke 18:24).

Christ's treatment of Zacchaeus, a corrupt tax collector, was significantly different. When confronted by Christ, Zacchaeus repented of his sins, offering to give half of what he owned to the poor and to repay fourfold anyone he had cheated. Said Jesus, "Today salvation has come to this house" (Luke 19:9). The point is, salvation, not political reform, was Christ's concern, "For the Son of Man came to seek and to save what was lost," he said (Luke 19:10).

Moreover, Christ's teachings emphasized the conversion of individual lives, not the reform of public institutions. Though genuine spiritual repentance has potentially far-reaching implications for how people relate in the civic sphere, that effect is only secondary. First, people are to love God with all their hearts; second, they are to love their neighbors as themselves. Jesus never went on to spell out any specific political changes that were to result.

Indeed, consider the Sermon on the Mount. There may be no more important set of Biblical standards nor a harder teaching to literally fulfill: the poor in spirit will have the Kingdom of God, the meek will inherit the earth, the mourners will be comforted, and so on. Jesus' emphasis was on changed personal attitudes, not government structures. Later on Christ told the crowd not to "store up for yourselves treasures on earth, where moth and rust destroy, and where thieves break in and steal," but instead to "store up for yourselves treasures in heaven" (Matthew 6:19, 20).

That the most important goal of Christ's message is to reform the individual is also evident from Jesus' discussion with Nicodemus, a member of the Sanhedrin. "Unless a man is born again, he cannot see the kingdom of God," said Jesus (John 3:3). Of course, deeds, including political involvement, are important: "faith by itself, if it is not accompanied by action, is dead," wrote James (2:17). But God still views a right heart as being more important than good works. "If I give all I possess to the poor and surrender my body to the flames, but have not love, I gain nothing," Paul explained to the Corinthian church (1 Corinthians 13:3).

Not surprisingly, then, nowhere does the Bible justify the use of coercion to enforce spiritual conformity. To the contrary, Christ's entire message suggested that coerced conversions, since they cannot transform the heart, are of no value. Paul wrote the church in Ephesus expressing his desire "that Christ may dwell in your hearts through faith," not force (Ephesians 3:17).

It is true that ancient Israel put many of its heathen neighbors to the sword. But the Israelites did so under divine direction. Christians have no similar mandate today. Instead, we are to "gently instruct" unbelievers "in the hope that God will grant them repentance leading them to a knowledge of the truth, and that they will come to their senses and escape from the trap of the devil, who has taken them captive to do his will" (2 Timothy 2:25, 26).

Moreover, the burning of the weeds, as Jesus referred to the final judgment will occur "at the end of the age," when God consummates history, not now (Matthew 13:41; see also

John 12:47, 48). And the Bible makes clear that the sorting out of righteous and unrighteous at that time is God's responsibility, not ours. "There is only one Lawgiver and Judge, the one who is able to save and destroy. But you–who are you to judge your neighbor?" wrote James (4:12). It is the Lamb of God who will open the scroll featured in John's apocalyptic vision (Revelation 5). Similarly, when John the Baptist told his followers about the one who was to follow him, he observed that Christ's "winnowing fork is in his hand to clear his threshing floor and to gather the wheat into his barn, but he will burn up the chaff with unquenchable fire" (Luke 3:17).[3]

Jesus was even more explicit in His parable of the weeds and wheat:

> The kingdom of heaven is like a man who sowed good seed in his field. But while everyone was sleeping, his enemy came and sowed weeds among the wheat, and went away. When the wheat sprouted and formed heads, then the weeds also appeared. The owner's servants came to him and said, "Sir, didn't you sow good seed in your field? Where then did the weeds come from?" "An enemy did this," he replied. The servants asked him, "Do you want us to go and pull them up?" "No," he answered, "because while you are pulling the weeds, you may root up the wheat with them. Let both grow together until the harvest. At that time I will tell the harvesters: First collect the weeds and tie them in bundles to be burned, then gather the wheat and bring it into my barn"(Matthew 13:24-30).

The danger of men "rooting up" the wheat as well as the weeds is exacerbated when the church focuses on intricate yet peripheral dogma that lack a clear Scriptural basis. The attempt of many clerics throughout the ages to develop extensive ecclesiastical doctrines in the absence of specific Biblical direction is not necessarily wrong. But judging people on such dubious criteria is likely to punish genuine Christians as well as nonbelievers. In fact, past church-initiated persecution of heretics and non-Christians was often motivated by just such a misguided commitment to extra-Scriptural standards.

The very gravity of God's requirements for salvation should prevent believers from trying to use civil government as an instrument of salvation.[4] For the most fundamental obedience demanded by God is spiritual: heartfelt personal repentance is the cornerstone of our relationship with God. Political action may follow, but it should never be thought to supersede the spiritual aspects of God's Kingdom.

God's unwillingness to hand over his "winnowing fork" to the state is, not surprisingly, a judgment supported by history. For two thousand years of practical experience have demonstrated again and again the danger of sinful men using corrupt worldly governmental structures to "sort souls." Indeed, Christian attempts to turn the state into a redemptive institution, whether independent of or subordinate to the church, have not only usurped God's authority, but have proved to be disastrous to the Body of Christ.

First, the politicization of religion has caused enormous injustice and harm to untold numbers of people. For the church has proved that it cannot be trusted with secular power. "Men never do evil so completely and cheerfully as when they do it from religious conviction," said the French moralist Blaise Pascal.[5]

The adverse impact of the shift in vision from spiritual reform to political action was evident almost from the moment the Roman Empire adopted Christianity as its official religion. Having been persecuted, the church began to persecute. Having been denied the support of the state, the church began to look to the state for support. Having viewed the emperor as the leader of a pagan system, the church began to view the emperor as the head of the Christian church. And so on.

Doctrinal disputes were rife during the early days of the church, so naturally the clerical establishment constantly turned to the state for help in suppressing heretics. Imperial Rome used the sword to settle conflicts between the orthodox church and the Donatists, Arians, and other splinter sects. Pagan worship, too, was often harassed; temples were forcibly closed, for instance. And though the church lost its access to secular power when Rome fell, Christians appeared to lose none of their enthusiasm for promiscuous state intervention when the church-state alliance was revived centuries later. Conversions were procured at the point of a sword by, among others, the Frankish emperor Charlemagne and Stephen I, Hungary's first king who was later canonized.

The abuses only seemed to increase as Europe was

"Christianized." Punishment and executions for heretics were widespread. The authorities even undertook a series of "crusades" in southern France during the early thirteenth century to root out unorthodox sects and, in an effort to formalize the process, established permanent inquisitional panels. Unconventional thinkers anywhere on the continent were in danger: The Antipope John XXIII had reformer John Huss burned in 1415, one of many Christians martyred by the corrupt Catholic hierarchy. Even Protestant Geneva, which represented spiritual liberation from the politicized papacy, executed the heretic Michael Servetus in 1553.

And there was, of course, the infamous Spanish Inquisition, which successively persecuted Jews and Protestants; as many as 400,000 Jews ended up as forced converts. The Inquisition was first established in 1478 to examine converts' faith. Children and grandchildren of those who had been condemned were denied the right to hold public office or enter a variety of private professions. Books by even orthodox Catholic writers were banned. The Inquisition financed itself by confiscating victims' property and selling positions as informers.[6] Though the persecution diminished in the late 1800s, the last execution for heresy–of someone who used "Praise be to God" instead of "Ave Maria" in his school prayers–occurred in 1826. Mexico, a Spanish colony, suffered under its own inquisition between 1536 and 1543.

The slaughter was international. The first crusade to roll back Islam ventured forth in 1095. Several more followed over the succeeding two centuries. Some of the expeditions had ephemeral success, including one directed more against the Christian Byzantine Empire than the Islamic powers, but by 1270 the eighth crusade had failed and the Middle East remained under Moslem control.

Later, within Europe itself, Catholics, Lutherans, and Calvinists all used state power against each other as well as other sects, like the Anabaptists. The Catholic king of France, Charles IX, inaugurated a massacre of the Protestant Huguenots in 1572. The Thirty Years War started in 1618 and involved much of Europe; the different Catholic-Protestant subconflicts and alliances were as confusing as they were changeable. (In the end, religious freedom was promised, but only for Catholics, Reformed, and Lutherans.) All told, between 1520 and 1648, there was just one brief respite from otherwise constant religious-based warfare. Observes historian Paul Johnson, "It is a tragic but recurrent feature of Christianity that the eager pursuit of reform tends to produce a ruthlessness in dealing with obstacles to it which brings the whole moral superstructure crashing down in ruins."[7]

Even today, religion plays a role in such conflicts as Northern Ireland. Real Christianity is, in fact, essentially absent from a dispute where Catholicism and Protestantism symbolize social and cultural differences more than doctrinal disputes. Nevertheless, throughout the ages the gospel of Christ has been used as an excuse for the most vicious sort of bloodshed imaginable.

The use of secular force to enforce ecclesiastical standards also did violence to one of the most important tasks of the church: the search for and enunciation of the truth. For a Christian, the gospel represents truth. Christ Himself said, "I am the way and the truth and the life" (John 14:6; see also John 1:14). And He instructed His listeners, "If you hold to my teaching, you are really my disciples. Then you will know the truth, and the truth will set you free" (John 8:31, 32).

Though Jesus is the truth, individuals must search before they discern God. Declared the prophet Jeremiah: "You will seek me and find me when you seek me with all your heart" (Jeremiah 29:13). Similarly, Christ stated that "I stand at the door and knock. If anyone hears my voice and opens the door, I will come in and eat with him, and he with me" (Revelation 3:20). A person must both hear Jesus and open the door to have fellowship with God—he cannot be pushed through. "How, then, can they call on the one they have not believed in?", asked Paul (Romans 10:14). True conviction cannot be coerced.

And if force cannot compel someone to accept the truth, that is, the gospel, there is no other possible warrant for coercing conversions, even as an attempt to consummate the Kingdom of Heaven. For trying to do so is a presumptuous effort to preempt God's perfect timing for another person's conversion. "There is a time for everything," and only God knows what that time is (Eccesiastes 3:1). In discussing His return to earth, Christ said that "No one knows about that day or hour, not even the angels in heaven, nor the Son, but only the Father" (Matthew 24:36).[8]

A review of Biblical texts also suggests that, in Richard John Neuhaus' words, "diversity in belief is inherent in, and not accidental to, the divine purpose."⁹ Neuhaus points to the Apostle Paul's letter to the Roman church in which he struggles with his own people's rejection of Christ. On the one hand, Paul stated that "I have great sorrow and unceasing anguish in my heart" (Romans 9:1). Nevertheless, he added that "It is not as though God's word had failed" (Romans 9:6). If the refusal of God's chosen people to accept the New Covenant appears to confound our understanding, that does not make it inconsistent with God's plan. For we cannot rely on human wisdom in assessing the will of God. The Lord asked Job, "Where were you when I laid the earth's foundation? Tell me, if you understand" (Job 38:4). And there is nothing that man can do, in or out of politics, to change or overturn God's plan. "It does not, therefore, depend on man's desire or effort, but on God's mercy," wrote Paul (Romans 9:16).

These fundamental truths apply with even greater force when the issue is civil punishment of alleged Christian heretics instead of pagans. The church may be able, with some certainty, to explain the bedrock aspects of the Christian faith, such as Christ's redemptive role, and consequently to assess a person's commitment to those doctrines. But formal religious institutions have failed miserably to reach agreement on many other issues that are important but not determinative for believers.

What is the proper role of baptism, for instance? It is commanded by Christ as part of the Great Commission; Peter included the procedure in his first sermon in Jerusalem. Though a few sects, including the Church of Christ, believe that water immersion is necessary for salvation, most denominations, like the Baptists and Catholics, argue instead about which procedure–infant baptism, adult immersion, or whatever–is the most faithful to God's intent. Ascertaining the Lord's will requires free dialogue; yet at one point the Catholic Church prescribed the death sentence for those who were rebaptized, such as the Anabaptists.¹⁰

Where the state is the ecclesiastical enforcer, erroneous church dogma becomes extraordinarily difficult to change. Indeed, in a sense Jesus faced the same sort of institutional resistance on the part of the ruling Jewish hierarchy: the ecclesiastical authorities ultimately relied on the power of the Roman Empire to oppose His mission to replace the Old Covenant. If God is truth, however, using state power to protect error is a particularly gross perversion of the church's role.

In any case, the attempt to turn to the state to settle ecclesiastical disputes and enforce church doctrine is flawed because the government is not the church–it is an agency that theoretically represents everyone, believer and nonbeliever alike, and not just the Body of Christ. As such, non-Christian influence in public decisions is inevitable.

Moreover, the state, no less than any other human institution, is run by fallen man. This was so in the Jewish provinces ruled by Rome when Christ walked the earth. It was so in imperial Rome and medieval Europe. And it is so today, even in this nation, which many Christians believe to be uniquely blessed of God. Writes Neuhaus: "Whatever the virtues of the American experiment, it is a society among other societies. It is part of the temporal order; it is in time as far short of the kingdom as is any other earthly kingdom. Its life is ordered primarily by power rather than by grace and love."[11]

In fact, given the many clear Biblical injunctions about the failure of public authority, it is hard to understand how Christians at any time could have turned to the state for official support. "None of the rulers of this age understood /the wisdom of God/, for if they had, they would not have crucified the Lord of glory," wrote Paul to the Corinthian church (1 Corinthians 2:8). He even urged Christians to avoid going to the civil authorities in secular matters: "If any of you has a dispute with another, dare he take it before the ungodly for judgment instead of before the saints?" (1 Corinthians 6:1) If the government is not always "the beast" described in John's Revelation, there is still no Scriptural basis for investing the system Paul commanded obedience to with ecclesiastical authority.

Moreover, the state that can promote a church's standards can also prevent it from enforcing unpopular doctrines. Constantine, for instance, was disinterested in the intricacies of theology. His primary objective was to ensure a universal and stable church that would buttress the Empire. For this reason he threatened the Bishop Athanasius: "As you know my wishes, pray admit freely any who wish to enter the church. If I hear you have stopped anyone claiming membership I will immediately send an official to depose you and send you into exile."[12]

Lastly, the church's involvement with secular power has

both damaged its outward witness to an unbelieving world and corrupted its inner being. The medieval church, for instance, constantly tarnished the name of Christ with its attempts at political aggrandizement. If the threat to the church's spiritual credibility is not quite so serious today, dangers nevertheless remain. In 1984 thirteen Baptist churches in Jackson, Tennessee, became deeply involved in a local referendum, opposing the sale of alcohol by the drink. They argued that their efforts stemmed from moral rather than political concerns, and refused to register as political campaign committees, which they said would be "repugnant." The Tennessee Supreme Court nevertheless ruled that they had to comply with the law. In short, he who plays politics will be treated just like any other political player, however distasteful it may be.

Appearances are not everything, of course, but they are important. Do non-Christians see the love and grace of God exhibited when the church grasps for secular power, using force to suppress those who hold unorthodox views? "The Christian view of political justice should be built directly on this understanding of God's gracious patience and love," writes James Skillen. "If this is done, Christian politics will not manifest itself as the Church's selfish attempt to control the state, or as an interest-group effort to 'get' benefits primarily for Christians, or as a campaign to flood political offices with Christians so that Christians can control the government for the enforcement of Christian doctrine on the populace."[13]

Even if Christians can directly benefit from using the state–and government has more often used religion than the other way around–they must not forget that their transcendent duty is to spread the Good News. If their reach for power inhibits their making "disciples of all nations" (Matthew 28:19), then they should abandon it. After all, Christ told the multitudes that "If your hand or your foot causes you to sin, cut it off and throw it away" (Matthew 18:8).

Moreover, an outwardly venal appearance usually reflects ongoing inner corruption. This phenomenon is symbolized by Constantine himself. Officially he became a Christian, and his conversion may have been genuine. But he continued to worship the sun, was cruel in war, and even executed members of his family. The Christ of the Gospels went from the Good Shepherd searching for the lost lamb to the head of a blood-stained imperial state waging war. As a result, the price the church paid for gaining imperial power, argues Vernard Eller, was "graciously taking unto itself every evil the empire had ever represented."[14]

Constantine essentially created a state-supported clerical class: bishoprics became prizes much fought over by competing ecclesiastical leaders because they could lead to a life of luxury. Bishops dressed, acted, and entertained like secular noblemen. Damasus, who served as Bishop of Rome from 366 to 384, made it a priority to formally convert wealthy individuals to Christianity. Important families even hired clerics much as medieval rulers underwrote court musicians.

There were good bishops, such as Gregory of Nazianzus, John Chrysostom, and Jerome, who criticized the debasement of the church. Indeed, officials like them struggled to prevent bishops from transferring from poor to rich sees. The ecclesiastical council meeting in Sardica in 341 adopted canons stating that "a rich man, or lawyer, or state official ... should not be ordained unless he has previously acted as a reader, deacon, or priest" and his "whole life has been under review for a long period, and whose worth has been proved."[15] Nevertheless, such efforts were unable to keep the church pure.

Moreover, the use of state power to essentially take over, wholesale, the temples and assets of paganistic cults inevitably compromised Christian doctrines. "Pagans came into the church with their paganism," writes Jacques Ellul.[16] For the many people who became Christians either to avoid imperial sanction or curry Rome's favor, their "conversion" essentially involved the mere substitution of deities–Jesus for Jupiter, for instance. In many cases Christianity seemed more to merge with local cults than to triumph over them.

Religious orthodoxy also became intermixed with geopolitics. The Donatist heresy, which involved the readmission to fellowship of those who had denied their faith during earlier imperial persecution, was very strong in the old Punic terrories of North Africa. Rome savagely suppressed the movement; though the underlying dispute was theological, the orthodox and Donatist churches split along class and territorial lines.

During the Hundred Years' War–really 118 years of intermittent conflict between France, England, and Scotland beginning in 1337–the papacy, located in Avignon, France, from 1305 to 1378, was inextricably linked to France. The Catholic Church's intervention in the conflict undermined its claim to universality, especially during the ensuing Great Schism when there were two and then three competing popes. Ultimately England broke with the Vatican, inaugurating the Anglican Church.

The Catholic Church also became entangled with the French monarchy; not surprisingly, when Louis XVI was displaced by violent revolution, the religious hierarchy came under attack as well. Tens of thousands of priests were exiled and imprisoned and thousands were executed; the Protestant churches, too, suffered grievously during the reign of terror. The leaders of the Revolution even tried to create their own religion, successively called the "Cult of Reason" and the "Cult of the Supreme Being." Napoleon Bonaparte, who took power in 1799, reached a new Concordat with the papacy, but the taint of the clerical class' alliance with aristocratic vested interests was not easy to remove from the church that was supposed to be representing the gospel of Christ.

Moreover, close collaboration between church and state usually resulted in the spiritual becoming subservient to the secular. Argues Alistair Kee, head of the Department of Religious Studies at the University of Glasgow, "Constantine achieved by kindness what his predecessors had not been able to achieve by force. Without a threat or a blow, and all unsuspecting, the Christians were led into captivity and their religion transformed into a new imperial cult."[17]

Constantine became involved in the most fundamental church disputes—such as the relationship between Father, Son, and Holy Spirit. Indeed, he, the secular ruler of an empire described as "the beast" in a divine revelation to an apostle, a worshiper of the Unconquered Sun who appeared never to entirely abandon his pagan heritage, played an important role in the deliberations of the Council of Nicea, which debated and rejected the views of Arius, who believed that Christ was not eternal but a created being. Constantine later changed his mind, ordering the readmission of Arius to communion in the orthodox church. A host of other heretical sects, including the Docetists, Sabellianists, Apollinarians, and Monarchianists, were also suppressed by state and church acting in concert, more to maintain domestic order than spiritual purity.

Unfortunately, this pattern repeated itself throughout history. Indeed, the problem became, if anything, worse as the papacy comported itself as a secular power, making alliances, conducting wars, extorting wealth, and suffering from unending power struggles.[18] At times the corruption of the church was almost total, as the clerical class flaunted wealth and immorality, using its influence to achieve materialistic rather than spiritual objectives. Bishoprics were sold to raise revenue, heavenly forgiveness was promised in return for the purchase of indulgences, extra-Scriptural doctrines were manufactured, and the Bible was withheld from the masses. Even the papacy itself was literally for sale, as Alexander VI purchased enough cardinals' votes to be elected Pope. It was said of him that "Alexander is ready to sell the keys, the altars, and even Christ himself. He is within his rights, since he bought them."[19]

Politics subverted foreign mission efforts as well. The Jesuits, Dominicans, Franciscans, and Calvinists all struggled against each other in Japan, inflaming the fears of the Japanese authorities by citing the political designs of the missionaries' home countries; the result was a brutal religious pogrom that destroyed the growing Christian church. The ordination of native priests and education of local peoples was sharply restricted in colonies like Mexico in part to pacify the ruling secular authorities at home.

The potential for corruption of the church today, if not so great because ecclesiastical access to power has been sharply circumscribed, nevertheless remains very real. American churches, for instance, allowed themselves to be caught up in the issues of "manifest destiny"—including the seizure of Mexican and Spanish territories—and slavery. Many of the churches that once opposed what a frankly aggressive campaign against Mexico joined in identifying with an action that opened a "door" for them into new territory, for instance. And some churches not only propagandized on behalf of slavery before the Civil War, but preached white supremacy, segregation, and Jim Crow laws a century later.

Even worse has been the ecclesiastical response to the totalitarian ideologies that have dominated different countries this century. The Lutheran church was supported by the state at the time of Hitler's rise to power and had, writes Paul Johnson, "no dogmatic or moral theology for an opposition role. Since Luther's day they had always been in the service of the State, and indeed in many ways had come to see themselves as civil servants."[20] The Catholic Church also shrank from confrontation, though for somewhat different reasons.

The church was used to operating in concert with government and worried about its ability to survive persecution; the Catholic authorities also feared communism above all else and looked favorably on any secular state that could act as a bulwark against the spread of Marxism. Explains Johnson, the church "became infused with an intense eagerness to demonstrate its loyalty to German ideals and aims and its total identification with Germanic society."[21]

Of course, Communist rule did come, first to the Soviet Union and then to Eastern Europe after the defeat of Nazi Germany. The Catholic and Orthodox churches largely accommodated the atheistic authorities, and, as a result, were dominated by the state and declined spiritually. In contrast, groups that held themselves apart–evangelical and Pentecostal sects, for instance, and the Polish Catholic church–generally maintained their integrity.

The more recent decline of liberal Protestantism in America is probably a result of those churches' increasing emphasis on the social gospel to the exclusion of spiritual issues. According to James Reichley of the Brookings Institute, between 1970 and 1980 the United Presbyterian church lost 21 percent of its members; declines for other sects included 15 percent for the Episcopal Church, 12 percent for the Presbyterian Church (largely located in the South), 11 percent for the United Church of Christ, 10 percent for the United Methodist Church, and 8 percent for the Lutheran Church. In contrast, those denominations emphasizing spiritual themes grew sharply: membership of Assemblies of God was up 70 percent, Seventh-Day Adventists increased 36 percent, and the Southern Baptist Convention rose 16 percent. The Catholic Church's rolls increased 5 percent, though primarily through Hispanic immigration.[22]

Though a host of demographic and social explanations have been offered for this phenomenon, the most important reason appears to be spiritual. Admitted Dean Kelley, a Methodist minister who works for the National Council of Churches, most people look to their churches to find "purpose, promise, and possibility" in "the human predicament." But the mainline churches, by focusing on political action, had abandoned "their unique and essential contribution to healing the world's wounds: meaning."[23]

Activists on the religious right face a similar danger. "We want to see a reformation in America," said Tim LaHaye, chairman of the American Coalition for Traditional Values, in December 1985. And he saw political action as the means to do so: "If every Bible-believing church in America would trust God to use them to raise up one person to run for public office in the next ten years, do you realize that we would have more Christians in office than there are offices to hold?"[24] But where in the gospel message does Christ suggest that all the disciples had to do to implement God's Kingdom was infiltrate the government?

In fact, some Christians appear to believe that the Republican Party offers the path to corporate redemption. "We've taken over the GOP in many areas," said Gary Jarmin of Christian Voice in 1984. "We intend to use the Republican Party as a vehicle."[25] But this vehicle, no matter how well driven by whom, cannot reform men's hearts. Instead, believers will be tempted to substitute a temporal, flawed political agenda for the eternal gospel of Christ.

It is this dismal history of the results of ecclesiastical access to state power that led Vernard Eller to admit that "my great fear about today's Christian revolution, out to transform and save the world for God, is not that it might fail but that it might succeed."[26] The church and the state are not the same; they are not even complementary institutions, one ruling the spiritual and one the secular realms. Instead, the government, though ordained by God, is run by sinful man. It is a compromise that will exist until God's eschatological promise–that is, the consummation of His Kingdom–comes to pass.

And until that time Christians must focus on their underlying spiritual duty. "Seek first his kingdom and his righteousness, and all these things will be given to you," Jesus told the crowds (Matthew 6:33). Christ commands obedience; political activism offers no substitute for losing one's life in the service of God. "What good will it be for a man if he gains the whole world, yet forfeits his soul?" asked Christ (Matthew 16:26). Believers must do all they can to prevent their neighbors from losing their souls.

In carrying out that duty Christians should infuse the political process, as well as all other human institutions, with Biblical values. For reliance on those principles is necessary for a humane society that respects religious freedom to exist. As Richard John Neuhaus has observed, "The force of virtue was thought to be both prior to and reinforcing of the polity. The polity presupposed a culture of virtue; it was not intended to replace it and it could not create a new one in its place."[27]

But the state cannot become an adjunct of the church, enforcing ecclesiastical rules. Christ Himself rejected Satan's offer of authority over all the kingdoms of the land, for to do so would have required Jesus to worship the Devil. Investing government with untrammeled coercive power and attempting to turn it, a human organization, into a redemptive instrument is, in essence, to create and worship an ungodly idol. Indeed, the gospel message exhorts individuals not to seek authority over their neighbors—even in God's name—but to subordinate their will to God. Jesus explicitly criticized the Gentile rulers who "lord it over" their people (Mark 10:42).

And given man's sinful nature, as long as the state is a flawed institution administered by sinful men, entrusting to it the preservation of spiritual purity will end in disaster. The long, bitter history of church-state relations has caused untold hardship and injustice, dampened the search for spiritual truth, and corrupted the church.

In fact, considering the degenerate nature of worldly government throughout history, there is a sense in which conflict between secular and ecclesiastical power is an inevitable result of following the gospel. For Christ came to challenge a humanistic worldview that included absolutist state authority; the Son of Man transcends rather than absorbs the public sector. Jacques Ellul may overstate the case, but his basic point remains valid: "What the recognition of the state and the entry of Christians and the church into politics have produced is a mutation that amounts to subversion. Revelation inevitably meant a break in the human order, in society, in power. Jesus came to cast a fire on the earth. He did not come to bring peace but a sword.... Just as conversion always means a break in individual life, so the intervention of revelation means a break in the whole group, in all society, and it unavoidably challenges the institution and established power, no matter what form this may take."[28]

To accept the fact that the government is not the repository of truth requires Christians to compromise their tactics, not their values. Yet in late 1985 Tim LaHaye made the astonishing assertion that "the only way to have a genuine spiritual revival is to have legislative reform."[29] Since when does Uncle Sam have a greater role than the Holy Spirit in man's regeneration? Political action may follow a change of heart, but it cannot cause that personal transformation. Indeed, the church grew most explosively when it was persecuted in the first century. The church's spiritual health and its reliance on government appear to be inversely related. In the end, believers' witness for Christ must flow from their personal actions, not their access to worldly power.

Christians should be politically involved. But as believers enter the policy-making process they must be careful to advance genuine Biblical standards when they are claiming to represent a Christian perspective. Believers must be especially careful to eschew the temptation to declare God behind every item on their personal political agenda, using their religious affiliation to advance positions that have little or no spiritual dimension. There are, in fact, political controversies that cannot be decided with reference to specific Scriptures; in such cases, the issue can be framed by Biblical principles, but Christians can, and do, differ on the particular policy advocated.[30]

"The Kingdom of God provides unique moral imperatives that can cause men and women to rise above their natural egoism to serve the greater good," writes Charles Colson.[31] And that includes avoiding the self-indulgent, even idolatrous, belief that one's own ideology is necessarily shared by God. The fact that this sort of humility has frequently been in short supply among Christians is demonstrated all too clearly by the history of the church's un-Scriptural yet persistent reliance on secular power, to which we now turn.

# Church and State: The Historical Experience

*C*hristians have spent the last twenty centuries trying to integrate God and government, without achieving any consensus. Truth, not unity, is a believer's proper goal, of course, but the failure of Christians to reach even general agreement on the goals of public policy highlights the many pitfalls in attempting to develop a Biblical political view. On a number of core theological issues there is little disagreement among believers: to be a true disciple of Christ, as He Himself defined it, for example, requires a belief in Jesus' divinity and redemptive role. Others may call themselves Christians, but it is in a modern secular, not Biblical, sense.

Similarly, though opinions differ on the exact purpose of baptism, no honest student of Scripture can deny its importance. The contours of the limited circumstances when divorce is justified occasion some debate, but God's view of the sanctity of the marriage covenant is not in doubt. And there is little controversy over the core role of the church–to evangelize all nations, administer the sacraments, and discipline errant believers–detailed in the Bible.

In contrast, on few of man's issues is there a similar accord. The Body of Christ has found itself badly riven over its proper stance on major issues such as when and on which side to go to war, slavery, economics, and poverty. Even on the issue of abortion there is surprising disagreement among believers who accept the authority of Scripture: one-fifth of fundamentalists and Southern Baptists back abortion "on demand," while another fifth support abortion on some vague showing of "need."[1]

While the specific policy outcomes of many issues are

simply beyond the Bible, the basic Scriptural principles that
should underlie every Christian's decision-making process are
ascertainable, as was discussed in Chapter Four. Yet even at
that level the Body of Christ has proved historically incapable
of constructing a consistent Biblical political perspective. On
the one hand, the lure of secular power has frequently caused
the organized church to dishonestly twist the Bible to justify
its use of government to promote and enforce moral and ecclesiastical rules: the result all too often has been an oppressive
clericocracy. Some Christians, horrified by the abuses of secular institutions, have advocated complete separation not only
of church from state, but also of believers from politics, thereby abdicating their duty to act as Christian salt and light for
the public square. Many other believers have struggled, with
varying degress of success, to find a better, Biblical balance in
between the two extremes.

## THE FIRST-CENTURY CHURCH

Jesus' ministry was devoid of any traditional political activity.
He paid what taxes were due and ultimately submitted to the
Jewish and Roman ruling authorities. Indeed, He purposefully
rebuffed those who would have made Him an earthly king, for
his spiritual mission was paramount. As He was being arrested
in the Garden of Gethsemane, He ordered Peter to sheath his
sword, saying: "Do you think I cannot call on my Father, and
he will at once put at my disposal more than twelve legions of
angels? But how then would the Scriptures be fulfilled that say
it must happen in this way?" (Matthew 26:53, 54). Similarly,
the Gospels do not record Jesus imparting any political advice
to the disciples before His ascension into heaven.

Nor do we have any evidence that the church's political
role was ever an issue during its formative years. In his
account in Acts, Luke paints a fledgling apostolic movement
struggling against both the traditional Jewish religious hierarchy and the paganistic Roman authorities. The battles are
almost entirely spiritual: Paul was willing to use his Roman
citizenship to demand the protections of the judicial process
due him, but he engaged in no lobbying on the public policy
issues of the day.

Moreover, his letters to believers in such important cities
as Corinth, Ephesus, and even Rome betrayed no interest in
secular political squabbles. Paul said nothing to discourage

Christians from holding office or participating in civic affairs, but he unveiled no religious policy agenda. Indeed, as Rome intensified its persecution of the church, ultimately executing both Paul and Peter, no normal political role was possible for Christians.

## PRE-CONSTANTINE ROME

Martyrdom set the tone for the church for decades as Christianity spread in spite of vigorous official attempts to stamp out what was seen as an atheistic cult which attacked worship of the traditional gods and the officially deified emperor. "Central to Christian martyrdom was a distinction between spiritual and political realms," writes Charles Villa-Vicencio. "For early Christians this was a distinction grounded in a theological suspicion of, if not hostility to, the state."[2] Though they believed they were obligated to honor the governing authorities, the early Christians did not believe in participating in political affairs. And their attitude naturally flowed from their circumstances—they expected no change in their status as a persecuted minority and looked for their rescue to come from Christ's early return, not a conversion of the emperor.

One of the early Christian theologians who articulated such a nonpolitical philosophy was Tertullian (who lived from A.D. 150-220). In his view, writes Paul Johnson, "Christians should limit their contacts with the state to the minimum: they should refuse to serve in the army, or the civil service, or even in state schools."[3] Given such an approach, confrontation between Rome, which commanded absolute allegiance, and the church was inevitable. Yet Tertullian was interested not in activism to achieve political reform, but in praying that the state ultimately fulfill its proper relationship in subordination to God, allowing the church full freedom.

## POST-CONSTANTINE CHURCH

There was perhaps no more dramatic religious upheaval in the ancient world than Constantine's conversion to Christianity. The general story of God's supposed sign to Constantine before his victory in the Battle of the Milvian Bridge near Rome is well-known, though the depth of his conversion is not clear: he never fully abandoned his heritage as a sun-worshiper, and his conduct while in power was less than pristine. But

Constantine's theological switch nevertheless almost instantaneously turned Christianity from an outcast cult into a state religion. Persecution had been sporadic but intense in the latter half of the third century; in 313, however, Constantine and co-emperor Licinius issued the "Edict of Milan," revoking previous anti-Christian decrees, returning confiscated church properties, and giving "the Christians and all others liberty to follow whatever form of worship they chose."[4]

For a time the state was neutral in the competition between different religions and Christian sects, but the end of imperial hostility toward the church caused believers to abandon the Tertullian policy of noncooperation with the state. In essence, the empire that had once done the work of Satan was now seen as an agent of God. "When the political structures were changed under Constantine, Christians apparently flocked to participate in the civil service and the army and to accept political office," writes Villa-Vicencio.[5]

And imperial tolerance soon turned into state support, as Christianity became the official religion and the church a buttress of the state. Constantine himself appeared to view himself as a priest-king; according to the Bishop Eusebuis, the emperor told a visiting group of bishops that "I also am a bishop, ordained by God to oversee those outside the church."[6] The distinction between church and state increasingly blurred as the Christian clergy received official support and Constantine ruled on theological disputes, such as the Donatist heresy. Eusibius exalted Constantine on the thirteith anniversary of his reign: "Our emperor, his friend, acting as interpreter to the Word of God, aims at recalling the whole human race to the knowledge of God. Our emperor, emulous of his Divine example, having purged his earthly dominion from every stain of impious error, invites each holy and pious worshiper within his imperial mansions, earnestly desiring to save with all its crew that mighty vessel of which he is the appointed pilot."[7]

Ironically, imperial Rome remained relatively tolerant of paganism. But it would not allow the spread of Christian heresies, ruthlessly suppressing the Donatists and Arians, for instance. By the fifth century more than 100 different laws restricted heretics; some even forbade religious discussions. In the end the state became the final guarantor of theological orthodoxy.

## THE MEDIEVAL CHURCH

The split in the Roman Empire led to two different church-state models. In the east Byzantium essentially continued Constantine's ecclesiocratic system; the emperor performed priestly as well as civil functions, and the Orthodox Church was an official adjunct of the government. In essence, the emperor was God's vice-regent, chosen to guard the orthodox faith and rule an earthly kingdom that prefigured the coming heavenly realm. This system persisted into the fifteenth century, when Constantinople fell to the Turks.

However, as the western empire gradually dissolved in the face of successive invasions by the Goths, Vandals, and other northern tribes, the relationship between church and state necessarily changed. Though the church initially lost power, its long-term influence was assured by the fact that it was the one imperial institution that survived Rome's fall. The church was generally not persecuted–many of the "barbarian" invaders were Arians who were tolerant of orthodox believers–and preserved hellenistic and Roman culture in the face of an essentially tribalistic society. Bishoprics eventually arose in cities, and the bishop often acted as the local chief magistrate. The church began to codify laws. Monastic orders arose, and the church gained a measure of economic power through large agricultural estates. Moreover, Christianity eventually permeated even the northernmost pagan peoples.

"In a general sense," writes Johnson, "we find the Christian bishops bridging the gap between the Roman world and the emerging world of the Dark Ages."[8] The clerical class, especially that in Rome, increasingly gained civil as well as spiritual authority. Church and state continued to work closely together as they had under Constantine, with the church eventually trying to dominate the partnership. In fact, a precursor to the political power of the papacy in medieval times was Bishop Ambrose's refusal to allow the Roman Emperor Theodosius communion until he repented of one particularly brutal campaign against Thessalonicans accused of sedition.

Similarly, Augustine, who lived in the end of the imperial period, developed a theology that came to permeate the medieval period. Augustine envisioned the total Christian society, with believers having essentially captured all nominally secular institutions, including the government. "Led by the elect, its duty was to transform, absorb and perfect all existng bonds of human relations, all human activities and institutions, to regularize and codify and elevate every aspect of life," writes Johnson.[9] Interestingly, Augustine's ideas seemed to shift somewhat as he aged and the empire deteriorated. In *The City of God* he sharply contrasted the earthly and heavenly cities, but he still believed that Christians, even as they kept their sights on God's realm, had an obligation to bring its earthly counterpart into conformance with God's law.

Augustine backed persecution of pagans and heretics. He believed that the use of force had successfully changed his own town's allegiance from the Donatist heresy to the orthodox church; he argued that Christ had used "great violence" to turn Paul into a disciple. In his view, the church, backed by the state, had a duty to compel the recalcitrant to come into the faith and his writings were cited by the later church inquisitors.

Thomas Aquinas expanded Augustine's theories, justifying the sort of ecclesiocratic society that emerged in medieval times. The state's power was not absolute; instead, it occupied a specific position in God's social hierarchy. Notably, government had no redemptive power. In this way the civil authority was clearly subordinate to the church. Wrote Aquinas: "The final aim of social life will be, not merely to live in virtue, but rather through virtuous life to attain to the enjoyment of God. If, indeed, it were possible to attain this object by natural human virtue, it would, in consequence, be the duty of kings to guide men to this end. We believe, however, that it is the supreme power in temporal affairs which is the business of a king.... But the enjoyment of God is an aim which cannot be attained by human virtue alone.... Only a divine rule, then, and not human government, can lead us to this end."[10]

The medieval model advanced by the organized church may have achieved its symbolic consummation on Christmas Day, 800, when Pope Leo III set the crown on Charlemagne, implying papal supremacy. The papacy had long played a role in worldly political struggles, though the state still dominated the relationship. Charlemagne, for instance, had won the throne on the battlefield and later said he regretted allowing the Pope to act as if the crown was the papacy's to give. In fact, Charlemagne placed Leo III on trial before allowing him to retain his position; the emperor considered himself to be the Lord's anointed on earth and the clerical class to be his agent.

But if there was disagreement over who was supreme, there was a unity of vision regarding the need to rule society along Christian lines. "Both the papacy and the strong-minded ecclesiastical element at the Carolingian court saw the new power-structure they had brought into existence not only as a restoration of the Roman empire in all its glory, but as a reconstruction from within of society in all its aspects, to produce a model of the Christian kingdom on earth. Charlemagne was to realize the Augustinian vision."[11]

The church took on many functions of normal civil authority: tithes were mandatory, for instance. The church regulated personal moral conduct, with clerics even visiting individual homes to ensure conformity with religious rules. De facto state enforcement of ecclesiastical moral standards lasted into the nineteenth century in some European nations. In such varying countries as Spain and England the monarch was the head of the church, and the clergy governed territories on behalf of that official. Though the system differed from the hierarchy in ancient Israel in many ways, the medieval structure was nevertheless essentially clericocratic.

Once the Carolingian empire began to deteriorate, church/state relations changed as well. Though for a brief period in the ninth century the papacy was generally viewed as the ultimate source of all power, the civil rulers–vested as they were with godly authority–largely reigned supreme until the eleventh century. But as the crown lost land, it also forfeited influence vis-a-vis not only other secular institutions but also the church. Around 1070 Pope Gregory VII asserted papal prerogatives when Henry IV attempted to appoint bishops in Italy. In Gregory's view, reports Johnson, "the State without the Church was nothing. Just as the spirit animated the body, so the Church ultimately determined the motions of the State. Indeed, the State, in carrying out its temporary functions, was merely exercising the authority delegated to it by the Church."[12]

In the ensuing centuries civil and ecclesiastical authorities struggled violently over the question whether the king was the Lord's anointed with the bishops as his lieutenants, or the Pope was God's highest representative on earth, entitled to choose the kings. The fight was bitter and prolonged, looking suspiciously like a brawl over secular power rather than godly justice. As a result, the Carolingian system–with a unified church and state to enforce personal morals–collapsed. Though the secular authorities were nominally Christian, they often resisted what they considered to be clerical meddling and over-reaching.

Nevertheless, the church remained uncompromising. Wrote Pope Boniface VIII in 1302: "Both swords, the spiritual and the material, therefore, are in the power of the church; the one, indeed, to be wielded for the church, the other by the church; the one by the hand of the priest, the other by the hand of kings and knights, but at the will and sufferance of the priest. One sword, moreover, ought to be under the other, and the temporal authority to be subjected to the spiritual."[13] In the end the papacy lacked the secular force necessary to impose its will, especially as the respective monarchies con-solidated their national power; the gap between ecclesiastical claims and actual authority grew steadily in the thirteenth century. But if the church did not reign supreme, it neverthe-less exercised significant influence at different times.

## THE CATHOLIC CHURCH

If the extravagant claims of earthly power made by the Catholic Church did not reflect reality, the church neverthe-less long held to Pope Gregory's position. Throughout the rev-olutionary 1700s and 1800s the church maintained its ulti-mate theoretical goal of a complete Christian society administered by the papacy, though in practice the church focused on resisting encroachments on its dwindling political influence. In 1864, for instance, Pope Pius IX issued the encyclical *Quanta cura*, which denounced any civil infringe-ment on the Church's expansive prerogatives. The encyclical went on to assert that the Pope was entitled to "a civil prince-dom" and that Catholicism "was the sole religion of the state to the exclusion of all others."[14] If the Vatican's civil power was in eclipse, the delay in forging a Christian society was assumed to be only temporary; in time it would complete the mission of the Vicar of Christ.[15]

But the Augustinian vision of a Christian society with civil and clerical authorities working together finally died on bloody battlefields throughout Europe as secular states were captured by vicious anti-Christian ideologies. The Catholic Church eventually accepted the reality of two separate king-doms, a process accelerated by Vatican II–the Twenty-First

Ecumenical Council convened on October 11, 1962.

The state's authority was still believed to come from above. Stated Pope John XXIII in his 1963 encyclical, *Pacem in terris*, "Such an order can have no other origin but in God, a personal God, our creator."[16] However, continued Pope John, "the attainment of the common good is the sole reason for the existence of civil authorities." Rulers were to "respect the hierarchy of values, and aim at achieving the spiritual as well as the material prosperity of their subjects," but government was no longer expected to be Catholicism's enforcer.[17] Today Pope John Paul II, though perhaps theologically more conservative than his recent predecessors, gives no indication of trying to return the church to a more ecclesiocratic vision.

## THE REFORMATION CHURCH

The theological revolution which rent the Catholic Church–symbolized by Luther's nailing of his Ninety-five Theses on the Wittenberg Castle's church door in 1517–also transformed the way in which many believers looked at the state. All of the major reformation sects broke with the Catholic Church's cleriocratic doctrines, though they achieved no unanimity among themselves.

For example, Calvin, like the Pope, believed both that the government's power came from God and that the civil authorities had a responsibility to order the world along Christian lines.[18] As a result, in Geneva, where Calvin held no political office but nevertheless wielded enormous influence, the civil government punished heretics, most notably the unitarian scholar Michael Servetus.[19] Calvin, however, differed sharply with traditional Catholic dogma in his belief that the state was answerable directly to God, and not through the organized church.

Luther preached submission to state authority, which he believed to be ordained by God, but he warned against allowing the temporal hand to "extend too far and encroach upon God's kingdom and government, ... for where it is given too wide a scope, intolerable and terrible injury follows."[20] Moreover, unlike Catholic theologians, Luther sharply distinguished civil from ecclesiastical government. Faith governed religious life; reason ruled public affairs.

The basic purpose of the state was to preserve order and contain human wickedness.[21] Thus, while Biblical values were not irrelevant to the political process, Luther believed that they should be introduced only to the extent that they were consistent with natural reason, which is why he once expressed a preference to be ruled by a competent Turk rather than an incompetent Christian. The civil authorities of his day, he wrote, were "to patch and darn as best we can while we live, punish the abuses and lay bandages and poultices over the sores" in a temporal kingdom that "God does not think as much of ... as he does of his spiritual realm."[22]

Condemned by the Calvinists and Lutherans, as well as the Catholics, were the Anabaptists. The Anabaptists arose when Conrad Grebel broke with Zurich Reformer Huldreich Zwingli; the name reflected their practice of rebaptizing believers who had been originally baptized as infants. There were many variants of Anabaptist thought, but they all emphasized personal rather than corporate responsibility to God, and many of them operated in the spiritual gifts discussed by Paul in his first letter to the Corinthian church.

A majority of the Anabaptists believed that the government was part of the ungodly world: the state had either been created or infiltrated by Satan. As such, it was opposed to God's Kingdom, and believers were expected to separate themselves from it—not to hold office, serve in the military, or even vote. Clerics who participated in government were denounced as "hirelings of the rulers."[23] The state was to be obeyed when possible, but Anabaptists believed that it had no real authority over believers. In contrast, the church was a voluntary community distinct from civil society, and was considered to be part of the process of establishing God's Kingdom in the earthly realm. The church was correspondingly believed to have no authority over non-Christians.

There was no question of the church operating through the civil authorities. Indeed, there could be no greater error than to ask the state to intervene in ecclesiastical matters. Wrote Pilgram Marpeck in 1532: "I admit worldly, carnal, and earthly rulers as servants of God in earthly matters, but not in the kingdom of Christ.... When such persons who hold authority become Christians (which I heartily wish and pray for) they may not use the aforementioned carnal force, sovereignty or ruling in the kingdom of Christ. It cannot be upheld by any Scripture. To allow the external authority to rule in the kingdom of Christ brings blasphemy of the Holy Spirit, who alone is Lord and Ruler without any human assistance."[24]

Another relatively radical outgrowth of the Reformation was the Puritans. Most of these "nonconforming Protestants," as they were called, had their spiritual roots in Calvin. Moreover, a variety of groups spun out of the Puritan movement, including Presbyterians, Quakers, Congregationalists, and Baptists. In general the Puritans believed that the Bible provided the absolute divine guide for church government, from which stemmed their duty to refashion the existing ecclesiastical structure. They believed in a strict separation of church and civil government; one of the reasons many of them withdrew from the Anglican Church was the influence of the secular authorities over its affairs.

In the Puritan view government was ordained of God and Scriptural principles were applicable in organizing civil government. The state was expected to enforce Biblical norms: the Massachusetts Body of Liberties, adopted in 1641, declared that "Civill Authoritie hath power and libertie to see the peace, ordinances and rules of Christ observed in every church according to his word. So it be done in a civill and not in an Ecclesiastical way."[25] Massachusetts' government punished and exiled religious dissenters, whether atheist, Quaker, or Anabaptist.

However, the state was not directly answerable to the organized church. Wrote Robert Browne, "In civil jurisdiction, the queen is second in power only to God, within her dominion."[26] The church was to resist attempts by the state to interfere in ecclesiastical matters, but it was to leave government alone in the exercise of its rightful power. Indeed, the civil authorities, wrote Browne, are only "subject to censure of the Church if they are Christians, and when they have sinned, they are to humble themselves in repentance, publicly and sincerely."[27]

Modern Baptists fall somewhere between the Anabaptists and the Puritans. The state is believed to be ordained of God, but its functions are thought to be almost wholly secular. Though in recent years the conservative Southern Baptist Convention has grown more active politically, the traditional Baptist stance—with some exceptions—has been to advocate strict separation between church and state and to avoid any organized ecclesiastical involvement in politics. Some early Baptists opposed the creation of congressional chaplains and church support for such political crusades as the temperance movement because, said John Leland, "he opposed making moral principles into laws violating the rights of the individual."[28]

## THE EASTERN ORTHODOX CHURCH

The Eastern Roman Empire essentially collapsed with the fall of Constantinople to the Turks in 1453, but the Orthodox Church survived in Greece, the Soviet Union, and elsewhere. The Eastern Orthodox vision is one of clericocracy, though with neither clear state nor church predominance. Instead, the church observes the "principle of synergy," writes Fotios Litsas: "it is to be distinguished from a sharp division of church and state, on the one hand, and a total fusion of church and state on the other hand. It recognizes and espouses a clear demarcation between church and state, while calling for a cooperative relationship between the two." The church, he adds, could become involved in politics in a number of different ways, "while retaining its clear distinction from and transcendence to it."[29]

Where the Orthodox Church has maintained some influence in government, it has used the state to punish religious minorities. In Greece, for instance, "proselytizing," even by Protestant groups, remains a crime today. However, as ecclesiastical influence over the state has waned, Orthodox teaching has tended to emphasize the role of the civil authorities in promoting justice rather than in establishing God's Kingdom. Moreover, the church relies more on the political involvement of individual parishioners than the organized church to influence government. In the 1982 Kiev declaration, for instance, the Orthodox Church refused to commit itself corporately to overturning existing political structures.

Necessity has forced the church to adopt a different stance in Communist lands. In the Soviet Union, for instance, the Orthodox Church has essentially been returned to pre-Constantine Roman status: a minority belief system oppressed by a totalitarian state. The result has been an uneasy coexistence between them, with the church awaiting the coming of God's Kingdom. In contrast to the first-century church, today's orthodoxy has not flourished under persecution, with the clerical establishment instead accommodating the atheistic civil rulers and bowing to state pressure in their public stance. In

1983, for instance, at the World Council of Churches assembly the Eastern Orthodox delegates opposed a resolution condemning the Soviet invasion of Afghanistan.[30]

## THE SOCIAL GOSPEL

The social gospel is traditionally viewed as a philosophy that developed in the context of modern, liberal Protestantism.[31] Starting in the late nineteenth century a number of churches began moving away from the spiritual gospel message, emphasizing political reform instead. "The Christian religion embraces humanity as well as divinity in its range–the whole mass of humanity, the poor, prisoners, laborers, infidels, all men," wrote Stephen Colwell in 1851.[32] The Reverend Edward Beecher spoke of bringing civil government under God's influence, while seminarian Samuel Harris argued that God's Kingdom required the reign of justice today.

Advocates of the social gospel held a radically different conception of the role of the state than did members of other more traditional faiths. Government, they believed, might still be ordained by God, but it was not subject to church control nor was it empowered to enforce Biblical principles. Instead, its chief duty was to promote a just society, and Christians, as believers in justice, were bound to work to advance that end. Advocates of the social gospel focused on reforming broad social conditions rather than promoting individual salvation. Writes sociologist James Hunter, "These advocates saw the basis of social reform not so much in the revival–where, so they believed, the 'hearts of men would be purged from sin'–as in the modification of the structural conditions related to social maladies."[33]

Most mainline Protestant denominations continue to operate in this tradition. Though the lay bodies of these churches are generally centrist in orientation, their leaderships have promoted an activist liberal agenda. Support for civil rights, social welfare spending, and arms control, and opposition to the war in Vietnam and most recently to intervention in Central America have all been treated as major theological priorities. America's Catholic bishops have been advancing a similar agenda in recent years. Though they support the separation of church and state, they have intervened on the liberal side of such issues as the economy and nuclear weapons; their major difference with the liberal Protestant denominations has been over abortion, of which the Catholic Church remains a staunch opponent.

There is no necessary conflict between following Christ and promoting liberal policies, but over time many of the social gospel churches have emphasized the latter task to the detriment of spiritual matters. Ultimately some of the mainline churches have come close to spiritual death, effectively subordinating the work of the Body of Christ to the affairs of government; they have substituted the temporal if worthwhile goal of improving worldly social conditions for their very raison d' etre–promoting God's Kingdom. Indeed, at its extreme the social gospel promises the onset of the Kingdom of God through political reform rather than personal spiritual regeneration, an idolatrous heresy.

## LIBERATION THEOLOGY

A movement has arisen within the Catholic Church to fuse the gospel with Marxist class analysis. Though its support is concentrated in Latin America, liberation theology has gained adherents all over the world, particularly in Asia and Africa. In practice, there often appears to be little difference between this religious doctrine and various leftist political ideologies. But "liberation theology is theology," writes Phillip Berryman, "that is, it is a systematic, disciplined reflection on Christian faith and its implications." The base point of its analysis, however, is "an interpretation of Christian faith out of the experience of the poor."[34]

In essence, liberation theologians argue that to truly follow Christ requires an identification with the materially poor and oppressed. In addition, they believe that genuine spiritual liberation requires emancipation from oppressive political, economic, and social structures. "To place oneself in the perspective of the kingdom means to participate in the struggle for the liberation of those oppressed by others," writes Peruvian Gustavo Gutierrez, one of the leading exponents of liberation theology.[35] These sentiments might be unexceptional were they not conjoined with a Marxist analysis of the causes of oppression–capitalism, colonialism, multinational corporations, the industrialized countries, and so forth. Thus, the liberation theologians' spiritual prescription is for political revolution, that is, the inevitably violent overthrow of existing systems.

Some Protestant clerics share this perspective. Argentinian José Miguez-Bonino, for instance, is a Methodist and former president of the World Council of Churches. Miguez-Bonino, who professes to acknowledge the Lordship of Christ, has praised Cuba and called for the destruction of capitalism. "Revolutionary action aimed at changing the basic economic, political, social and cultural structures and conditions of life is imperative today in the world," he writes.[36]

## THE BLACK CHURCH

Another form of liberation theology has arisen within some black churches, particularly those in the United States. During the 1960s and 1970s a number of black clerics spoke of the need for radical change, even violence, to free blacks from an oppressive white society. This view, explains Villa-Vicencio, rested on the belief that "black people in the United States are an oppressed minority divested of their spiritual and cultural identity, which means that even the structures from which they are excluded are white and therefore unacceptable. It is this struggle against white values and structures which provides black theology with its appeal in a vast number of colonial and neocolonial countries around the world."[37]

This perspective differs from Latin American liberation theology through its reliance on racial rather than Marxist analysis. Many black liberationists view the Latin version as essentially a white doctrine, while many of the Latins consider black theology to be limited to America, seeking national equality but not international justice.

As the bitter civil rights struggles of the 1960s have given way to increasing racial cooperation, with blacks participating ever more in an integrated American society, a new, moderate form of black theology has developed. Though political action remains important, black theology has moved back towards the traditional gospel. In December 1984, for instance, a group of black clerics and theologians gathered in the so-called Richmond Consultation and issued a formal declaration that "in the final analysis the test of apostolicity is the experiencing of the life, death and resurrection of Jesus Christ in our daily struggle against demonic powers that seek to rob us of our inheritance as children of God redeemed by the blood of Jesus Christ. Our deeds, more than our creeds, determine whether we have fully received and acted upon the faith of the apostles." Added the assembly, "holiness in the Black Church is not coterminous, as in some expressions of White liberalism, with frenetic social activism.... The Black Church is sustained by prayer and praise. It exists in and for the glory of God and not the glorification of human institutions."[38]

## THE SOUTH AFRICAN CHURCH

The church in South Africa is suffering the same sort of division that rent American denominations before the Civil War. Different white churches have split over the validity of apartheid, the government-enforced policy of racial separation.

For years the predominantly black English-speaking churches opposed apartheid while the white Dutch Reformed Church, to which roughly 70 percent of Afrikaners belong, backed the ruling establishment and white supremacy. The Dutch Reformed Church even set up separate "daughter" churches for blacks and Asians to maintain racial segregation. However, in October 1986 the Dutch Reformed Church admitted that its support for apartheid had been an error; the church has been steadily biblicizing its doctrines, opening the church to all races and allowing inter-racial marriages, for instance. So in mid-1987 whites committed to strict racial separation broke off to form the Afrikaans Reformed Church.

On the more general issue of church and state, there has been little divergence from modern Protestantism. Writes Villa-Vicencio, the major South African churches "have generally affirmed a similar doctrinal perspective on church-state relations: the need for legitimate government capable of instituting justice and good order; the obligation of the church to exercise a prophetic ministry in relation to the state; and in certain circumstances the possibility of conscientious disobedience to the laws of the states."[39]

## MODERN EVANGELICALS

Though evangelicals involved themselves in politics early in America's history, defeats over Prohibition and the Scopes trial caused many churches to withdraw almost entirely from politics. For a variety of reasons, including the rise of the electronic church and the perception of increasing secular attacks, aided and abetted by government, on religious values, evangelicals became more active in the political process in the latter half of this century. By the 1970s evangelicals were more likely than any other religious group to vote.

The massive influx of evangelicals into the American political process in the 1970s and 1980s constitutes a clear rejection of the Anabaptists' refusal to countenance political involvement. Similarly, evangelicals, given their reliance on faith to determine their positions on issues such as abortion and pornography, do not share Luther's belief that faith should play no role apart from reason in the political process. However, few evangelical activists seem committed to subordinating the state to the church, as in the traditional Catholic view, or to have government enforce Biblical norms, in line with Calvin's Geneva.

In short, there is no clearly articulated evangelical view of the role of the state and public policy. Most churches enjoin their members to be active politically as part of their citizenship duty; believers are encouraged to look to Biblical principles in deciding how to vote. Opinions as to the role of the organized church differ more sharply. Some clerics–most notably Pat Robertson and Jerry Falwell–have directly entered the political process, though Falwell has since returned to his ministerial roots. Other religious authorities have chosen to support established political figures who speak to their concerns. In fact, surveys by the National Association of Evangelicals in 1987 and 1988 found that Robertson lagged behind several of his Republican opponents.

Though most evangelical political activism has been conservative in nature, there are some leftist evangelicals, represented by Ron Sider and Jim Wallis, among others. This group also advocates political action based on Biblical principles. Its focus, however, is not on the social issues, such as pornography and homosexuality, but on themes of "economic justice" and foreign intervention. The leftist evangelicals share the religious right's concern over abortion, but their emphasis on poverty more closely resembles the position of the liberation theologians, though without the overt Marxist class analysis. Nevertheless, despite their dramatic policy differences, evangelicals on both the right and left share a commitment to Scripture-based political action.

## A CHRISTIAN POLITICAL PERSPECTIVE?

The church has struggled with the proper relationship between church and state for nearly 2,000 years. While Islam has almost continuously been a state-supported religion, Christianity spent three centuries as an outcast sect, often brutally persecuted by the civil authorities. Since then different faiths have promoted ecclesiocracy, complete separation, revolution, peaceful political activism, and any number of variants in between. In short, if unity within the Body of Christ is hard to achieve on many theological issues today, the issue of politics has proved to be even more divisive.

The consistent inability of Christians to agree on a Biblical political view does not mean that believers today should give up trying. But past failures should make us more cautious. Christians need to approach the task with abundant humility, recognizing both the honest efforts that have been made by so many committed believers before us and the risk of mistaking our own ideology for God's plans. "For now we see through a glass, darkly," wrote Paul, and our political vision is no less cloudy today (1 Corinthians 13:12, KJV). But that lack of clarity should not stop us from trying to apply Kingdom principles to every aspect of our lives, including politics.

# SEVEN

# Applying
# Biblical Principles

*A* Christian automatically has a different perspective on politics than a nonbeliever, for he has submitted his whole life to the Lordship of Christ. But the mere fact that followers of Jesus view government and public policy differently does not mean that there is a unique Biblical legislative agenda, one set of specific policies that all Christians should support.

First, the Bible does not speak to every human problem. Of course, it deals in great detail with the most fundamental issue of man's existence, his relationship with God. And if everyone zealously followed God, we would face far fewer of the problems that people now try to resolve in the public square. But it is not true, as President Reagan once told a conference of religious broadcasters, that the answer to every question is contained in that one book. There are a host of specific issues–the intermediate nuclear forces arms control treaty, for instance, and the relative benefits of a parliamentary and presidential governmental system–to which God does not spell out a solution. We should seek wisdom from God as we search for the answer to current public policy questions, but that doesn't mean there is only one Biblical answer.

Second, though God has laid out some very clear principles to govern man's relationship with his neighbors, the exact application of those standards to the sort of coercive relationships entailed by government activity is not so obvious. Support for justice and assistance for the poor are fundamental to Christian discipleship, for example, but there is no Biblical proof-text available, despite the passionate advocacy of Christians on the right and left, to establish that the one proper divine policy is private charity, a subsistence level public welfare program, or widespread wealth redistribution. In such an area we should be exceedingly cautious before claiming to speak for the King of Kings and Lord of Lords.

Third, the Bible never authorizes the church to enforce any sort of political orthodoxy. Paul's epistles reflected his continuous effort to root out doctrinal heresy within the Body of Christ and to maintain believers' spiritual purity, to preserve what Vernard Eller calls "the integrity of the Gospel."[1] Nowhere, in contrast, did Paul suggest that the apostles or the church had a similar role to play in terms of political ideology. He commanded submission to government, but in none of his many letters did he ever detail even one policy for the local church to urge on public institutions.

What Scripture does provide is a set of fundamental moral precepts, such as justice and righteousness, as well as a few well-defined duties, largely regulating the harmful conduct of sinful man, that government is to fulfill. The Bible also proscribes the totalitarian state, but in between that and the minimalist structure mandated by Scripture lies a large area where believers must grapple with the prudential application of general Biblical principles to human problems, just as their secular counterparts must apply their humanistic philosophies to common social ills.

What policies in practice promote the godly role of government–to maintain a just and righteous order, one in which people can live peaceful lives and worship God? In ordering society, Christians need to recognize that many of the common, public responsibilities that we have to our neighbors are not in the first instance political matters. Instead, writes Richard John Neuhaus, "the things that matter most happen in the 'mediating structures' of our personal and communal existence. These structures–family, neighborhood, church, voluntary association–are the people-sized, face-to-face institutions where we work day by day at our felicities and our fears."[2]

Indeed, the Bible concerns itself far more with our personal interaction within these forums than our civic involvement. Not surprisingly, then, the Puritans who originally settled in America subsumed within the general concept of "government" a variety of institutions that were to help order society. The church and family, for instance, were believed to be ordained by God and to have their own specific roles; so too did subsidiary institutions like school, business, and voluntary groups, which operated on authority delegated from the other "governments."

The Puritans believed that the state, or civil government, also had important responsibilities, but it was viewed as only one among many organizations that were to support a godly social system.[3] In fact, the state's role was considered to be largely restricted to the maintenance of justice; the civil authorities were not supposed to interfere with the proper activities of the other institutions. This analysis remains valid today. Writes R.J. Rushdoony: "Government is a broad concept; justice is a strict and narrow one; by restricting law to justice, and the state to the administration of law as justice, both salvation, which is left to God, and vast areas of self-government, which are left to man, are kept out of the hands of the state. If the state is not restricted to justice, it will relentlessly claim to be the only government of man, a claim made repeatedly in history."[4]

Thus, one important way that believers can infuse the public square with Biblical principles is through their involvement in the wide variety of nonpolitical institutions that perform important social functions. Christians have an obligation to exhibit the fruit of the Spirit in their personal dealings with their neighbors. And believers should reflect godly virtues in the activities of their families and the mediating structures of which they are a part: though God's calling for every Christian is different, all believers should participate in community affairs.

The bedrock social unit of society is the family. Husbands, wives, and children all have mutually reinforcing responsibilities to one another(Ephesians 5, 6; 1 Corinthians 7). One of the parents' most important biblical obligations is to discipline their children (Proverbs 13:24; 23:13, 14). Effective government in the home is important, first, for the spiritual health of its members. For instance, God chose Abraham "so that he will direct his children and his household after him to keep the way of the Lord by doing what is right and just" (Genesis 18:19). Moses instructed the Israelites to "impress" God's commandments "on your children" (Deuteronomy 6:7). And Paul told fathers to bring up children "in the training and instruction of the Lord" (Eph. 6:4).

Moreover, family oversight helps prepare members for church leadership: A deacon, wrote Paul, "must manage his children and his household well" (1 Timothy 3:12). In fact, Paul included the bringing up of children among the "good deeds" expected of widows who were eligible for church assistance (1 Timothy 5:10).

The family unit has other public–though not political–duties as well, including the care of needy family members. Wrote Paul to Timothy, "If anyone does not provide for his relatives, and especially for his immediate family, he has denied the faith and is worse than an unbeliever" (1 Timothy 5:8).

That charitable obligation extends beyond blood relatives. Of particular concern to all Christians must be the welfare of the community of believers. The early Christians, recorded Luke, "shared everything they had" (Acts 4:32). Paul spared no effort to collect an offering from the Greek churches for believers in Jerusalem (2 Corinthians 8-9). Denial of assistance to a fellow Christian drew a rebuke from James that was as sharp as Paul's criticism of the man who would not help his family: "Suppose a brother or sister is without clothes and daily food" and you do nothing to help them, your faith "is dead" (James 2:15-17).

Finally, the duty to assist those in need applies outside of the Body of Christ. Jesus told the parable of the separation of the sheep and goats, when the latter will be cursed and sent away "into the eternal fire prepared for the devil and his angels. For I was hungry and you gave me nothing to eat, I was thirsty and you gave me nothing to drink, I was a stranger and you did not invite me in, I needed clothes and you did not clothe me, I was sick and in prison and you did not look after me" (Matthew 25:41-43).

Some theologians believe that this passage refers to helping fellow Christians rather than the needy generally. Jesus did talk of "these brothers of mine" and he apparently told the parable to the disciples rather than the larger crowd that usually followed him. Even if this exegesis is correct, however, Christ taught that the second most important commandment was to "love your neighbor as yourself" (Mark 12:31). And he used the parable of the Good Samaritan to illustrate the fact that one's neighbor was not limited to one's religious or ethnic kin. Moreover, while Paul stated that Christians were to be especially concerned about "those who belong to the family of believers," he wrote the church in Galatia: "let us do good to all people" (Galatians 6:10).

Another important social institution, or government, is the organized church. Among its most important duties are preaching the gospel and administering the sacraments, but it, like the individual and the family, has important public duties to carry out. For instance, the church must nurture the spiritual growth of its members, encouraging them to maintain the purity of their walk with God, and disciplining them when necessary.

That means teaching and promoting the fundamental values that underlie Christianity–standards of honesty, charity, and public spiritedness which even many nonbelievers now recognize are sadly lacking in modern society. The primary responsibility for transmitting such moral precepts lies initially with the family and the church, rather than with civil government institutions such as the public schools and the courts. For instance, Paul charged the Corinthian believers not to associate with Christians involved in immorality, idolatry, and greed (1 Corinthians 5:11). Values like these, which reflect a person's spiritual state, are beyond the reach of an institution such as civil government. The state can punish those who act criminally, but it cannot point the way to redemption. For this reason the church's public role in promoting Biblical morality is particularly important.

Activists on the political left have made a powerful case that much of the modern evangelical church has sold out to the values of the world. For instance, Andrew Kirk, associate director of the London Institute for Contemporary Christianity, denounces the failure of the church to be a "servant community," particularly to those in need.[5] Some middle-class congregations seem comfortable with the emphasis that the world places on money, status, and success; the "health and wealth" gospel, in particular, has perverted Christ's message and defused his demand to renounce the earthly status quo.

However, Kirk, for one, goes awry when he demands state intervention to redistribute wealth and quash consumerism. Government action is no substitute for Christ's modern disciples rediscovering the radical challenge posed by the gospel–and spreading that message throughout society. The solution to today's problems is preeminently a spiritual one, fostered by the Body of Christ, not a matter of political reform instituted by the civil authorities. Only God, not the state, can cure the pervasive greed, envy, and materialism that rightly concern Kirk and similar thinkers.

The church also has several public duties that are now routinely thought of as matters for the civil authorities. It is, for example, to punish members who transgress their proper relationship with other people, believers and nonbelievers alike. Paul, for example, enjoined Christians in Ephesus not to steal (Ephesians 4:28). In his letter to the Corinthian church Paul mandated expulsion for swindlers and slanderers, activities which today could also by punished by civil government (1 Corinthians 5:11).[6]

Moreover, Jesus instructed believers to attempt to settle their differences between themselves, and if that effort failed, to then go to the church (Matthew 18:15). Paul taught that the church's purview extends to judging any sort of dispute between Christians. He discouraged lawsuits among believers, instead urging that such disagreements be brought before church members (1 Corinthians 6:1-8).

The church also has a corporate responsibility to care for its indigent members. The Jerusalem body provided for a daily distribution of food; Paul elaborated on the proper procedures for helping needy widows (Acts 6:1; 1 Timothy 5). And as was discussed in Chapter Four, God mandated a variety of specific procedures to help the poor in the early covenant nation of Israel.

Since the church has commensurately greater resources today than it did when the apostles first began proclaiming the Good News, it has the ability to fulfill Paul's teaching to "do good to all people." This should translate into a passion for helping non-Christians in need—for feeding the hungry, clothing the naked, housing the homeless, and healing the sick. While the religious left, including the National Conference of Catholic Bishops and Protestant groups like Evangelicals for Social Action, can be rightly faulted for its coercive and often counterproductive political platform, it has exhibited a godly zeal over relieving the plight of this nation's underclass. In contrast, many middle-class Christians would appear to prefer to ignore any unsightly bits of human wreckage.

In fact, mainstream believers in this country were once known for their commitment to the needy. "The church-going classes, those who have come under the influence of evangelical Christianity," observed liberal educator John Dewey, "embody and express the spirit of kindly good will towards classes which are at an economic disadvantage."[7] Half of the nation's 330,000 church congregations are believed to provide some form of social assistance, ranging from shelters to soup kitchens. Charitable efforts are estimated to have doubled since 1980, but much more still needs to be done.

The organized church, as a godly form of "government," has an obligation to act irrespective of the response of civil government. That responsibility should cause every Christian group to regularly rethink their activities. Writes Ron Sider: "Imagine what would happen if evangelical institutions–youth organizations, publications, colleges, seminaries, congregations, and denominational headquarters–dared to undertake a comprehensive two-year examination of their total program and to answer this question: Is there the same balance and emphasis on justice for the poor and oppressed in Evangelical programs as there is in Scripture?"[8]

And the church should move to meet human needs before it lobbies the civil authorities for action. America's Catholic bishops have, for instance, been leading proponents of activist government programs to promote "economic justice." But William McManus, a retired bishop from Indiana, forthrightly acknowledges that many parishes have fallen short in applying to their own members the very theories which they would have the civil authorities impose on people and institutions outside of the Catholic Church.[9]

Indeed, the organized church and other Christian groups should provide a model of voluntary social organization for the rest of society, one that is dedicated to helping people, whether it be through mediating disputes, rehabilitating criminals, or providing for the poor. The church is to reflect God's love for man; it is to support and encourage its own members and light the path of truth for unbelievers. The community of faith is to be a truly classless society that represents God's Kingdom in a fallen world.

Believers need to apply Biblical values in the other non-civil governments in which they are involved. Christians should eschew dishonesty and greed in their economic relationships; a firm has a responsibility to fulfill godly obligations to workers, other firms, and consumers, irrespective of the reach of government regulation. Similarly, for believers matters of social responsibility, such as environmental protection, are in the first instance issues to be resolved by voluntary "government," such as a private firm. Whether or not the state eventually intervenes, a Christian should base his work on Scriptural principles.

A particularly important aspect of Christian self-government is the godly instruction of one's children. Responsibility for their education naturally flows out of the family's Biblical role; indeed, the home itself provides an important environment for learning. Much of that instruction, of course, is moral: "Train a child in the way he should go" (Proverbs 22:6). But the education is also practical–most children learn to speak from their families, not in school. And the parental role was protected in the young American republic; even the early "common schools," which were supported both publicly and privately, were not seen as displacing the family's role.

However, the state has increasingly usurped control of the education process, at times with the active encouragement of Protestant denominations that saw public education as a way to reduce the influence of religious minorities, particularly the Catholic Church. And the goals of some advocates of public education were fundamentally anti-Christian–to mold young people to serve the collective polity rather than God. For instance, Orestes Brownson, a Universalist minister who eventually converted to Catholicism, worked with the Working Men's Party and other groups to promote universal public education in the early 1800s. "The great object was to get rid of Christianity," he later wrote. "The plan was not to make open attacks on religion, although we might belabor the clergy and bring them into contempt where we could; but to establish a system of state–we said national–schools, from which all religion was to be excluded, in which nothing was to be taught but such knowledge as is verifiable by the senses, and to which all parents were to be compelled by law to send their children."[10]

Perhaps the sharpest assault on private education occurred earlier this century when the Oregon legislature passed a statute requiring parents to send their children to public schools. The U.S. Supreme Court voided the law as a violation of the Fourteenth Amendment: "The fundamental theory of liberty upon which all governments in this Union repose excludes any general power of the State to standardize its children by forcing them to accept instruction from public teachers only. The child is not the mere creature of the State; those who nurture him and direct his destiny have the right, coupled with the high duty, to recognize and prepare him for additional obligations."[11]

Though private schools remain legal, those who wish to educate their children privately must pay twice–both property taxes and private tuition. Moreover, many states tightly regulate private institutions, setting curriculum and teacher certification requirements. A number of jurisdictions also discourage home schooling.

Nevertheless, despite these obstacles, private schools are an important option for parents, particularly Christian ones. In addition to the nation's many Catholic schools, there are some 18,000 non-Catholic religious institutions, most of which are evangelical. While enrollment in parochial schools has been falling, the number of students in evangelical ones has jumped 149 percent since 1965, to 2.5 million. Moreover, an increasing number of parents are educating their children at home.

The Bible does not require organized Christian schooling, whether through a church or at home, but it does obligate parents to take an active role in the formal teaching process. And that means monitoring the curriculum, reviewing textbooks and course materials, and getting involved in school decision-making. Christians cannot expect what is a universal, nonsectarian institution to advance our specific theological views, but we can demand that the public schools honestly present issues and history, treat religion with respect, and not propagate un-Christian philosophies. Where parental and political involvement proves inadequate to guarantee a child an education consistent with godly values, withdrawal from the public school system may become the only option.[12]

However, believers should not waste time attempting to insert formalistic, ceremonial religion into public institutions. Nondenominational prayer led by an unbelieving teacher is not only meaningless, but is also unfair to non-Christians who must attend public institutions. Parents can easily teach their children about prayer at home as long as their values are not being undermined in school. The quality, both intellectual and moral, of the instruction, not the existence of hypocritical pretenses of religiosity, should be the standard by which parents judge the acceptability of the public schools.

The Scriptural imperative for proper education of children combined with the duty to assist those in need yields another implicit Biblical obligation: to help ensure that poor parents have an opportunity to provide for schooling for their children that is consistent with Christian tenets. The most helpless victims of the current system are the poor, who must pay property taxes (either directly or indirectly, as part of their rent) to maintain public institutions, but who cannot afford to send their children to a private school. Believers, as individuals and through their churches and schools, should provide scholarship aid for the needy. Moreover, Christians should support political initiatives, such as tuition tax credits and vouchers, that would increase parents' freedom of choice by effectively returning to them a portion of the taxes they paid to support the public schools if they send their kids to a non-state school.

Finally, Christians have an important role to play in the organization that most people think of as "government"–the state. Indeed, believers have a Biblical obligation to be involved in civic affairs, since that sphere, no less than the private realm, is subject to God's rule and requires a generous dose of Christian "salt."

Today's disciples of Christ need not all become politicians, of course. Writes Vernard Eller, there are "no scriptural or gospel arguments indicating that political channels offer such unique possibilities for serving one's neighbors and doing good for the world that all Christians have a sacred obligation to be politically active."[13] But believers should take an interest in public affairs. That may simply mean voting regularly and occasionally writing letters to the editor. Or perhaps attending a local party caucus or protesting the use of city funds to finance abortions in the local hospital. Believers should be especially willing to act when Christian organizations are challenged, showing up at functions such as a county hearing on a church's zoning request, for instance. The specifics of our involvement are less important than our readiness to hold political leaders accountable for their conduct.

Where vigorous political involvement of Christians both individually and through the organized church is mandatory is in matters of conscience, where the moral underpinnings of the society are at stake. The Body of Christ should act as the polity's conscience, calling it to account for attacks on human life, dignity, and property. For if moral precepts based on Biblical principles do not not provide the framework for government action, other values based on other standards will.

The problem may be both fundamental and structural, like the moral collapse of Nazi Germany. Biblical justice is likely to be almost completely absent in a totalitarian state that claims godlike status. In the face of that kind of pervasive moral evil, believers must take a stand, however costly it may prove to be to us personally and to the church institutionally. Resistance by the Confessing Church to Nazism was checkered, but these Christians provided some godly leadership for their countrymen, in contrast to the generally obsequious behavior of the mainline denominations. Indeed, widespread protests over euthanasia, joined in by clerical leaders, caused the government to temporarily retreat–an important, if limited, victory.

In a society that comes closer to the Biblical ideal, like our own, the loss of social moral tone may be localized, with one or more specific issues warranting sustained attention. Only issues involving the most fundamental values can make a mandatory claim for Christian involvement: there may be important reasons to support a balanced budget amendment or oppose the MX missile, for instance, but these issues raise prudential more than justice/righteousness concerns. In contrast, the civil rights movement of the 1960s should have been a priority for all Christians; in this case many mainline churches did more to promote biblical justice than did evangelical congregations.[14] Today abortion and euthanasia are similar issues, since they reflect a nation's treatment of and respect for human life.[15]

However, in most cases a Christian's political involvement will be far more mundane. The cornerstone of a believer's vision of government should be that it is an institution with the essential purpose of regulating relations among sinful men. Humanity will not climb to perfection if it finds just the right earthly utopia; instead, only God can inaugurate the Kingdom of Heaven. Thus, the state's objective is justice, not salvation. And for functions best done by other institutions, such as the church, believers should only turn to the civil government as a last resort.

At the same time, Christians should never allow the idea of political liberation to obscure attainment of the more important goal of spiritual freedom through Christ. An interesting example of this principle at work is provided by Paul's letter to Philemon.

Paul was no friend of the institution of slavery–he condemned slave traders as being among "the ungodly and sinful,
the unholy and irreligious," and for acting "contrary to the
sound doctrine that conforms to the glorious gospel of the
blessed God" (1 Timothy 1:9, 10). He also counseled slaves to
gain their liberty if they could. But Paul never launched a
quixotic political campaign against the practice that would have
been bound to fail. Moreover, he didn't even order Philemon to
free the runaway Onesimus. Instead, after Onesimus met Paul
and apparently gave his life to Christ, the apostle sent the
slave back to his erstwhile earthly master requesting that
Philemon "have him back for good–no longer as a slave, but
better than a slave, as a dear brother" (Philemon 15, 16).

The very inclusion of this letter in the New Testament
suggests that Philemon complied with Paul's request, thereby
demonstrating his willingness to sacrifice worldly wealth for
God. As for Onesimus, a letter written by Syrian Bishop
Ignatious around the year 110 A.D. refers to a Bishop
Onesimus of Ephesus. We don't know for certain that they
were the same person, but the circumstantial evidence, including the text of the letter, strongly suggests that they are. If this
is the case, writes Vernard Eller, "the example of Onesimus
marks the truer freeing of more slaves than all the emancipation proclamations ever proclaimed and all the class warfare
ever warred."[16] Indeed, Paul urged slaves to obey their masters
"so that in every way they will make the teaching about God
our Savior attractive" (Titus 2:10). Spiritual, not political, salvation must always remain a Christian's highest goal.

Nevertheless, there is a role for civil government. What
should such an institution based on Biblical principles look like?

First, the state's powers should be limited. Through the
prophet Samuel, God warned the Israelites of the dangers of
having a king. Indeed, the Scriptures tell us to "not be surprised" at official corruption and injustice (Ecclesiastes 5:8).
Christians therefore have an obligation to support a governmental framework that will neither allow the emergence of
the satanic-state nor widespread injustice and oppression.

There is no Biblical list of restrictions that should be
placed on government action. But the procedural emphasis on
fairness under the Old Covenant–and the Lord's decree that
Israel's king was not to "turn from the law to the right or to
the left" (Deuteronomy 17:20)–suggests that modern civil gov-

ernment, too, should be one of law rather than men.[17] That is, the state's power should be objectively defined, rather than set subjectively by individual leaders or oligarchies. And that implies a constitution, whether written or unwritten, which acts as the citizens' specific grant of authority to the civil government.

To be effective, such a system should limit the state's power to interfere, without compelling justification, with the actions of individuals and other, private "governments," such as the family and the church. The Biblical basis for imposing stringent limitations on the civil authorities is particularly strong when it comes to the worship of God, management of the home, and governance of the church.

Moreover, the state should be organized so as to dilute the opportunity for sinful men to abuse public authority. This suggests that political leaders be accountable to those they govern; that the civil power be decentralized and disaggregated, so that a broad consensus is necessary for government to act; and that all laws be equally applied.

An important model of the kind of government that may result from the application of Biblical principles is provided by the American constitutional system. It is not uniquely God's scheme–the Bible provides a single basic theological message, not a specific political theory. Indeed, the exact mode of civil government, whether monarchy, empire, or democracy, appears to be almost a matter of indifference to God. Whatever system exists is to be submitted to God and to implement God's purposes.

But in practice the sort of limited government like that established in the American colonies appears to have come closer than most systems in ensuring that the civil authorities act in a manner generally consistent with Scriptural principles. Which should come as no surprise, since the people in colonial and revolutionary times were religious and their beliefs helped shape the government that they formed. Writes A. James Reichley: "The single most influential cultural force at work in the new nation was the combination of religious beliefs and social attitudes known as Puritanism. At the time of the Revolution, at least 75 percent of American citizens had grown up in families espousing some form of Puritanism. Among the remainder, more than half had roots in related traditions of European Calvinism."[18]

The country's political leadership was also largely Christian. Thomas Jefferson was a deist, and Benjamin Franklin doubted the divinity of Christ, though he appeared to believe in a personal God. But most of the other men who played such an important role in forging the new nation—"Founding Fathers" such as James Madison, George Washington, Roger Sherman, and Patrick Henry—were probably, in today's parlance, born-again Christians.[19]

This is not to say that the Constitution which underlies our society's political organization was intended to create a Christian republic in the sense of a modern Israel.[20] The civil government was legally separated from any ecclesiastical structure. The federal regime's functions were nonreligious, involving making wars and treaties, regulating commerce, coining money, and the like.

Moreover, the Constitution set no religious requirements for either officeholders or voters; in fact, Article VI explicitly states that "no religious test shall ever be required as a qualification to any office or public trust under the United States." The main purpose of that provision may have been to prevent a majority denomination from disenfranchising smaller sects, but by its terms it protects nonbelievers as well. And Jefferson's authorship of the Declaration of Independence as well as his subsequent election as President demonstrates that even then Americans were willing to entrust non-Christians, at least those who shared the nation's general religious-based moral consensus, with high political office.

Nevertheless, the Constitution's framers, including Franklin, who admired the wisdom of the Bible despite his doubts about Christ's status within the Godhead, relied on Scriptural principles in forming a civil government. "We have no government armed in power capable of contending with human passions unbridled by morality and religion," wrote John Adams: "Our constitution was made only for a moral and religious people."[21] Indeed, a study of political writings between 1760 and 1805 found that one-third of their citations were to the Bible.[22]

Not surprisingly, then, the Declaration of Independence included an appeal to "the Laws of Nature and of Nature's God." This was not a paganistic notion, an appeal to the natural human condition. Instead, it refers to a higher law, divinely inspired but reflected in the world.[23] In the same way Paul, in his letter to the Roman church, speaks of the Gentiles doing "by nature things required by the law," and thereby showing "that the requirements of the law are written on their hearts, their consciences also bearing witness, and their thoughts now accusing, now even defending them" (Romans 2:14, 15). The Declaration's signers also closed "with a firm reliance on the protection of Divine Providence."

Perhaps the most important Biblical theme implemented by the nation's founders was stringent limitations on government authority. In the Declaration America's revolutionaries contended that the state was to derive its powers from the governed. Otherwise the sort of despotism represented by, in their view, the British Crown–and prophesied about by Samuel thousands of years before–would result.

In fact, the nation's founders explicitly acknowledged the danger of creating powerful, coercive structures to be run by sinful man. During the great debate over ratification of the Constitution Madison wrote of the problem of factions, the greedy coalitions that are even more active today than in 1787, and the way the Constitution was intended to constrain their power. For example, in the *Federalist Papers* (No. 51) he observed that "In framing a government which is to be administered by men over men, the great difficulty lies in this: You must first enable the government to control the governed; and in the next place, oblige it to control itself."

The practical constitutional framework adopted by the new nation reflected these general Biblical principles. It established a federal government only of limited authority; the Tenth Amendment "reserved to the States respectively, or to the people" any "powers not delegated to the United States."

The framers then added a number of specific restrictions on the authority of the executive and legislative branches, barring passage of, for instance, bills of attainder (which stripped individuals of their property or other civil rights) and limiting suspension of the Writ of Habeas Corpus. Moreover, the Bill of Rights, passage of which was promised to increase support for ratification of the Constitution, guaranteed religious and press freedom, protection from abusive searches, procedural safeguards for those accused of committing a crime, and property ownership.

The Constitution also spread public authority between the federal and state systems and, within the federal government, provided for three separate branches to check the potential for abuse. Further, the legislative branch was split into two chambers whose members represented separate constituencies, were elected in dissimilar ways (Senators were originally chosen by state legislatures), and served different terms in office. And procedures were established to remove errant public officials from office.

Moreover, several specific constitutional provisions appear to have have been rooted in the Bible. The Eighth Amendment prohibition against "cruel and unusual punishment" reflects the requirement under Mosaic law that punishment be proportional–"an eye for an eye." Old Testament rules barred penalizing family members of criminals (Deuteronomy 24:16). The Constitution prohibits bills of attainder, except in the case of treason, but even then forfeiture can be imposed only on guilty parties (Article III, Section 3/2/). Article III, Section 3(1) requires two witnesses or a confession in open court to convict someone of treason. Similarly, Mosaic law, which established strict procedures for trying cases, mandated testimony from at least two witnesses to convict a defendant "of any crime or offense" (Deuteronomy 19:15).

Though there is no similar one-to-one relationship between Mosaic and constitutional law in the economic realm, both systems were generally concerned about protecting the right to possess and use property. For instance, God forbade theft and covetousnous; he similarly warned the Israelites not to move their neighbor's boundary stones (Exodus 20:15, 17; Deuteronomy 27:17). The Fifth Amendment, part of the original Bill of Rights, prohibits government from confiscating private property. And the so-called Commerce Clause, in Article I, Section 8(3), bars federal regulation of economic transactions within states. (This provision was intended to protect state sovereignty as well as individual rights.)

Both Biblical and constitutional law also take personal oaths very seriously. Occupation of the Promised Land, for instance, was part of the Lord's covenant with the Israelites: "Be careful to follow every command I am giving you today, so that you may live and increase and may enter and possess the land that the Lord promised on oath to your forefathers" (Deuteronomy 8:1). David wrote that God honors one "who keeps his oath even when it hurts" (Psalm 15:4). In the same way, the Constitution protects contracts, which are essentially mutual oaths. Article I, Section 10(1) prohibits Congress from "impairing the Obligation of Contracts." (The Supreme Court has gutted this requirement, along with the Commerce Clause, mentioned earlier, but the original purpose of these provisions was unambiguous.)[24]

A Christian's political tasks today differ from those in 1787, of course, since he is not in a position to create, *de novo*, a governmental system. But the original constitutional scheme can help inform his judgment on current issues. The importance of limiting the power of public officials to do evil, which has steadily expanded over the last two centuries, could take the form of redefining the separation of powers, giving new life to constitutional restrictions now largely ignored by the courts, amending the Constitution to limit presidential and congressional authority, applying ethics laws to Congress, and so on.

Beyond supporting restrictions on state power, Christians must decide what are proper state responsibilities. In short, what does the Bible mandate as duties for the state? As was detailed in Chapter Four, rulers are to promote justice and righteousness; that entails protecting life and property from domestic and foreign lawbreakers and preventing oppression of the weak by the strong. The state is also to maintain impartiality in its dealings with people, whether rich or poor. Moreover, the civil authorities may have some responsibility, though secondary to the obligation of individual believers and the organized church, to provide for the needy. Government is not barred from performing other functions, but no others appear to be Biblically required.

Again, the original American system provides a good example of the practical implementation of these broad Scriptural principles. The philosophical framework for the Constitution was developed in the Declaration of Independence: "all men are created equal" and "are endowed by their Creator with certain unalienable Rights," including "life, liberty, and the pursuit of happiness."[25] And the purpose of the government was to secure those rights–in effect, to implement Biblical justice. The basic objective of the American federal government was, according to the Constitution's preamble, "to form a more perfect Union, establish Justice, insure domestic Tranquility, provide for the common defence, promote the general Welfare, and secure the Blessings of Liberty."

The Constitution established the framework necessary to regulate sinful man: a military to guard the nation and a court system to punish criminals and to adjudicate disputes. No specific aid program for the poor was established. At the time such a role was considered to be the responsibility of another level of civil government, the states. Nevertheless, the Constitution contains no bar to federal assistance for the needy. The document does not, however, authorize Congress to raise taxes for just any purpose: Article I, Section 8(1) requires that the "general Welfare of the United States," not the comfort of one or another avaricious interest group, be at stake.

Christians should use these functions as guideposts in evaluating whether government is currently fulfilling its Biblical role. Not that the federal government's programs either then or now are the only ones consistent with Scripture: the Bible does not provide a specific policy agenda. Again, Scripture gives us overall principles, but we have to use prudential judgment to apply them. However, the relative success of the U.S. constitutional system suggests that we should consider the founders' wisdom in judging policy today.

For instance, the civil authorities, at both the federal and state level, are authorized to punish wrongdoing. Does the criminal justice system convict the guilty while protecting the accused from false prosecution and conviction? Is the system just, treating everyone equally? Is punishment proportional to the crime? Do the civil courts operate impartially, with fair judges who will give the widow in Christ's parable "justice"? If not—and the judicial system today is overloaded, slow, and often unfair to all participants—a Christian should support reform.

The Bible provides no specifics on how the military should be organized, but its purpose is properly one of defense. Intervention abroad has to be judged on two important standards: is the action necessary to protect this nation, and is it consistent with basic concepts of Biblical justice and righteousness? America's support for foreign dictatorships of left and right and its extensive alliance system raise both moral and prudential questions, covered in chapter 9.

More fundamentally, has the state itself become a tool of domestic injustice, misused by influential individuals and interest groups to enrich themselves and steal from the body politic? God expects the civil authorities to stand against oppression but warns us not to be surprised if they are corrupt instead. Christians have an obligation to see that government fulfills its Scriptural responsibilities in this area.

As for assistance to the needy, programs should be judged, first, on whether they are consistent with private–individual as well as church-led–charitable efforts.[26] Second, any welfare system should respect Biblical tenets regarding work and the recipients' responsibility to try to better their own condition. Lastly, programs for the needy should preserve beneficiaries' dignity and provide them with the tools to become self-supporting. As will be discussed in greater detail in chapter 8, our current system performs badly on all three counts, and therefore requires fundamental change.

In considering the appropriateness of government activities beyond the few specifically mandated by the Bible, Christians have to apply both general Scriptural principles, such as justice, and common sense. Believers can, of course, act on God's promise to give wisdom "generously" to those who ask for it (James 1:5). But their application of reason within revelation will yield no predetermined policy positions; Christians must grapple with the same prudential arguments as nonbelievers and, as a result, may disagree in the judgments that they reach.[27]

Moreover, Christians must seek to build coalitions with those who do not share their theological concerns, being careful to frame their arguments in what has become a very secular civil political arena in moral rather than religious terms. Writes Vernard Eller: "*Religiously* derived moral ideals are welcomed and needed in the political marketplace–although not in the form of *religious* claims. So, how about it?–*Christians* with their Christianly derived values active in the public arena? Yes. But, *divine sanction* introduced as *political* recommendation in a secular, pluralistic setting? Inviting the secular public into an intramural squabble over which Christians represent the true Christian morality and which an immoral perversion? This is where I have been insisting that religion and politics must be kept strictly separate."[28] For instance, the ideologically divergent Just Life Education Fund and Biblical News Service have both made the Strategic Defense Initiative a litmus test for Christian political activism, but have come down on opposite sides of the issue.

Finally, believers should approach issues systematically:

• Is there a Scriptural principle on point? While justice is an imperative, the Bible does not speak to the appropriateness of federal grants to states and localities. Scripture recognizes a role for the military, but fails to detail what factors should determine whether a particular missile system is constructed.

Moreover, verses must be considered honestly in context. Just as statistics, if tortured long enough, will confess to anything, Bible verses, if twisted the right way, will back any argument. For instance, the Presidential Biblical Scorecard, published by the Biblical News Service, purports to give "accurate, true, inside information on where presidential candidates stand on the biblical-family-moral-freedom issues." The Scorecard attacks comparable worth, which involves government wage-setting. Though the publication's analysis is correct on policy grounds, it adduces unrelated Scriptures as purported Biblical support for its stand.[29]

• Does the Scriptural reference apply today? God instructed the Israelites to hold a Jubilee Year to provide for the redemption of property every fifty years and to cancel all debts every seven years. During his presidential campaign Pat Robertson proposed adding a debt cancellation amendment to the Constitution. Yet does rigorous Scriptural exegesis suggest that God intended to institute the same formula in today's secularized, industrial society as He devised for the covenant nation of Israel, an agrarian and ethnically homogenous society devoted to following His law? The principle of debt avoidance is still valid today—"the borrower is servant to the lender" (Proverbs 22:7). But the specific system created under Moses is no longer applicable.[30]

• Is the Biblical rule mandatory or advisory? Mosaic law provided for the death penalty in several situations, including murder, adultery, sorcery, and disrespect for parents. Thus, it is impossible to argue that

Scripture forbids capital punishment. However, whether the death penalty should be used today by secular authorities that have little regard for God's Law is a different matter. Such a punishment for a moral offense like adultery would be inappropriate since the civil government both governs and is run by nonbelievers. (Of course, the church, which has taken the place of the ancient nation of Israel as God's covenantial people, still has an obligation to discipline its members for transgressions of divine Law, though it does not possess the power of criminal punishment.)

Even in the case of murder, the Biblical principle, which remains valid, must be applied in a prudential matter. Is the state today too corrupt and the criminal justice system too imperfect to warrant the use of the death penalty?[31] It is not enough for Christians to demand strict punishment of lawbreakers; they must also work to ensure that the truth-determining process is both fair and accurate enough to warrant taking someone's life. For instance, Old Testament law required the testimony of more than one witness to invoke the death penalty (Numbers 35:30).

- If there is no Scriptural principle on point, is the proposed policy consistent with the Biblical pattern of government? Scripture says nothing of price supports for beekeepers. However, as detailed in Chapter Two, in December 1987 Congress lifted the $250,000 limit on payments to individual producers: some fourteen beekeepers were expected to collect an extra $6 million. This sort of transfer, by which the rich used government to tax the poor and the middle-class to get richer, would appear to be a modern form of "oppression" that the prophets of old regularly railed against.

- Does the proposal, if not barred by the Bible, weigh costs as well as benefits? Using tax revenue to subsidize some small firms through a Small Business Administration (SBA) obviously helps some individuals. But the evidence is that such a program hurts not only taxpayers, but also other small businesses, which lose access to loans as a result of the SBA's activities. No government activity harms no one, and all the costs should be taken into account.

- If a policy's objectives are consistent with God's mandate for civil government, does the specific measure actually promote those goals? Good intentions are not enough: James, for one, decried believers who wish their hungry brother or sister well but offer them no food (James 2:15-17). Thus, while help for the needy is a persistent Biblical theme, a Christian needs to ask whether, say, a proposed increase in the minimum wage would actually assist the poor. In fact, as is discussed further in Chapter Nine, experience has shown the minimum wage to price out of the job market those who most need an entry-level job—minority teens with a poor education, no training, and little experience. The major beneficiaries are higher skilled union workers for whom the minimum wage operates as a wage floor.

- Is the proposed policy the most cost-effective way to achieve the godly objective? Providing housing for the poor is a major concern of government today. However, some programs work better than others. For instance, public housing and so-called Section 8 subsidies for construction of low-income units have proved to be incredibly costly, even while providing often substandard shelter for those in need. In contrast, a federal effort to override exclusionary local zoning laws, which make the private construction of cheap housing virtually impossible, combined with vouchers for poor people to use in renting private apartments, would likely improve the access of low-income individuals to housing at a lower cost to taxpayers.

- Does the Bible give primary responsibility for the issue to a different "government"? The disciplining and education of children is clearly a family responsibility. Government provision of education may be consistent with, though not required by, the Bible—

as long as the public system neither attacks Christian values nor excludes parents from the educational process. But onerous restrictions on parents' rights to educate their children in private institutions and at home are not Scriptural. Similarly, as mentioned earlier, welfare is primarily an individual, family, and church responsibility. Government action should not inhibit these activities.

Christ said His yoke was light, but His followers are, no less than unbelievers, fallen creatures who must struggle daily to live up to the perfection that He represents. And applying Biblical principles to the political arena is no easier than living up to them in any other area of a Christian's life. Believers must look first to God's revelation through the Bible. Then they should review the role of the other "governments" that God has ordained, particularly the family and church. Lastly, they need to use simple prudence in applying Biblical principles to current policy issues.

As a result, there is no Christian legislative agenda per se. On some fundamental moral issues, such as abortion, which is discussed further in Chapter Eight, it would be hard for anyone who takes the Bible seriously to disagree. But on most matters of public controversy Christians can differ in the same ways that nonbelievers do. Though Christians' shared worldview should make the gap between them somewhat smaller than that among their secular neighbors, the variance remains large. Nevertheless, there is a uniquely Christian perspective in which issues should be framed. The following chapter reviews a number of specific subjects, suggesting the broad arguments that a Christian should consider in judging policy. The positions I reach reflect not a Christian legislative agenda for the next Congress or President, but the judgment of one believer who takes the Bible seriously. For this reason, the specific conclusions are less important for other Christians than the way in which the matters are assessed.

# EIGHT

# Applying Biblical Principles: Some Examples

*T*here is hardly an issue on which one cleric or another has not offered his opinion. In fact, some church denominations seem to spend more time critiquing the annual federal budget than analyzing Scripture; instead of urging people to voluntarily help their neighbors, pastors sermonize about the need for government to create new programs. On economics, farm price supports, foreign aid, plant closings, taxes, nuclear weapons, comparable worth, South Africa, welfare, and many other topics, religious leaders constantly purport to speak for God.

All of these are important subjects, of course, and Christians, both as believers in godly justice and as citizens of a worldly republic, have an obligation to speak out. Indeed, writes Madeleine L'Engle, "it is impossible to listen to the Gospel week after week and turn my back on the social issues confronting me today."[1]

But believers also have a duty to act responsibly. Christians must review Scripture as honest seekers of God's Word rather than as political partisans, whether conservative or liberal, in search of a contextless verse to support their opinions.[2] Not every issue is a matter of godly justice; Christians must exercise prudence as well as moral outrage in judging competing policies. Moreover, believers need to recognize that we speak not as God's agents, authorized by Heaven to settle worldly policy disputes, but as individual citizens who happen to be submitted to the Lordship of Christ.

Nor should Christians tie our faith to particular public officials or political parties. Salvation is achieved through God, not the state. Moreover, partisan political involvement can threaten the church's credibility as a representative of the impartial God who, wrote Peter, is patient, "not wanting anyone to perish, but everyone to come to repentance" (2 Peter 3:9). Warns former White House aide Charles Colson, who now heads Prison Fellowship: "Politics is not the church's first calling. Evangelism, administering the sacraments, providing discipleship, fellowship, teaching the Word, and exhorting its members to holy living are the heartbeat of the church. When it addresses political issues, the church must not do so at the risk of weakening its primary mission."[3]

Nevertheless, believers, including those who hold church positions, need to think about politics and policy. A few issues are easy: an impartial court system; a war of conquest against a peaceful, democratic neighbor; genocide; racial discrimination; and so on. In most cases, however, matters are not so easily resolved. Thus, as developed in Chapter Seven, Christians should consider the following questions in judging proposals for government action or inaction:

- Is there a Scriptural principle on point?
- Does the Scriptural reference apply today?
- Is the Biblical rule mandatory or advisory?
- If there is no Scriptural principle on point, is the proposed policy consistent with the Biblical pattern of government?
- Does the proposal, if not barred by the Bible, weigh costs as well as benefits?
- If a policy's objectives are consistent with God's mandate for civil government, does the specific measure actually promote those goals?
- Is the proposed policy the most cost-effective way to achieve the godly objective?
- Does the Bible give primary responsibility for the issue to a different "government"?

In applying these criteria to current issues, Christians may still disagree about the appropriate result. After all, disputes over the likely costs and benefits of legislative proposals are legion; while believers start from a common understanding of man and his relationship with God, we, no less than anyone else, may be unable to reach a consensus about the desirability of a particular policy. However, what is needed is not a godly framework within which to judge issues and candidates. The cornerstone of such an approach is a commitment to Biblical justice, a passion for the plight of the unfortunate, and a respect for individual liberty, property, and dignity.[4] All policies should be measured as they affect these three broad principles.

There are obviously scores of issues that citizens and public officials are now struggling with in the public arena. Only a representative sample of them can be dealt with here. This chapter continues with a discussion of eight issues where Scripture is not silent: abortion, birth technologies, criminal justice, divorce, drugs, education, pornography, and welfare. Often the Bible is clearer about the duty of the individual Christian–in the case of drugs and pornography, for instance–than it is on the government's role in responding to the problem. But in all these cases there are Scriptural references that must be applied.

In contrast are matters where Scripture provides us with little guidance. We can often inform our analysis with general Biblical principles, but the specific issues cannot be decided by simple reference to a verse or two. Fourteen of those issues are covered in chapter 9.

## ABORTION

Evangelicals and Catholics are generally pro-life, while the liberal Protestant denominations–despite significant dissent among the laity, especially in the Lutheran Church–have supported legalization of abortion.[5] This issue may be the most emotional controversy now present in the public arena, rivaling slavery in the passions that it inflames.[6]

There is no one Scripture that speaks directly to the issue of abortion. However, the Bible offers us substantial guidance on the question, for life is clearly sacred in God's eyes. Man was, for instance, created in God's image (Genesis 1:27). And the child that results from conception is a gift from God (Genesis 4:1). For this reason, the Lord declared that he would "demand an accounting for the life of his fellow man" (Genesis 9:5). The Sixth Commandment proscribes murder, and death was fixed as the penalty for that crime (Exodus 20:13; Numbers 35:16).

Are the unborn considered life worth preserving? Neither Moses nor the apostles discussed the issue, presumably because either the idea of inducing an abortion was widely considered to be an anathema not worth mentioning or because few women had a serious opportunity to prematurely end their pregnancies. Mosaic law did, however, offer some protection for the fetus in another context: if a man struck a pregnant woman causing her to deliver prematurely, he "must be fined whatever the woman's husband demands and the court allows" (Exodus 21:22). If serious injury occurred, the Bible prescribed "life for life" retribution; the best exegesis suggests that this rule applied to the life of the unborn child as well as that of the mother, but the matter remains a issue of some disagreement.[7]

There is also an obvious Biblical concern over the plight of the helpless–which a fetus certainly is. The Old Testament prophets frequently attacked Israel's leaders for ignoring the plight of widows and orphans, while Christ's parable about the Good Samaritan exhibited the enormous reach of Christian love. (In fact, with at least one parent committed to ending his life, an unborn child is rather like an orphan.)

Moreover, Scripture relates manhood back to conception, suggesting that that instance, rather than birth, is the point when life begins in God's eyes.[8] For instance, the Lord told Rebekah after she had conceived Esau and Jacob that "Two nations are in your womb, and two peoples from within you will be separated" (Genesis 25:23). God's word to Jeremiah was that "Before I formed you in the womb I knew you, before you were born I set you apart; I appointed you as a prophet to the nations" (Jeremiah 1:5). The angel who visited Mary told her that "You will be with child and give birth to a son, and you are to give him the name Jesus" (Luke 1:31). And the unborn John the Baptist "leaped" in his mother's womb when Mary visited Elizabeth (Luke 1:41).

Similarly, as he was being afflicted, Job lamented: "Let the day perish on which I was to be born, and the night which said, 'A boy is conceived'" (Job 3:3, *New American Standard*; the *NIV* repeats the word "born," but other translations, such as the *King James* and the *New English* also use "conceived"). And Job observed later: "Your hands shaped me and made me.... Did you not ... clothe me with skin and flesh and knit me together wih bones and sinews?" (Job. 10:8-11) Though human development continues after birth, the creative process that Job is describing is almost surely occurring in the womb.

David, too, wrote on this theme. "Surely I have been a

sinner from birth, sinful from the time my mother conceived me" (Psalm 51:5). David went on to state that God taught him wisdom "in the inmost place," which may mean the womb.[9] Similarly, in a later Psalm David wrote: "you knit me together in my mother's womb.... When I was woven together in the depths of the earth, your eyes saw my unformed body. All the days ordained for me were written in your book before one of them came to be" (Psalm 139:13-16).

In short, God apparently sees life beginning at conception, with birth perhaps only the most significant incident in a constant developmental process which continues until death.[10] The fetus, even at the moment of conception, is a life being molded by God. As such it deserves protection.

Of course, the fact that God considers life to be precious does not mean that it can never be taken. Life is sacred, not inviolate: Mosaic law prescribed death for a variety of offenses, including murder and adultery. In these cases other fundamental interests were considered to be more important than the right to life. The unborn child, however, is innocent of any crime. Thus, only the most compelling of reasons could justify taking his life.

A number of rationales have been advanced for abortion, two of which can be dismissed with little discussion, for they have neither Scriptural support nor are they consistent with the tenets of Biblical justice. For instance, some people contend that abortion should be legal since desperate women would otherwise go to illegal practitioners. However, the fact that some people will violate the law does not change the moral imperative of protecting the lives of the unborn.[11]

Another argument is that abortion is necessary to prevent the birth of unwanted children. That Christians should be as concerned about the welfare of the born as the unborn is an important point often made by abortion supporters–and a matter recognized by Jerry Falwell and others who have established homes for unwed mothers. However, the argument that an unborn child should be killed because he might be abused if allowed to live is fundamentally evil. After all, should one-year-olds be evaluated to determine if they are happy, and, if not, be "aborted"?

Finally, there is a life/liberty/privacy interest on the part of the mother-to-be. That interest can be substantial, most obviously in the rare instance when the woman's life is at stake. Most people who oppose abortion believe that there should be an exception when the mother's life is in danger: they have implicitly treated the established life as more valuable than the developing one. There is no Scriptural basis for making such a choice, and some pro-life advocates believe man is not authorized to make such a decision. In the end, this judgment seems to be a logical and appropriate one, for the established life is fully developed and has an immediacy lacking in the fetus, but that is more a prudential than a theological consideration.[12]

Another hard case is a rape victim who desires to be rid of an unwanted baby. She, like the unborn child, is entirely innocent, having become pregnant without voluntarily engaging in the act that naturally leads to pregnancy. The high esteem in which God holds every life and the strong Biblical injunctions against killing suggest that it would be difficult for a Christian to justify an abortion even in this traumatic circumstance, but it is far easier for a man or even a nonpregnant woman to deliver an arm-chair lecture than for a pregnant rape victim to listen to one.

There is also the issue of a woman's concern about bearing a seriously deformed or defective child. Aborting a fetus simply because he is "abnormal" is inconsistent with the value that God accords all human life; nothing in Scripture suggests that man, whether through government or not, has been authorized to destroy life that is believed to be less intelligent or physically capable than average. Of course, there are some defects which leave a baby with little potential for anything that we consider to be life—such as anencephalus, where the brain fails to develop—but giving some people, whether parents, doctors, or government officials, the power to choose who is normal enough to live is enormously dangerous. In fact, the great strides that have been made in working with children with Down's syndrome, who were once automatically institutionalized, demonstrates man's inability to accurately assess the value of any life.[13]

Finally, there is the issue of abortion "on demand," based on a woman's not wanting, for whatever reason, to have the baby. Though a woman's desire not to carry the unborn child to term is an important one—the nine-month burden is substantial and the privacy interest in such a family matter is real—the life at stake should have primacy. Especially with adoption an attractive alternative, the desire to be rid of human being that resulted from a voluntary sexual union pales compared to the right to life of the unborn child, who David described as "fearfully and wonderfully made" (Psalm 139:14).

Even if abortion is wrong, does that justify government restrictions? Sodomy and adultery involve transgressions against God's Law, but generally do not threaten the rights of others; therefore, as was argued in Chapter Four, they are not properly within the reach of the state today.[14] Abortion, in contrast, involves not only a violation of godly standards, but also an infringement of the rights of another human. Since the unborn are unable to assert their rights, government has an obligation, as a matter of justice, to intervene–to fulfill the Biblical duty of preventing a form of "oppression."[15]

Not that government action alone should be looked at as the answer. "If we make abortion illegal, without doing much more than that, it won't solve anything" since "we will not be addressing the reasons that abortion was a desirable option in the first place," warns Thomas Klasen, the founder of Heart-Light, which is building a Memorial to the Unborn Child.[16] Christians should do their best, through educational efforts, counseling centers, facilities for unwed mothers, support services for single parents, and efforts to streamline the adoption process, to create a social ethic that values all life, including that of the unborn. State involvement in what is a very personal and family matter will always remain less than a perfect solution.

Indeed, allowing government to restrict abortion raises a host of other disturbing issues about the proper reach of state intervention. Should pregnant women be prohibited from taking any action, such as exercising or smoking, that could conceivably harm the unborn? The threat to the fetus seems too small to justify such government micromanagement of a mother's life, but the principle is related to the one governing abortion. Nevertheless, the difficulty in determining the line does not mean that one should not be drawn: killing the unborn is clearly wrong and should be prohibited.[17]

## BIRTH TECHNOLOGIES

Surrogate motherhood has become a legal issue, with the New Jersey Supreme Court simultaneously voiding the surrogacy contract but effectively upholding most of its terms in the well-publicized case of Baby M. In vitro fertilization–resulting in "test tube babies"–and artificial insemination have become increasingly common practices. The exact nature of the procedures, and their ethical implications, vary widely: artificial insemination may be by a husband or another donor, for instance. How should a Christian view such practices?

There are no Scriptures that directly deal with these subjects. After all, such advanced technologies only appeared this century. But the issues involve such basic matters as God's purpose for marriage and sex and have, not surprisingly, occasioned serious controversy within the Christian community. The Catholic Church denounced artificial insemination as early as 1949 and in 1987 criticized in vitro fertilization as well. Evangelical Protestants have split over these questions.

The Vatican's opposition to the new birth technologies stems from its view that "the unitive meaning and the procreative meaning" of sexual intercourse are inseparable. Yet, argues Christian ethicist Stanley Grenz, sex also can be seen as "an expression of the self-giving of the marriage partners," a "spiritual metaphor," and a "'sacrament' of the marriage covenant."[18]

Moreover, there is nothing to suggest that another purpose of sex is not to provide pleasure for God's creatures. Paul, for instance, wrote of spouses' "marital duty" to one another, enjoining them, "Do not deprive each other" (1 Corinthians 7:3, 5). Similarly, though he praised celibacy as allowing one to better serve God, Paul stated that "it is better to marry than to burn with passion" (1 Corinthians 7:9). Paul's concern was not apparently with procreation, but sensual desire. And rather than denounce that feeling, he cited marriage as a means of satisfying it.

Under these circumstances it is hard to see an objection to artificial insemination by a husband or to in vitro fertilization when his wife carries the pregnancy.[19] In these cases the process does not include another person within the marital relationship and both partners are performing their usual roles, albeit with the assistance of one or another advanced technologies.

Artificial insemination by donor and surrogate motherhood, in contrast, do allow for the intrusion of another party into the marital relationship. The emotional effect of the third party on the marital union, especially in a case like New

Jersey's Baby M, where the natural mother wanted to renege on the contract and keep custody of the child, is potentially enormous. However, neither of these practices involve actual adultery, which causes the most serious violation of the marriage covenant, and the consent of both parties shows that the parents, at least, believe the action to be in the best interests of the family.

Yet given the importance placed by God on the marriage covenant and the family, Christians should be wary of involving a third party, even indirectly, in those relationships. Infertile couples should especially consider adoption as an alternative. But the Bible does not specifically forbid believers from relying on one or more of the new birth aids.

Are there prudential concerns that justify either promoting or forbidding the use of advanced birth technologies? Few problems are likely to arise if the process is kept within marriage, but the introduction of third parties may raise a number of serious questions. Should a child be told that his real father, for instance, is an anonymous donor to a sperm clinic? Is the family prepared to handle potentially divisive emotional crosscurrents? The issue of surrogate motherhood is even more complex. Should the birth mother be able to claim the child? What if the baby born by a surrogate mother is seriously retarded or handicapped? And so on.[20]

As serious as these problems may be, they must be balanced against an infertile couple's joy in gaining a child. Indeed, it is hard to imagine an interest, including even overwrought fears of "baby-selling," that would outweigh the value of that child to them. So personal are these decisions that no legislature is really qualified to try to balance the competing interests in deciding which is more important.

Thus, in an intensely private area like this, where civil government is not well-equipped to act, Christians probably should leave the issue to other levels of "government"–the family and the church. Since Scripture is not clear, church leaders, in Protestant denominations as well as the Catholic Church, should help their members ascertain God's will. And the best Biblical guidance may very well be against surrogate motherhood and even artificial insemination by donor.

But there is no Biblical imperative that government enforce any church's doctrinal views. Legislatures and courts are necessarily drawn into disputes like the Baby M case, but what is required there is a stable set of legal rules to wisely govern the new birth technologies, not a prohibition. Instead, the basic decision whether to use one of these new practices seems best left up to the family rather than the state.

## CRIMINAL JUSTICE

Mosaic law provides a thematic starting point for determining both specific crimes and appropriate punishments. Force and fraud, for instance, were prohibited. Murder, rape, kidnapping, and theft were all treated as crimes, as was false testimony in a trial. Since these actions involved violations not only of one's personal covenant with God, but also an individual's relationship with his neighbors, they appropriately remain forbidden today.

Not all Old Testament crimes are properly matters of secular justice, however. As discussed in Chapter Four, moral violations that infringe not the rights of others but one's personal responsibility to God—such as sodomy, which was punishable by death—no longer appear to be properly within the mandate of the civil government.[21] Similarly, the special Mosaic standards of economic responsibility, most notably the Year of Jubilee and property redemption, were uniquely tied to Israel's status as a covenant nation and God's gift of the land to the different tribes.

Nor does Mosaic law restrict what may be properly punished by the criminal law. The limited use of the criminal sanction in ancient Israel may yield a presumption that activities that do not fall into the general categories of fraud and force, of which embezzlement, for instance, is a subset, are best not handled through the criminal process. An example might be violations of the so-called Ethics in Government Act, which sets highly technical limits on when former government officials can lobby on issues they worked on. Violations of this law neither involve traditional moral norms nor a direct assault on the rights of others, and thus probably should involve civil rather than criminal penalties. Nevertheless, Old Testament law does not prevent Christians from expanding the criminal law for prudential reasons.

Similarly, the range of Biblical punishments included restitution, beating, banishment, and death. Given the differences between the covenant nation of Israel and the secular state of America, and the corresponding contrasts between a judicial system that operated directly under God's guidance and the decrepit, failing process that exists today, Mosaic law would appear to be more a guide than a mandate for present law. As observed in Chapter Seven, a racist judicial system in the South earlier this century turned the death penalty into a hideous weapon of injustice; under such circumstances it may have been better not to have had the penalty at all, even though it was used in Old Testament times.

Nevertheless, the Scriptural principles can guide us in important ways. First, punishment for serious violations of the rights of other individuals–murder, rape, kidnapping–was severe. The very sacredness of life in God's eyes required retribution. However, the sentence was to be proportional to the crime, an "eye for an eye." And even the guilty appear to have been treated with dignity; though Mosaic Israel apparently did not have prisons, it is inconceivable that the ancient Israelites would have countenanced the overcrowded and dangerous institutions in which inmates are incarcerated today.

In Mosaic times it also appears that guilt was ascertained and punishment imposed swiftly. The reasons are not surprising, for justice delayed is truly justice denied, particularly for the innocent defendant and the victim.

Finally, Biblical justice emphasized a criminal's repentance and his making victims whole. Theft of oxen or sheep was to be repaid four- or fivefold (Exodus 22:1). Similarly, someone who stole from or cheated his neighbor was to provide restitution plus one-fifth of the value, and to make a guilt offering before a priest (Leviticus 6:1-7). One organization putting these principles into practice today is Justice Fellowship, an offshoot of Charles Colson's Prison Fellowship, which works with states and communities to promote alternatives to imprisonment, such as house arrest, community service, and restitution.

Thus, while there is no uniquely Christian answer to crime, believers can seek to insert Biblical principles into the criminal justice process. And given the severity of the problems that now face both the court and prison systems of most states and the federal government, a more limited reliance on the criminal sanction, an emphasis on swift and sure punishment, and a search for alternative sentences that make victim and criminal whole through restitution and repentance could only improve matters.

## DIVORCE

God's position on divorce is not in doubt: "anyone who divorces his wife, except for marital unfaithfulness, causes her to commit adultery, and anyone who marries a woman so divorced commits adultery," preached Christ on the mount (Matthew 5:32). What position, then, should a Christian take on the civil law to govern divorce? In Catholic countries like Italy, Spain, and Argentina, for instance, the church has publicly opposed proposals to allow divorce.

However, Christ did not forbid divorce, or argue that the Pharisees should ban divorce, but simply said that remarriage constituted adultery. Moreover, even in the covenant nation of Israel divorce could be procured–not because doing so was right, but, explained Jesus to the Pharisees, "because your hearts were hard" (Matthew 19:8). Men are no less unfeeling today, and the state must govern a population which includes only a minority of people who have submitted themselves to Christ's teachings. In this situation it would appear to be best for Christians to work through their religious "government" (the church) to promote the institution of marriage; indeed, the church has an obligation to uphold God's standards by refusing to sanctify an adulterous union. But believers should recognize that the roles of ecclesiastical and civil authorities differ in this case, and should not try to use the state to override people's hard hearts.

This does not mean that divorce should be quick and automatic: a minimum separation period before the granting of a divorce would help ensure that both parties have seriously considered the consequences of their decision. Moreover, the settlement needs to provide for an equitable distribution of property and the needs of any children. For the most important cause of poverty among female-headed households today is divorce. While families that have been severed emotionally should not be held together legally, the law can and should enforce the parental obligations that have come out of that union.

## DRUGS

America faces a crisis over drugs, both licit and illicit. Cigarette abuse costs some 350,000 lives a year; alcohol use is estimated to cause nearly 100,000 deaths annually, including 25,000 traffic fatalities. Illegal drugs, such as cocaine, heroin, and marijuana, kill 3,600 people a year, ruin the lives of a host of users, and finance criminal gangs that stage gun battles in the streets of cities like Washington, D.C., New York, and Los Angeles. Is there a scriptural answer?

The Bible warns us against drug abuse. One of "the acts of the sinful nature," wrote Paul, is "drunkenness" (Galatians 5:20). And Peter directed his readers not to live as the pagans, "in debauchery, lust, drunkenness, orgies, carousing and detestable idolatry" (1 Peter 4:3).

Similarly, Paul described the body as the temple of the Holy Spirit; though he was particularly critical of sexual immorality because it was practiced "against" one's own body, while other sins occurred "outside" of the body, he nevertheless admonished his readers generally to "honor God with your body" (1 Corinthians 6:18-20). Moreover, at another point Paul instructed the Corinthian church: "Don't you know that you yourselves are God's temple and that God's Spirit lives in you? If anyone destroys God's temple, God will destroy him; for God's temple is sacred, and you are that temple" (1 Corinthians 3:16, 17).

It is clear that a Christian's first responsibility is to respect his own body; he should also work within the church to encourage other members to live up to this Scriptural requirement. And believers should discipline fellow members of the body who refuse to repent, but continue to engage in immoral activities, such as drunkenness (1 Corinthians 5:11).

However, Paul made no policy recommendations. While Christians were not to act as nonbelievers, he didn't urge them to lobby for a government prohibition of sinful behavior. In fact, Paul didn't even tell his readers to avoid immoral pagans, for to do so "you would have to leave this world" (1 Cor. 5:10). He hardly seems likely, then, to have backed the use of civil authority to regulate the activities he criticized.

Thus, drug policy is more a matter of reason than revelation. Companies have an obvious interest in restricting their workers' on-the-job use of drugs, licit or illicit, but they can do that without the government's help. There are obvious policy grounds for the civil authorities to proscribe the use of mind-altering substances while driving, for instance; if "second-hand smoke" is found to endanger bystanders, a much contested issue, there would be grounds for some restrictions on public smoking.

However, outlawing personal consumption of these and similar substances raises far more difficult issues. Alcohol prohibition earlier this century did reduce demand–though current consumption is above pre-Prohibition levels–but it was unable to prevent those determined to drink from doing so. Moreover, the ban created a criminal underworld and financed the activities of organized crime. In fact, mobsters openly fought for control of the alcohol trade. There were more than 1,000 gangland murders in New York City between 1920 and 1933.

A similar pattern has emerged with the current attempt to regulate such drugs as heroin and cocaine. Battles between competing drug gangs in New York City have resulted in 359 to 523 deaths between 1983 and 1987. Young men are being gunned down in the nation's capital as groups fight over the drug market; 60 percent of D.C.'s homicides in 1987 were drug-related.

Government officials are largely helpless. The best the Washington, D.C., Board of Education could come up with in early 1988 was to consider introducing school uniforms so that kids wouldn't have to earn extra cash selling drugs to buy the latest fashions to wear to school. Other, more draconian proposals included drafting the military in the drug war, calling out the National Guard, shooting down planes piloted by suspected drug smugglers, strip-searching tourists at the border, and spending more on interdiction efforts. But even as the federal government spent $21.5 billion between 1981 and 1987 to enforce the drug laws, the supply of cocaine, the latest drug of choice, doubled.

There is no uniquely Christian solution to the problem of drug abuse. Believers should work individually and through their churches and other community institutions to educate the young and counteract deleterious peer pressure. As long as there is a demand for drugs, the drug trade will continue.

In fact, the failure of current policy requires a fundamental rethinking of current enforcement strategies. The reason that gangs fight over city turf, pushers invade schools, and drug overlords terrorize foreign nations is that selling drugs is one of the world's most profitable enterprises, a criminal entrepreneur's dream. And if the government further tightens the supply, the price, and the potential profit, will only go higher.

One possible approach–prudential, not Biblical–would be to refocus efforts toward protecting children rather than adults from drug use, similar to how the government now regulates alcohol and cigarette consumption.[22] Decriminalizing adult drug use would cause the violent drug empires to collapse overnight. With the criminals most willing to ruin youngsters' lives for a buck out of business, kids would face at least one less pressure to use drugs. R. J. Reynolds, for instance, neither stages gun battles in residential neighborhoods nor puts tobacco pushers in elementary schools.

Of course, dropping sanctions against adult drug use would not lead to a perfect world. Total drug consumption might increase, though drugs now appear to be readily available to anyone who really wants them. But even then the problem could be better treated as a social problem, like alcoholism, rather than prosecuted as a crime. Anyway, we've run out of answers: politicians who are promising, for the tenth or hundredth time, to control the drug trade are merely engaging in wishful thinking. Indeed, more of the same enforcement programs will only make the drug trade more profitable, increasing sales in schools and crime in the streets. Many Christians will undoubtedly disagree with this proposal, and there is no clear Scriptural answer. Instead, we must preach the gospel as the ultimate solution and search for the most prudent government policy to limit the damage caused by sinful man.

## EDUCATION

As discussed in chapter 7, the Bible vests primary responsibility for education with the family. While formal schooling need not be provided by a Christian institution, parents have a responsibility to be actively involved in the education process. Moreover, given the hostility of many public schools to Christian values, believers need to work to protect parents' rights to educate their children at home or in a Christian school, preventing government from either banning or controlling, through detailed regulation of teachers' credentials, curriculum, and other matters, private instruction.

Believers also have an obligation to get involved in the operation of the nation's dominant public schools. Though the Bible gives us little guidance on how to improve public education, the system's decrepit state should concern all citizens,

Christian or not. Indeed, the public schools, which mold personalities and philosophies of, as well as impart knowledge to, the vast majority of children, are both too important and influential to be left unsupervised.

One issue is educational quality. Average SAT scores have only recently stabilized after years of decline; American children do far worse on science and math skills tests than kids in many other nations. Moreover, U.S. children are appallingly ignorant of history. A 1987 survey by the National Endowment for the Humanities found that two-thirds of seventeen-year-olds could not place the Civil War within a half-century of its occurrence. Nearly half had no idea when World War I took place and almost as many didn't know when the Constitution was drafted, even though they were questioned during the bicentennial year of the constitutional convention.[25]

The educational establishment, naturally, constantly asks for more money, but inadequate funds is not the issue. Total public outlays on schools run more than $160 billion annually and the U.S. devotes a larger share of its Gross National Product on education than any other nation except Sweden. The federal government alone spent $20 billion in 1987, nearly 50 percent more than when Ronald Reagan took office.

Instead, the problem is the lack of competition. The public schools are a monopoly, one that is especially powerful in poor areas, where people are less able to afford to educate their children privately. As a result, schools have less incentive to innovate, spend money cost-effectively, and meet parental concerns. Indeed, students in private schools routinely outperform their counterparts in government institutions, even after accounting for socioeconomic differences.

Not surprisingly, then, 49 percent of parents whose children are in public school say they would send their kids to a private school if they could afford to do so. Minority parents, a disproportionate number of whose children are trapped in inferior inner-city institutions, are even more desperate to escape the public educational system than are whites.

The problem is, most parents have to pay twice–first in taxes for government education, and second in tuition for private schools. The solution, then, is to empower parents by providing them with tax credits and/or vouchers. (The latter provide greater assistance to lower income people who pay less in taxes.) The Supreme Court has restricted the use of vouchers and tax credits, treating them as a de facto subsidy of religious schools, but that argument is badly flawed: the money goes to all private schools, whether religious or not. Moreover, the immediate beneficiaries are parents, not the schools, and a tax credit is merely a partial refund of the payment the parents had to make to subsidize the public schools. Vouchers and tax credits eliminate the injustice of forcing parents to pay twice to provide a good education for their children.[24]

The Reagan administration proposed to turn one federal educational grant program into vouchers for parents of disadvantaged children; congressional opponents argued that the resulting payment, roughly $600, would be inadequate to keep a needy student in a private school. Yet the average annual cost of a parochial education in predominantly black Washington, D.C., where thousands of black Baptist families send their children to Catholic schools, is about $600. Poor parents around the nation already sacrifice to place their children in private schools; even a small tax credit or voucher would enable many more to bear the cost.

Such a policy would not only increase the number of good private schools, but would also ultimately enhance the remaining public ones. Organizations rarely perform well unless they are under pressure to do so. As long as urban poor families have nowhere else to educate their children, the public schools have little institutional incentive to reform. If parents had both additional educational alternatives and the means to exercise those options, the public schools would have to improve or shrink.

Christians have another Biblical duty, to ensure that government does not use its educational power to promote injustice of any kind. There is no room for racial or ethnic discrimination, for instance, and believers should have been in the forefront of the campaign to eliminate segregation. Moreover, believers should demand fair treatment for their beliefs, opposing the use of textbooks that exclude Christianity from history or promote alternative philosophies such as secular humanism.[26] Believers should also press for equal access to public facilities; in early 1988, for instance, two different federal courts barred prayer groups from meeting in public high schools even though organizations like the scuba club were free to use the same facilities.

However, Christians should always remember God's injunction to the Israelites to treat aliens justly. Secular parents, too, are forced to send their children to public schools, so believers should not try to use the state to forcibly evangelize.[26] Our goal should not be to use religious textbooks, but ones that fairly reflect the role of Christianity in people's lives and on the founding of our nation. Voluntary Bible clubs should be able to meet in school buildings; mandatory Bible readings are not appropriate.

Moreover, evangelical activists should rethink their commitment to organized school prayer. Nondenominational prayer led by an atheist teacher is but meaningless formalism: it also could put enormous social pressure on religious minorities and would stir up unnecessary fear and resentment, particularly among Jewish Americans. Far from advocating corporate prayer in public institutions, Christ told His listeners, "when you pray, go into your room, close the door and pray to your Father, who is unseen. Then your Father, who sees what is done in secret, will reward you" (Matthew 6:6). In short, the Bible does not mandate organized school prayer and prudence suggests that it would do more harm than good.

## PORNOGRAPHY

The making and use of pornography is sinful. The Apostle Peter criticized those who, "by appealing to the lustful desires of sinful human nature," misled other people (2 Peter 2:18). Similarly, wrote Paul, God gave those who rejected him "over to shameful lusts" (Romans 1:26).

Thus, Christians should work through their families and churches to discourage the spread of pornography. They should preach against it, as well as organize boycotts. Pressure from anti-pornography activists caused Southland Corp., which owns many 7-11 stores, to stop carrying skin magazines. A number of other drugstore chains, including People's Drug, Dart Drug, and Rite Aid, have also dropped the pornographic materials they once carried.

As with drugs, however, there is no Scriptural mandate for the civil government to ban sexually explicit material. Paul wrote the Corinthian church, telling its members "not to associate with sexually immoral people–not at all meaning the people of this world who are immoral.... In that case you would have to leave the world. But now I am writing you that

you must not associate with anyone who calls himself a brother but is sexually immoral" (1 Corinthians 5:9-11). Admittedly
the early Christian church had little influence with the Roman
authorities and a lobbying campaign to ban sexual immorality
was doomed to failure, but Paul did not even order Christians
to stay away from immoral pagans. Would he have advocated
jailing them?

Without explicit Biblical direction on the issue,
Christians must rely on more general Scriptural principles and
simple prudence, exercising their God-given reason within revelation. For instance, people have a right not to have sinful
activity literally thrust in their faces; thus, the state should
limit the invasive aspects of pornography, the public displays
of sexually explicit material, such as movie marquees and side-
walk magazine racks, that essentially force the material on the
unwary. Government should also protect minors from being
used in pornographic films and from acquiring obscene materials.

However, as strongly as believers object to obscenity–for
good reason–we should think carefully before attempting to
control what our non-Christian neighbors can read and watch.
The effectiveness of state action diminishes rapidly as it
moves from issues involving conduct toward others to matters
of personal conscience. While government might be able to
keep an obscene magazine out of someone's hands, it can not
make his heart any purer. Indeed, 2,000 years' worth of
attempts by the church to use the state for moral ends have
produced an enormous amount of harm.

Nor do any of the arguments for censorship seem persua-
sive. While pornography is evidence of declining moral standards, it is hard to prove that the availability of sexually explicit materials itself threatens society. The real problem is that
people want to look at such material, not that it is available.
(Of course, government should not promote the spread of
pornography by funding lewd poetry, for example, as it has
done in the past through the National Endowment for the
Humanities.)

In fact, the most serious "pornography" problem facing
us is probably not obscene materials, which can be legally
banned today, but the soft-core sexuality that dominates TV
programming and print ads. Most people are revolted by, say,
Hustler magazine. But it is the soft-porn that permeates our

culture which is probably doing the most to erode traditional sexual mores.

Moreover, simple sexual erotica has no apparent effect on violent crime. Pornographic films have caused some study groups of male viewers to say they might attack a woman, but only if the movies were violent; most obscene material, however, is nonviolent. (In fact, Sweden censors movies based on the level of violence, not indecency.) Nor do rape rates correlate with the availability of pornography. Some sexual offenders have been found to possess lewd materials, but most consumers of smut commit no crimes. In short, there is no empirical evidence for banning pornography on this basis.[27]

Christians should promote a moral climate in which pornography would be viewed as unacceptable. However, believers should remember that civil government is not a redemptive institution; it should be used to regulate interpersonal relations, not to try to make men into angels. While government has a role in insulating minors, for instance, from obscene materials, the availability of pornography to adults determined to have it is a price we pay for living in a secularized society with a non-Christian majority. In sum, neither Biblical nor prudential arguments justify arresting people who commit this sin.

## WELFARE

Overall, the Reagan years were economically good to America–employment rose and average incomes increased. But still, not all is well in the U.S. Though the poverty rate has been declining, falling from 14 percent in 1985 to 13.6 percent in 1986, that still left 32.4 million people poor.[28] And particular segments of the population suffer disproportionately: in 1986 31.1 percent of blacks were below the poverty line, more than in 1978. An incredible 45.6 percent of black children under the age of six lived in poor households. Hispanic poverty is increasing five times the national average.

Nor is the problem of poverty only inadequate income. It is also personal dependency on government. Today nearly three-fourths of all single women under twenty-five who go on welfare remain on the rolls at least five years. Their *average* stay is more than nine years. And most of these women have children who are growing up poor. Indeed, the proportion of births to black single mothers jumped from 15 percent in 1959 to 57 percent in 1982. Female-headed households have become the norm in inner-city ghettos; most of these women, despite their best efforts, will never be able to provide either financially or emotionally for their children in the same way that the traditional intact family can.

There is a clear Biblical perspective on welfare. Christians are commanded to help the needy. Indeed, believers should demonstrate the same passion as did Jesus in reaching out to the poor, the hungry, and the homeless. We should give generously, both as individuals and through our churches and other community organizations.[29] Indeed, there may be no parable that sears the conscience more than Christ's description of Judgment Day, when he will tell the accursed that "I was hungry and you gave me nothing to eat, I was thirsty and you gave me nothing to drink, I was a stranger and you did not invite me in, I needed clothes and you did not clothe me, I was sick and in prison and you did not look after me" (Matthew 25:42, 43).

Scripture is less precise about the government's role. As discussed in Chapter Four, there is one verse that suggests the state is required to help provide for the poor, but most of the injunctions about giving apply to individuals and the Body of Christ collectively. Nevertheless, there is nothing prohibiting government assistance to the poor, if provided in a manner consistent with Biblical principles. The problem, of course, is that our political system seems incapable of designing a program that does not violate other Scriptural norms.

Christians should first work to remove public barriers to private, self-help efforts. In many areas government actually inhibits community-based programs; for instance, the Davis-Bacon Act, which sets minimum construction pay scales for federally subsidized work, effectively precludes the hiring of local youth in neighborhood rehabilitation projects. Black activist Robert Woodson, president of the National Center for Neighborhood Enterprise, has recommended a number of reforms to encourage local self-help, including allowing tenant management of public housing, lowering regulatory and licensing barriers to black enterprise, and placing day-care decisions in the hands of welfare recipients rather than social workers.[30]

As for welfare itself, drastic reform is needed. Existing programs both discourage work by and degrade the dignity of beneficiaries. The program is also highly complex, involving dozens of specific programs involving cash transfers, food assistance, medical care, and housing. Finally, welfare is expensive–roughly $130 billion is transferred annually to the poor.

A separate book could be written solely on the problem of welfare, but the goals of reform for a Christian are simple. The least important is to save money. There is no justification for waste, of course, and the program should be structured to better protect the right of taxpayers to the fruit of their labors, but the twin goals of physically saving lives and helping people become independent should be paramount.

Perhaps most important, existing programs should be reshaped so that they don't encourage family break up. For instance, benefits to teenage mothers could be conditioned on their remaining with their parents.[31] Moreover, the federal and state governments should place greater emphasis on enforcing child support obligations on the part of fathers. Though an unemployed black teen may be unable to contribute much to meet his child's needs, any action that would make him feel responsible for the life that he has helped create would be a step forward.

Welfare should also require work by recipients. This fits the Biblical pattern, where beneficiaries of charity had responsibilities to individual donors and the community, such as gleaning the food from the fields and assisting the body of believers. Moreover, there is no better preparation for work than a job, and other than marriage, employment for the head of the household is the most important way that welfare families escape poverty. Requiring work would also force welfare recipients to face the same incentives and constraints as the nonpoor. For this reason even mothers should be expected to work. Instituting such a policy would obviously be a burden on those with children, but it is imperative to reform policies to reflect this sort of "tough love." Otherwise, welfare will continue to provide an easy subsidy for an unmarried teenager who wants to have a baby.

An integral part of welfare should be job training and employment banks, though past program failures prove that there is no simple policy panacea for people who tend to have few skills and often have not finished high school. Nevertheless, the ultimate goal of welfare should be to enable the poor to lead fulfilling, independent lives.

Even as policies are changed to place greater responsibility on the poor, they should be given more authority over their own lives. In particular, federal benefits should be turned into vouchers, where possible, to enhance the beneficiaries' power to choose. Today, provider groups, such as legal aid attorneys, control the type of services received by the poor; with vouchers poor people could search for the producer who would best meet their needs. Such an approach could work with housing, legal services, and education, among others.[32]

"The poor you will always have with you," Jesus warned us (Matthew 26:11). But we still have an obligation to help as many people as possible who suffer from the enormous pain and hardship that accompanies poverty. The ultimate Scriptural solution is a change of worldview, a decision by people, rich and poor, to get right with God. We live in a fallen world, however, and we need to search for imperfect, temporary solutions for human problems. While the Bible does not provide us with specific policy answers–like which type of job training program will work best–it does offer us the experience of charitable measures implemented in both the Old and New Testament periods. More important, Scripture mandates a commitment to the dignity and well-being of all men, especially those who are least able to fend for themselves. Christians should bring the full force of God's abiding love for those in need into the welfare debate.

## THE BIBLE AND POLICY

In judging any political proposal, a Christian should first consult the guidebook for his life, the Bible. For there are some issues, like abortion, to which Scripture directly speaks. In most cases, however, God's Word merely provides the starting-point for analysis; the Bible tells us that divorce is wrong, not what the state's civil statute should say. To decide that issue, we must use our God-given reason to apply the Scriptural principles. And the role of prudential judgment becomes even more important in assessing policy where the Bible is largely silent, an area to which we now turn.

# NINE

# Applying Biblical Principles: More Examples

*I*f Scripture gives us some particularized guidance, though not necessarily a specific legislative proposal, for issues like abortion, drugs, and welfare, there are a host of other matters where only the broadest of Biblical principles apply. They may cause us to be generally skeptical or supportive of certain policies, but we must utilize a heavy dose of reason within God's revelation to judge them. Examples of issues which, though illuminated by the Bible, must be decided largely on prudential grounds, are agriculture, Central America, comparable worth, the draft, economic regulation, environment, foreign aid, income redistribution, Israel, military alliances, the minimum wage, nuclear weapons, protectionism, and taxes.

## AGRICULTURE
All levels of government are now heavily involved in regulating and shaping the agricultural market in two different ways. Many localities preserve farmland through zoning and tax measures, while the federal government simultaneously subsidizes and limits agricultural production.

Where should a Christian stand on such issues? In contrast to a question like abortion, the Bible says very little on the appropriateness of the current, or any, government agricultural policy. Men are stewards of the earth's resources, which obviously includes agricultural land (Psalm 24:1; Leviticus 25:23). Mosaic law also provided for redemption of land–primarily property outside of walled cities–by those who had sold it (Leviticus 25).

Our role as stewards mandates a respectful attitude toward the earth and the rest of God's creation; surely destruction for its own sake would violate God's trust. But the Lord did not expect his world to remain a pristine wilderness: man was to "fill the earth and subdue it" (Genesis 1:28). Nor is there any indication that God wants land that was once in agricultural production to remain permanently in that use. God does not, for instance, say that farms are more important than homes, that picturesque agricultural scenes are better than crowded suburbia.

Similarly, the Year of Jubilee demonstrates more the importance of family ownership of land–which had been distributed by God to the twelve tribes–than its particular use. There were no apparent limits on how far walled cities, which are treated differently under Mosaic law, could expand in ancient Israel. And there were fewer alternative uses for land then than there are now: agriculture and livestock production were the country's most important economic activities, and land was the prime form of wealth. For reasons that he does not fully explain, God was concerned about maintaining a family balance in land ownership within the covenant nation of Israel. But there is nothing in that goal that helps us decide whether or not to restrict the conversion (or ownership transfer) of farmland today.

Given no theological imperative for government intervention, is there a prudential reason for backing controls over farmland? The Association for Public Justice argues that three million acres of cropland are disappearing each year and that the demand for food will increase in the future, requiring the state to act.[1] However, there is no crisis. In fact, contrary to the common myth, the stock of prime agricultural land appears to be shrinking "well under one million acres per year, and there is reason to believe that the rate will decline over the next several decades. Consequently, when measured against present and potential cropland of some 540 million acres, prospective rates of conversion to nonagricultural uses would seem to pose little threat to the future supply of cropland."[2]

Nor should the possibility of higher future demand for food be a concern. Today, as part of its subsidy program, the federal government requires significant "set-asides" of farmers' land; were those restrictions lifted, production would jump. Moreover, existing domestic crop surpluses are huge. In December 1986, federal warehouses contained 2.7 billion bushels of wheat, 10.3 billion bushels of corn, and 325 million bushels of oats and barley. And "the green revolution" throughout the Third World has greatly increased foreign production. Inadequate agricultural supplies is not likely to be a problem.[3]

Lastly, there are neither Scriptural nor prudential reasons to favor farms over homes. An unregulated market allows the interplay of all factors–projected future demand for food and housing, the relative value of particular pieces of land for grazing and building, and so on–to determine which property is used for which purpose. Indeed, if expectations of a possible food shortage grew, farmland prices would rise, halting the conversion process and bringing back into production land put to other uses, such as grazing. There is no evidence that a federal or state bureaucracy, which could never collect and assimilate the volume of information that is inherent in market prices, could make a better determination. Moreover, the Bible's warnings about the possibility of politicians' abuse of power should bias one against entrusting authority over such a basic resource as land to political authorities.

The second issue is government support for farmers. The National Conference of Catholic Bishops, for instance, advocates government aid to "moderate-sized farms" and the preservation of "the opportunity to engage in farming."[4] However, nothing in Scripture justifies the forced redistribution of resources from all taxpayers to a few farmers. If poor farmers deserve help it is because they are in need, not because they either grow crops or raise livestock. Indeed, a transfer system based on criteria other than privation is more likely to violate than to promote Biblical justice, for such a program does not provide for equal economic treatment under the law. Instead, the government is providing special privileges to a group that accounts for less than 2 percent of the population. This influential community is using its disproportionate political power to oppress their fellow citizens.[5]

Are there other, nontheological reasons to subsidize crop production? There is no shortage of food in the world, even though poor Third World citizens often lack the resources necessary to buy more crops. Agriculture is an uncertain business, but that alone is no justification for a policy that cost $70 billion between 1986 and 1988 alone. Anyway, the wild swings of government policy have brought no stability to farmers.

Another concern–one that has motivated many socially activist religious groups in the farm belt–is the survival of the family farm. However, the desire of small operators to stay in business has to be balanced against the right of taxpayers to the fruit of their labor. Many Americans retain a soft spot in their hearts for the small farm, but that institution is no more deserving than a family dry-cleaner, or a "family minister" for that matter. Individuals and churches may feel a real burden to help their struggling neighbors, but as a matter of public policy Christians should hesitate before demanding that others outside of their voluntary community be forced to keep farmers in their preferred occupation.

Moreover, existing policy has proved incapable of helping the farmers most in need. The bulk of farm subsidies are distributed according to production; thus, farms with sales over $500,000 collect almost half of the federal money. Barely 17 cents of every dollar in government support goes to those farmers in greatest financial need. And proposals by legislators like Senator Tom Harkin (D-Iowa) and Representative Richard Gephardt (D-Missouri) to sharply limit production through agricultural cartels–and to jail farmers who try to grow more crops than their neighbors want–would not only prove to be economically ruinous, but would transfer control over peoples' livelihood to the state.[6]

There is no Christian position on agriculture, but there is a strong practical case to be made against turning Uncle Sam into the Farmer-in-Chief. Thus, before backing such a role, believers should honestly balance the costs of current policies against their benefits and the rights of general citizens to justice against the material desires of farmers.

## CENTRAL AMERICA

Perhaps the most divisive issue within the religious community today is the question of American support for the Nicaraguan contras, the anti-Sandinista resistance movement. Left-leaning evangelicals associated with *Sojourners* magazine, for instance, have joined with Catholic groups and liberal Protestant denominations in attacking U.S. intervention. In contrast, many conservative evangelicals, including former presidential candidate Pat Robertson, advocated American support for the Nicaraguan resistance.

The Bible offers little in the way of specific guidance for Central American policy. Foreign affairs is clearly a proper activity of government; the covenant nation of Israel used military force to create and defend its territorial boundaries. What should be the goals of today's Christians in foreign policy? We are clearly called to be peacemakers, but the exact parameters of that duty are not clear. Moreover, the government's actions internationally no less than domestically should be consistent with Biblical tenets of justice.

How to implement these principles is primarily a prudential matter. Active Christian backing for the Sandinista regime is certainly hard to justify. It is made up of Marxist-Leninists who long ago shoved aside other members of the broad-based, eclectic coalition that drove Anastasio Somoza from power. The press has been suppressed, elections controlled, opponents arrested, and evangelistic Christians harassed. The refusal of what is widely touted to be a "progressive, revolutionary" government to grant conscientious objector status to would-be draftees alone should unsettle those on the religious left. The Sandinistas' brutal treatment of ethnic minorities like the Miskito Indians, use of mobs to break up opposition rallies, and vow to retain effective power even if they lose an election show them to be as autocratic as Somoza, if not as ostentatiously venal.

Nor is support for the Sandinistas justified on grounds of social or economic justice. The economy is in shambles–partly in response to the insurgency and the U.S. trade embargo, of course, but primarily as a result of the Sandinistas' own collectivist policies that have failed wherever else they have been tried. The improvement in literacy rates is welcome, but the government's use of education to indoctrinate the young is not. And in Nicaragua, as in other revolutionary states, class distinctions remain as sharp as ever, with Sandinista apparatchiks flaunting their access to special stores; only the members of the ruling elite have changed.[7]

On the other hand, Christians should be wary of aiding the contras. The insurgents represent a mixture of genuine democrats and old Somoza supporters; they have garnered substantial popular support within parts of Nicaragua, but have also treated civilians harshly at times. Distinguishing Sandinista propaganda and contra apologies in the argument over "atrocities" has proved difficult, but the contras seem to be something less than the moral equivalent of America's Founding Fathers. In short, neither side in this guerrilla war has behaved any differently from most combatants involved in other insurrections.

The U.S. has two different interests at stake: regional peace and its own security.[8] First is the question of peace in Central America. There is evidence of Nicaraguan support for Communist guerrillas in El Salvador, a group that has been more brutal than the contras. However, while Nicaragua's other neighbors are nervous about the Sandinista military buildup, they apparently view an invasion as unlikely and face no serious domestic insurgencies of their own. Polls suggest that citizens in most Central American nations back the contras, but the much-publicized peace plan advanced by Costa Rican President Oscar Arias and backed by other Latin American leaders proposed ending U.S. assistance to the contras.

The second American concern is security. Though Nicaragua does not itself threaten the defense of the U.S., it contains both naval docking facilities and air bases that could serve the Soviet Union in a time of war. The value of such facilities is unclear, since Cuba already provides the Soviets with access to military bases in Latin America; but increasing Soviet military flexibility would obviously not be in American interests. Fears have also been expressed that an aggressive Nicaragua could undermine Mexico's government, sparking a Communist revolution that could harm the U.S. However, that scenario is an extremely unlikely one. For all of Mexico's many problems, Marxist influence in the country appears to be very low.

How can the U.S. satisfy these two interests? One form of "peace" could be established by the contras' defeat. That would stop the bloodshed, an important consideration, but it would also lead to a peace in which Sandinista rule and repression would become institutionalized. U.S. security interests would remain unprotected.

A far different peace would result from a contra victory. However, even before the cutoff of U.S. funds, the insurrection, despite localized successes, appeared to have little chance, at least in the near-term, of toppling the Ortega regime. Moreover, there is no assurance that an anti-Sandinista government, though presumably allied with the U.S. like the Somoza dynasty, would be a just one. The contras would be more likely to allow full religious freedom, an important consideration, but other important rights might go unprotected.[9] The Sandinistas squeezed out centrist members of the coalition that defeated Somoza because the Sandinistas controlled the guns; it is not clear that the contras now controlling the guerrillas' weapons are any more democratically minded.

Thus, U.S. influence, short of a military invasion, is limited: additional American aid to the contras would help the insurgency grow, but probably not triumph. In effect, the U.S. might be able to prevent a full potemkin peace that would leave the Sandinistas firmly in power, but it cannot impose what could turn out to be a disappointing peace under contra rule. Sadly, furthest from American reach is a peace that would lead to the establishment of a just, democratic government.

What is the best of the imperfect alternatives? There is simply no Biblical answer. One approach–my proposal, not *the* Christian answer–would be for the administration to abandon its attempt to overthrow the Sandinistas and encourage the Arias plan's democratization proposal. The moral ambiguities seem too great and the practical chances too slight to warrant continued funding of the guerrillas. Second, as part of an American willingness to pledge its nonintervention in Nicaragua's internal affairs, the U.S. should work toward a regional security arrangement to limit Central American subversion, particularly Nicaraguan assistance to the El Salvadoran guerrillas. Third, this country should tell Nicaragua that it is prepared, if the Sandinistas both maintain a close relationship with the Soviets and build military facilities that could be used by Soviet forces in a war, to take out those military assets preemptively in any superpower conflict.[10]

Such an approach is not perfect–it withdraws aid from a group that is fighting an oppressive regime, and it may be unable to curb potential Nicaraguan aggressiveness, evidenced by the Ortega regime's plan to continue expanding its military.[11] But the Central American struggle is one with no easy answers, whether reflexive endorsement of the Sandinistas or funding of the contras. In considering different policy options Christians must deal with a host of ethical dilemmas and practical imponderables; they must use their reason within God's revelation, requesting the full dose of wisdom that he has promised to give them.

## COMPARABLE WORTH

An increasingly important issue is comparable worth, which involves the government setting wages based on some evaluation of the "comparable worth" of different jobs. The concept has been advanced by feminist groups as a means of upgrading the pay of primarily female occupations, such as nurses, compared to blue collar, male-dominated work.

There are many instances of people being paid for their labor in the Bible, but God tells us little about how salaries should be set.[12] The Lord does promise to "reward each person according to what he has done" (Psalm 62:12). But nowhere does God detail precisely how wage rates are to be determined or by what measure our work is to be compensated.

There are three general Biblical themes that should cause us to view government wage-setting based on its assessment of the value of different occupations with at least some skepticism. There is, for instance, an element of covetousnous involved in expecting the state to increase one's own wages merely because someone else is making more. People are certainly justified in seeking the salary warranted by their work, and comparisons can be useful in determining what level is proper, but imposing comparable worth throughout society would come close to legislating envy.

Moreover, to the extent that advocates of comparable worth want to apply the concept to the private sector by government fiat, they risk violating the Eighth Commandment against theft. It would obviously be wrong for an individual who favored restructuring pay scales to menace his employer with a gun to get a raise; we would say he was stealing. A government threat to imprison a businessman unless he changed his pay scales would have the same moral character, since comparable worth is neither a matter of promoting the general welfare nor of helping the poor. Instead, state-enforced comparable worth would involve the use of government by one group to seize resources from others. Christians should think carefully before supporting coerced wealth transfers that serve no genuine public purpose.

Which brings up the third Biblical principle. Scripture warns us about the danger of overarching state power. The right to set wages has always been considered fundamental to the freedom of both employers and employees. Granting that authority to the state would involve an enormous shift in power, which could easily be abused. Indeed, advocates of comparable worth should themselves be wary of such a transfer: wages could just as easily be lowered as raised.

These general Scriptural principles, though not determinative, should cause Christians to be distrustful of comparable worth proposals. At the very least, there should be strong practical arguments for implementing the concept. On prudential grounds, then, does comparable worth make sense?

Today wages, like other prices, are largely set in the marketplace. Water, a necessity, costs less than diamonds, a luxury, because the supply of the former is more abundant. The interaction of supply and demand helps signal people about which occupation they should enter–as salaries rise, more people study to be engineers, and as salaries fall fewer people try to become makers of whale oil. If some wage differentials don't seem fair, there is no objective standard of what is right.

Indeed, the experience of the many states and localities that have tried to implement comparable worth to some degree is that it is a pseudo-science that takes wage-setting from a marketplace in which all individuals interact and places it in the hands of a few obscure consultants. For instance, Vermont judges photographers to be twice as valuable as does Iowa; Minnesota treats a nurse, social worker, and chemist as equivalent positions, while Iowa rates the nurse as 29 percent higher than the social worker, who in turn is considered to be 11 percent more valuable than the chemist.[13]

Women do get paid less on average than men, but the gap continues to shrink. Anyway, aggregate figures are almost meaningless, as women work fewer hours on average and are more likely to interrupt their careers–especially to have children. To the extent that a largely female profession like nursing is discriminated against, it is because legislators, at the behest of doctors interested in reducing professional competition, have restricted the work that nurses can do. In none of these cases is government wage-setting a solution.

In contrast, Christian churches and organizations certainly have the right, and indeed the responsibility, to set salaries for their employees at what they consider to be just levels. Similarly, a Christian businessman can properly take noneconomic factors into account. In fact, doing so might be an effective way of providing charity to a needy family while preserving the worker's dignity. But this is an area where government action is not a solution.

## DRAFT

Scores of nations use conscription to raise their armed forces; the United States maintained a peacetime military draft from

1948 to 1973. And some congressmen and military leaders have never been happy with the move to a volunteer military. As a result, legislation is regularly introduced in Congress to restore the draft.

The Bible tells us that the ancient nation of Israel often went to war; it records many instances of soldiers marching off to fight the country's foes. Scripture even reveals some instances where God intervened to choose which men would serve and how the battle would be fought. But the Bible does not tell us precisely how Israel normally raised its army. Though there may have been an expectation that all able-bodied males were subject to military service, many were not called up. In one case, at least, anyone who had newly built a house, planted a vineyard, been pledged in marriage, or was "afraid or faint-hearted" was excused (Deuteronomy 20:5-8). Moreover, Mosaic law specifically prohibited sending a man to war within a year of his marriage (Deuteronomy 24:5).

Though there is no explicit Scriptural bar to coerced military service, a draft was one of the abuses that Samuel warned the Israelites of when they demanded a king: the ruler "will take your sons and make them serve with his chariots and horses" (1 Samuel 8:11). Interestingly, Samuel seemed to predict broader forced service—rather like current proposals for universal national service—warning that the king would press daughters into service as "perfumers, cooks and bakers" (1 Samuel 8:13). Finally, the prophet Jeremiah denounced the Israelite King Shallum for "making his countrymen work for nothing, not paying them for their labor" (Jeremiah 22:13).

These Scriptural admonitions suggest that Christians should view conscription warily, avoiding the practice if possible; some important, even compelling, prudential circumstances, such as the survival of a society in the face of foreign threats, should be required to override the Biblical caution on forced service. And if a draft is imposed, it would appear that the government must offer fair pay as well as exemptions for cause. Though God recognizes a communal responsibility for defense, he also obviously desires to protect the dignity and rights of the individual and family.

Are there pragmatic reasons today for implementing a draft? The all-volunteer system is working extraordinarily well: the military is meeting its recruiting quotas with a better caliber of youth than the population at large.[14] There are a host of issues, such as costs, representativeness, and citizenship obligation, that could be discussed at length, but America's voluntary military appears to be the most cost-effective means for meeting this nation's defense needs. A draft would, in fact, be more costly and less representative; the volunteer system also encourages those who are the most patriotic and committed to the common good to serve.[15] In short, there is no practical justification to move toward a draft today.

## ECONOMIC REGULATION

Economic policy is a highly contentious issue for Christians. Liberation theologians forthrightly attack capitalism as an oppressive institution deserving destruction; many mainstream Catholic bishops and leftist evangelicals don't explicitly use Marxist analysis, but nevertheless advocate extensive government regulation of the economy. For instance, Andrew Kirk, associate director of the London Institute for Contemporary Christianity, while arguing that both capitalism and Marxism "are but different expressions of the follies of the modern age," endorses Marxist class analysis and speaks warmly of some virtues of socialism.[16] In contrast, many Protestant denominations have been inextricably linked to the Western commercial system, and groups like the Moral Majority have been consistent defenders of a relatively unregulated market economy.

However, the Bible does not speak to the proper degree of government intervention in the economy. As with any other ideology, it is critical not to confuse a human form of economic management with the Kingdom of God. The Bible reveals no holy ideology; neither capitalism nor socialism is uniquely of God. The relevant issue is, which is more consistent with Biblical principles?

The covenant nation of Israel appeared to allow relatively free economic exchange, with some restrictions placed on debts, interest, and property transfers. The Gospels and epistles are remarkably free of any policy recommendations as to economic affairs. Indeed, writes Paul Heyne, a professor at the University of Washington, "What we do find in the New Testament is an extraordinary disregard for almost everything in which economists are interested."[17]

The message of Christ and the apostles makes it clear that believers are not to place their faith in Mammon, but that does not imply that economic decision-making should be placed in the hands of a coercive institution such as government. The early Christians, at least in Jerusalem, shared their material goods with the needy in the community of faith. However, the believers never attempted to forcibly redistribute the assets of non-Christians. Jesus' love for one another, not any ideological impulse, apparently motivated this voluntary practice. Indeed, the apostles consistently taught that giving was not required. Peter stated that Ananias and Sapphira did not have to sell their property and turn over the proceeds to him, while Paul refused to order the members of the Corinthian church to provide assistance for the believers in Jerusalem (Acts 5:4; 2 Corinthians 8:8).

There are, however, some broader Biblical principles that should cause Christians to be wary of placing too much economic power in the hands of the state.[18] The first is the danger of government abusing its authority–voiced by the prophet Samuel, among others. For Socialist states are, in the main, anything but humane: like the beast of Revelation, they control political, religious, and economic life.

And economic liberty is a prerequisite for other freedoms. According to the human rights rankings of the New York-based human rights group Freedom House, half of the world's sixty-three capitalist nations are free; another twenty-four are partly free. The proportion of free countries falls as the degree of state involvement in the economy rises. Of the 24 Socialist states, only one, Hungary, is even partly free.[19]

The reason for this relationship is quite simple: private property is necessary for the exercise of other rights. If you can't buy a printing press or TV, hire a hall, or sell newspapers, you have no press freedom. Government paper monopolies in Mexico and Nicaragua restrict supplies to opposition publications; Romania registers typewriters.

Moreover, widespread private ownership of economic resources allows the development of alternative centers of power, ranging from corporations and labor unions to think tanks and universities. These essentially economic institutions can play an important political role. In contrast, those who lose political struggles in Socialist states–like the Soviet Union's Grigory Romanov, for instance, who was the first rival pushed off the politburo by Mikhail Gorbachev–are relegated to oblivion.

Another Biblical reason to generally favor a market system is concern for the poor. Kirk makes the astonishing assertion that "Marxism has exalted collective freedom–the freedom of everyone to enjoy a basically dignified life." But that freedom is nowhere evident in practice in countries where the state controls all economic resources.[20] There is no longer any doubt that market-oriented economies outproduce Socialist ones. This is true even in the Third World, where Taiwan and South Korea have vastly outperformed not only collectivist ethnic neighbors such as China and North Korea, but also the statist Latin American economies which only two or three decades ago had much higher per capita incomes than the Asian countries.

The truly free market societies, in contrast to statist systems like Brazil, have also done well in enhancing the economic status of all their citizens. Taiwan, for instance, has seen an increase in literacy, life expectancy, and equality of income distribution as it has expanded economically.[21]

Does this mean that all Western-style economic systems are always just? Of course not. But it is important to realize that the mere existence of private property rights does not make a market society. The Philippines under Marcos, for instance, was a kleptocracy, where state power, not the free play of market forces, directed economic policy. In this case influential groups used government economic regulation to enrich themselves.

Indeed, the liberation theologians properly challenge what is an oppressive system. But the free market essentially does not exist in South America. If government does not own all of the major means of production, as it does in Eastern Europe, the state does control an enormous portion of the economy in countries such as Brazil and Mexico, and directs most private activity through special interest regulations, public monopolies, subsidies, and the like. The Latin American countries are built on a system of government privilege, where those in power distribute economic opportunity to a favored few. It is the antithesis of genuine capitalism.[22]

And it is this sort of statist system which hurts the poor the most. For in a market economy, those with the least influence still can gain access to economic opportunity. Where the government monopolizes economic decision-making, it is those who are in power who make decisions for their own benefit and in the interests of their political allies. The Marxist systems that Kirk says preserve man's "collective dignity" are not only national gulags, but also economic sink-holes: life expectancy in the Soviet Union is falling, there are few goods that are not rationed in Romania, and huge numbers of China's billion people live in abject poverty. In fact, the rapaciousness of the Nomenklatura, the Soviet ruling class, is unparalleled. One cause of the fall of former Gorbachev ally and Moscow Communist party boss Boris Yeltsin was his challenge to such upper class privileges as special stores.

Thus, a less regulated capitalist system both places greater limits on the state, a coercive institution that has been continually abused by evil men, and provides a larger productive base from which to meet everyone's needs.[23] Whether income redistribution should be great or small and what kind of programs are needed to help the poor are different questions, but as a practical matter they can be asked only if there is some production to redistribute.[24]

One further issue is of importance to those who take the gospel message seriously. Does a system with more or less economic regulation better foster spiritual values? Kirk, for instance, contends that capitalism assumes "that the main purpose of man's life is the pursuit of happiness to be achieved by the constant expansion of goods and services," which is thereby "the basis of our daily political and economic life."[25]

However, all men are fallen and sinful; greed and envy are common to man, not products of particular social systems. Capitalism allows those who have dedicated themselves to the pursuit of Mammon to live that way, but it also lets believers like Kirk decide how to fulfill their own lives. Kirk, for one, is affiliated with a religious institute; he could not make that same choice in Eastern Europe. Capitalist America has similarly proved receptive to communal religious sects like the Hutterites.

The hallmark of a relatively unregulated market economy is freedom of choice, and some people will undoubtedly use their liberty to go grievously wrong. But Marxism is profoundly materialistic, and political life in such societies revolves around gaining access to a relatively small pool of consumer goods–thus the ubiquitous lines in the U.S.S.R. The average Soviet citizen does not care any less about possessing shoes, a washing machine, or a car than an American; he is simply less able to satisfy his desires.

On prudential grounds a market economy is superior to socialism for these same reasons: it better protects other human rights, better feeds and houses its citizens, and better preserves people's opportunity to pursue noneconomic objectives. Though even believers in a market economy may argue about whether laissez-faire capitalism or the welfare state is the best model, and over the exact parameters of the state's regulatory responsibilities, it is hard to find a practical argument for extensive state economic control today, especially as the main adherents to Marxist doctrine, such as China and the Soviet Union, have repudiated much of that ideology.

Is capitalism Christian? No. It neither advances existing human virtues nor corrects ingrained personal vices; it merely reflects them. But socialism is less consistent with several important Biblical tenets, for it exacerbates the worst of men's flaws. By divorcing effort from reward, stirring up covetousness and envy, and destroying the freedom that is a necessary precondition for virtue, it tears at the just social fabric that Christians should seek to establish.[26]

## ENVIRONMENT

The Bible sets forth no specific environmental agenda. Instead, man has to meld two separate injunctions: to act as stewards of God's resources and to "fill the earth and subdue it" (Genesis 1:28). That implies a respect for all of God's creation, a refusal to engage in purposeless destruction of resources, and a careful balancing of environmental preservation and economic growth.

Beyond such general principles, environmental issues are largely prudential. Should additional controls be placed on air polluters? Should additional lands be designated as wilderness? Should energy or mineral exploration be allowed offshore? Should part of Yellowstone Park be shut down to protect the grizzly bears? And so on.

The practical failures with current environmental policy are many and can be but summarized here.[27] The underlying clean air standards are flawed; the emissions monitoring system is inadequate. The law makes no distinction between major and minor health defects and allows no trade-off between marginal health improvements and economic cost. Most important, Congress has focused on means rather than results–that is, it has mandated the use of specific technologies rather than set pollution reduction goals.

As prudent citizens, Christians need to be open to alternative strategies that could provide better environmental protection at less cost. One simple example would be to tell firms how much to reduce emissions rather than what technologies to use, and then to allow them to buy and sell their "duty" to cut pollution. Firms with very high environmental control costs then could pay companies which could reduce effluent more cheaply to decrease their output. The result would be an equally clean environment, but focusing clean-up efforts on those who could do so most efficiently would slash total compliance expenses by anywhere between 50 percent and 90 percent.[28]

Similar unconventional means could be used to help protect the federal government's 720 million acres of land. In many cases Uncle Sam has engaged in enormously destructive environmental practices–subsidizing uneconomic logging throughout the Northwest and Alaska, for instance, and "chaining" land, that is, tearing out brush and trees to create additional rangeland. Turning over parks and wilderness areas to private environmental groups would provide for more permanent protection and better land-use management.

Christians should be at the forefront of efforts to protect both the health of Americans and the beauty of the outdoors. However, they should also press for policies that are consistent with man's "filling" of the earth. And they should choose policies based not only on purity of intentions, but also cost-effectiveness.

### FOREIGN AID

The Bible says nothing directly about assistance to other nations, though, as discussed in Chapter Seven, the Scriptural injunction to help the needy is not limited by religious or national bounds. In fact, Paul collected money from the Greek churches for the brethren in Jerusalem. However, the duty to help is largely a personal and a church matter–believers have an obligation to support both foreign missions that evangelize and organizations that minister to the material needs of the poor. In contrast, the civil government's Biblical role in helping even its own citizens is not clear, and there is no explicit Scriptural basis for supporting or opposing government-to-government assistance.

Nevertheless, foreign aid is a perennial favorite of liberal clerics. In early 1988, for instance, the Pope issued an encyclical letter, "The Social Concerns of the Church," which reiterated his oft-repeated call for more international assistance for poor countries. And the evangelical left has similarly supported increased global wealth transfers. "The people of the nonindustrialized world are poor because we are rich," charges Jim Wallis, editor of *Sojourners* magazine.[29]

However, though the issue is an involved one, the overwhelming evidence is that Third World poverty results more from domestic rather than international failures. First, not all Third World countries are poor. As noted earlier, Taiwan and South Korea have industrialized rapidly, in contrast to their much poorer neighbors, China and North Korea. The development of Japan, Hong Kong, and Singapore, and the relative success of countries such as the Ivory Coast compared to their neighbors, also demonstrate that domestic legal institutions, cultural attitudes, and economic policies are more important than either natural resource endowment or foreign aid flows.[30]

Second, cultural factors, such as man's view of the value of effort to overcome nature, also play a critical role in a nation's economic progress. Bernard Bududira, Bishop of Bururi in Burundi, has written of the deleterious impact of passive cultural systems on Africa's economic development; in his view, Christianity, by increasing a person's sense of individual responsibility, is an antidote to harmful tribal ways of thinking.[31]

Third, studies by academics and such international organizations as the World Bank have found a clear correlation between economic growth and market-oriented economic policies, particularly looser controls over prices, marketing, interest rates, and trade, as well as fewer public enterprises and smaller government sectors. The general inefficiency of statist economic policies is exacerbated by the lack of legal and political stability in many of these nations–they often become family oligarchies, as in Marcos' Philippines. Not surprisingly, then, foreign aid flows do not correlate with relative economic success of recipients. Tanzania, for example, has received more foreign assistance per capita than any other nation, and its economy is in shambles; India is a favorite aid beneficiary, and it remains one of the poorest states on earth.

Indeed, assistance has become a problem in many countries by propping up venal autocrats who squelch both political liberty and economic development. In this way American assistance has probably played a negative role in such nations as Haiti, Nicaragua, and the Philippines.

The enormous, indeed overwhelming, problems of Third World poverty and hunger are impossible for the typical middle-class American to fathom. The crisis in Ethiopia brought mass starvation into American homes, but some thirteen million to eighteen million people die of starvation every year. Another half billion people are seriously malnourished and double that number live in serious poverty. No one who takes the gospel seriously can remain unmoved by this pervasive human devastation.

There is no easy answer, such as more money, however. Christians need, first and foremost, to preach the gospel overseas. To the extent that government aid programs continue, we need to search for ways to transfer resources that do not strengthen brutal regimes that are actually inhibiting development; it is also critical that new aid not be wasted, like so much of the $1.2 trillion that Third World states currently owe Western banks. Possible new approaches include conditioning aid on fundamental policy reform in recipient nations, funneling assistance through the indigenous private sector, lending money generated through Food for Peace sales to local enterprises, and using federal crop surpluses to encourage Third World reforms.[32] These are not Christian policy proposals, of course, but represent practical attempts to overcome the demonstrated failures of past aid programs.

## INCOME REDISTRIBUTION

"There is a biblical imperative to redistribute wealth on a regular basis," argues Andrew Kirk.[33] Thus, Kirk proposes that the government fix incomes and own most major industries.

In fact, however, the Bible neither creates a personal duty to equalize wealth nor mandates government to engage in such a practice. As discussed in chapter 4, Christians have a very clear duty to help the needy, but the Bible presents such transfers as a believer's obligation, not a beneficiary's right. In urging members of the Corinthian church to give generously, for instance, Paul pointed to the example of Christ, who "though he was rich, yet for your sakes he became poor, so that you through his poverty might become rich" (2 Corinthians 8:9).

And the end goal of such charitable transfers is not equivalence of incomes, but both the alleviation of the recipient's physical poverty and promoting the donor's spiritual growth. Paul instructed Timothy to command the wealthy "to be generous and willing to share. In this way they will lay up treasure for themselves as a firm foundation for the coming age, so that they may take hold of the life that is truly life" (1 Timothy 6:18-19).

Scripture also challenges all people to follow Christ rather than money; wealthy believers face an especially stiff challenge in avoiding the temptations posed by riches. But again, God's objective is not to make everyone financially equal; instead, it is the wealthy man's salvation. "It is easier for a camel to go through the eye of a needle than for a rich man to enter the kingdom of God," explained Jesus (Matthew 19:24).

Nor does Scripture suggest that the Biblical definition of justice includes income redistribution simply to promote equality. The rich are not to oppress the poor or acquire money through force, theft, or fraud; instead, the wealthy are to help the needy. But there is no Scriptural principle that mandates income transfers that are unrelated to these sort of issues. In fact, even the Year of Jubilee is not a matter of wealth redistribution, but of family land redemption. Sale prices were to be based on the number of years remaining until the Jubilee Year; in effect, the Bible provided for the leasing rather than the sale of the property. The underlying wealth of neither lessor nor lessee was altered (Leviticus 25:14-17). In fact, God distributed the Promised Land unequally. The tribe of Joseph, for instance, complained that its allotment was too small (Joshua 17:14, 16).

There are, however, two important Biblical principles that discourage income transfers unrelated to helping the poor. The first is that, as was detailed in Chapter Five, a believer's primary goal must be to promote his neighbor's spiritual transformation; material well-being should never be confused with salvation. The former is important, but it is not the fundamental norm upon which Christian political action should be based.

Second, redistributing wealth for the purpose of satisfying personal envy—where the issue is not that people lack shelter, but that their home isn't as big as someone else's in another neighborhood—comes perilously close to institutionalizing a continuous and society-wide violation of the Tenth

Commandment against covetousness. "You shall not covet your neighbor's house. You shall not covet your neighbor's wife, or his manservant or maidservant, his ox or donkey, or anything that belongs to your neighbor" (Exodus 20:17).

Similarly, John warned, "Do not love the world or anything in the world. If anyone loves the world, the love of the Father is not in him. For everything in the world–the cravings of sinful man, the lust of his eyes and the boasting of what he has and does–comes not from the Father but from the world" (1 John 2:15, 16). A poor person who turns to government to seize the possessions of his richer neighbors, no less than a wealthy man who devotes his life to making money in the marketplace, has fallen in love with the world. Though Kirk and others on the religious left may not be motivated by greed, most of the redistributionist demands evident in modern American politics are. The 1988 presidential campaigns of Richard Gephardt and Jesse Jackson, for instance, were fueled not by a professed commitment to a just economic order, but by an angry demand that their listeners get more.

Are there prudential reasons to engage in widespread income transfers?[34] Support for the needy may improve social stability as well as alleviate individual hardship, but making sure that no one earns more than $30,000 or $50,000 or whatever serves no public purpose, other than to assuage envy. And there is a serious economic disadvantage to pervasive economic redistribution: it creates a disincentive to innovate and work. Some people get rich by entertaining the rest of us, whether by singing or throwing a football. Others do so by creating a product, such as a car or a copying machine, that greatly benefits everyone else. In a fallen world money is an important motivator, and we would all be worse off if people with special gifts were unwilling to put them to use because they were unable to reap some financial reward for doing so. Expropriating their earnings to satisfy the envy of a few would impoverish our culture and lower our standard of living–and make us less free.

Christians should exalt neither wealth nor the pursuit of any sort of worldly gain. And they are personally bound to engage in a limited form of income redistribution by giving, generously, to those in need. But there is no Scriptural basis for believers to use the civil government to transfer other people's wealth to promote some vague standard of equality; indeed, the prohibition on covetousness warns against such a program. And there is no convincing prudential reason to confiscate money from people simply because they have high incomes.

## ISRAEL

There may be no more obvious an insoluble problem for man than bringing peace to the Middle East. The Bible does not speak to the specifics of a divine peace settlement, but many fundamentalist Protestant groups have zealously supported Israel on what they believe to be Scriptural grounds.

God established a special covenant with the Jews through Abraham, of course, and promised to give "the whole land of Canaan" to Abraham "as an everlasting possession to you and your descendants after you; and I will be your God" (Genesis 17:8). What that promise means today is not so clear, however.

For the Jewish people violated their obligations to God—to follow Him and His Law—and lost their land as a result. There is a good exegetical case that the prophecies regarding Israel, which have spawned so much interest in the sort of dramatic "end-times" theology popularized by Hal Lindsey's *The Late Great Planet Earth* and similar publications, actually refer to the Body of Christ rather than the new nation state of Israel. That is, the geo-political entity occupying the historic lands of Judah and Israel may not have the special place in God's eschatological plan that some people believe.

Nevertheless, even if we assume that the prophecies do refer to the country of Israel, they still offer us little guidance on how to deal with the intricacies of Mid-East politics—whether, say, the West Bank should remain under Israeli control. After all, God blessed not only Jacob but also Ishmael, saying that he would "make him into a great nation," namely the Arabs (Genesis 17:20).

Moreover, even if the re-creation of the nation state of Israel is the fulfillment of prophecy, we have no assurance that there could not be another dispersal and reconcentration of the Jewish people, as unlikely as that may seem. In taking a position on the Middle East, it is critical that we not act as if we can advance God's timing. "For prophecy never had its origin in the will of man, but men spoke from God as they were carried along by the Holy Spirit," wrote Peter (2 Peter 1:21). Supporting Israel's territorial boundaries will not speed up the ultimate conflict that many interpret Daniel and Revelation to predict. God will use our actions in His eschatological scheme, but we should not base our decisions on whether or not we believe they fit His consummation of history. To act as if we can know and promote the Lord's plan is the ultimate in arrogance.

Scripture does, of course, warn against anti-semitism. "I will bless those who bless you, and whoever curses you I will curse," God told Abraham (Genesis 12:3). But rejection of the hideous anti-Jewish violence of the Spanish Inquisition, the Czarist pogroms, and the Nazis' Final Solution, for instance, does not mean reflexive political backing for the secular state of Israel. Christians have a special obligation to support the human rights of all people, including Jews; that duty, however, does not help us determine the proper disposition of the Gaza Strip.

What position should Christians take toward the Middle East? They need to be peacemakers and search for a settlement that provides justice for Jew and Arab alike. In doing so, believers should be skeptical of unthinking support for or opposition to any of the countries involved. A general bias towards Israel is not unreasonable: it is, after all, a democratic state with a better record of dealing with residents of the occupied territories than some of its neighbors, particularly Syria, have in treating their own people. Moreover, terrorist groups like the Palestine Liberation Organization, by focusing on civilian rather than military targets, have forfeited any claim to moral legitimacy. Nevertheless, Palestinians living in the West Bank and the Gaza Strip have legitimate grievances, since they have no political and only limited civil rights; Israeli brutality in confronting the 1988 riots was deplorable.

Christians need to work with nonbelievers to try to develop a proposal that would simultaneously meet legitimate Israeli security concerns and provide for measurable self-determination for the Arabs residing in the occupied zones. Drafting and selling such a package would be no easy task, especially when there are innumerable partisans on both sides who are not interested in any settlement which requires any concessions. But believers need to try to forge such a plan, concentrating on being peacemakers rather than on fulfilling Biblical prophecy.

## MILITARY ALLIANCES
The United States has developed an alliance network of forty-one countries, 1,600 military installations, and 492,500 ser-

vicemen aground and another 244,800 afloat around the globe.
It is these defense commitments which account for the bulk of
the Pentagon budget; high military spending is the price we
pay for an activist foreign policy.

Is there a Biblical perspective on the validity of such
expansive military involvement overseas? Israel and Judah
both entered into alliances with neighboring nations as part of
the perpetual political struggles in the region. However,
nowhere does God provide any theological guidance on the
appropriateness of military pacts.

Thus, a decision to forge an alliance must satisfy more
general Scriptural principles—the government's duty to promote justice and peace. An agreement with the Soviet Union
to, say, jointly invade Canada would fail on both these counts.
Other cases are more ambiguous: by supporting the unjust
government of Nicaraguan Anastasio Somoza the U.S. may
have, for a time at least, helped preserve peace. (In a similar
way, as mentioned earlier in this chapter, cutting off aid to the
contras may promote peace at the expense of justice.) The
interplay between justice and peace, especially where fundamental American security interests are at stake, can become
very complex.

However, most of this nation's current overseas commit-
ments, in contrast to its financial backing of many Third
World regimes, are broadly consistent with these general
Biblical guidelines. The North Atlantic Treaty Organization
(NATO), for instance, is made up of democratic states. South
Korea is another beneficiary of U.S. military support; though it
has a heritage of authoritarian rule, that country appears to be
moving toward genuine democracy. And so on.

In cases like these, the issue is largely one of prudence.
Are the alliances necessary to preserve a just peace? Are the
benefits worth the cost?

There is no doubt that the American presence in Europe
and Korea has had a deterrent effect; on the other hand, it
insures U.S. involvement in any war that might break out.
Moreover, foreign commitments, since they rely so heavily on
costly conventional forces, are very expensive. NATO, for
instance, accounts for between 42 percent and 58 percent of
the defense budget.[35] That's between $119.8 billion and $165.5
billion in 1988. The annual price for protecting Korea is in the
range of $24 billion.[36]

The first question is whether U.S. involvement is necessary to prevent foreign aggression. A good case can be made that, given time to build up their militaries, America's allies could defend themselves. Western Europe's combined Gross National Product exceeds that of the Warsaw Pact countries and Soviet Union combined; their populations are equivalent. NATO spending exceeds that of the Warsaw Pact and the Europeans could do far more: they currently spend less than half as much per capita as does the Soviet-led alliance.[37]

The case of the two Koreas is similar. The South has a GNP nearly five times that of the North and a population twice as great. Though South Korea's military currently lags behind that of Pyongyang, it is catching up fast. And as the South continues to spurt ahead of North Korea economically, its military potential will grow.[38]

Even if permanent American military involvement–which was not contemplated when NATO was formed–is deemed desirable, the burdens of defense should be more equally shared. In 1987 the U.S. devoted 6.4 percent of its GNP to the military; the Europeans averaged only 3.4 percent, and West Germany, the country most at risk, planned to let that figure fall below 3 percent in 1988. Only in 1987 did Japan exceed the 1 percent level. America's allies are effectively free-riding on the U.S., expecting this nation to subsidize their defense so they can spend their money in other ways. We should consider this behavior to be unacceptable, since whatever the ultimate strategic importance of Japan, Korea, and Europe to the U.S., their defense is, first and foremost, their responsibility.

There is probably no greater enemy of Biblical justice and the gospel than war. More than 100 million people–half of them civilians–have died in conflicts since 1700.[39] But Christians will never achieve world peace. Jesus told the disciples that they would "hear of wars and rumors of wars" in the end-times (Matthew 24:6). Nevertheless, believers have an obligation to strive for peace. And that requires a thoughtful, common-sensical review of particular circumstances, always searching for alternatives to the use of force, but never naively ignoring threats from powerful states committed to the destruction of not only the democratic values of the West, but also of Christianity.

## MINIMUM WAGE

Christians are to help the needy; their responsibility is not dependent upon or absolved by any public welfare programs. Though Scripture does not clearly delineate the role of civil government, there is nothing to prevent believers from supporting state assistance as a prudential matter. Both Mosaic law and the New Testament spell out some forms of Biblical assistance; a minimum wage set by government is not one of them, but it is not forbidden either.[40] Thus, the question a Christian needs to answer is whether the minimum wage is a prudent way to help the poor.

There are two basic problems with government wage-setting. The first is that if the state is going to care for the needy, it is a general social responsibility, not just the obligation of the labor intensive businesses that hire the least-skilled workers. In fact, the minimum wage operates as a tax on precisely those firms, many of them small, which are bringing younger and less well educated workers into the marketplace. This approach may not quite rise to the level of Biblical injustice, but it would seem to be, in common parlance, unfair.

The second difficulty is that the minimum wage doesn't really require employers to pay workers at the official level. Instead, it tells companies not to hire anyone who lacks the training, skills, and schooling necessary to make his work worth the minimum wage. The most marginal members of our society–precisely the ones who most need to get onto the economic ladder of opportunity–lose their jobs as the legal minimum rises. In fact, the minimum wage is one reason that black teenage unemployment regularly runs around 40 percent.

Economists have long made the practical case against the minimum wage. But even the Minimum Wage Study Commission, which was dominated by liberals, estimated that every 10 percent hike in the minimum wage reduced teenage employment by 1 percent, or about 80,000 jobs. And many studies figure the average loss to be two to three times higher. In any case, people who desperately need work are losing their opportunity to gain the experience and learn the job skills that are necessary for advancement. Because of these concerns even the National Conference of Black Mayors has endorsed a sub-minimum wage for young people.[41]

Christians intent on helping the poor should never forget

that good intentions are not enough. Prime responsibility for assisting the needy lies with individuals and mediating structures, such as churches. Any government support for the poor should involve transfers from all taxpayers, not just a few businesses. And such a program should be structured so it doesn't create unemployment and cause poverty. Unfortunately, the minimum wage has proved to be counterproductive, even destructive.

## NUCLEAR WEAPONS

Entire books have been written on the proper Christian perspective on war and peace.[42] There is, however, simply no Scriptural mandate for pacifism and unilateral disarmament. The entire pacifist case essentially rests on Jesus' Sermon on the Mount and his statements, "Do not resist an evil person" and "Love your enemies" (Matthew 5:39, 43). However, as was discussed in Chapter Four, there is a critical distinction between personal righteousness and godliness and the authority and duties of civil government. In fact, only individuals, not governments, can love. Christ's message was clearly directed at transforming lives, not altering the state's legitimate role.

Moreover, the Sermon on the Mount must be read in the context of Jesus' statement that He came to fulfill the law. Israel of old was not only entitled to defend itself; God ordered it to attack its enemies. And Paul later wrote that government was to be "an agent of wrath to bring punishment on the wrongdoer" (Romans 13:4). He does not limit his statement to domestic criminals.[43]

A subsidiary issue is whether nuclear weapons are permissible. A number of Christians advocate negotiations to eliminate all nuclear weapons. Writes Mennonite Myron Augsburger, "Nuclear weapons, as the greatest destructive evil, must be rejected and removed from the human scene."[44] Some believers would reject nuclear weapons unilaterally. Argues Jim Wallis of Sojourners, "Christian faith in our day must include a complete turn away from nuclear weapons. It is a sin to build nuclear weapons."[45]

It is true that nuclear weapons pose a serious moral dilemma because of their enormous destructiveness and potential for killing and injuring noncombatants. But that problem is not unique. The allied bombing raid on Dresden in

1945 killed an estimated 100,000 civilians: it was the most destructive aerial attack in history, carried out without nuclear weapons.

Because nuclear weapons, particularly tactical warheads, can be directed at military targets, the more fundamental issue is the validity of a deterrent strategy that holds cities hostage, so-called Mutual Assured Destruction (MAD). Is it moral to threaten the mass destruction of civilian population centers to prevent war?

Given the horror of a nuclear holocaust, Christians have an obligation to search for alternatives. Arms control should be a priority, though not just any agreement will necessarily promote peace and reduce the chance of a nuclear exchange. Defensive strategies, such as the Strategic Defense Initiative (SDI), deserve consideration. SDI is an enormously complex issue, and the feasibility and likely cost of a comprehensive system are highly controverted issues. But peace activists should not reflexively reject a weapon that would protect American cities rather than threaten to destroy Soviet ones. Indeed, trying to develop at least some sort of thin network that could destroy a missile launched erroneously would seem to be a moral imperative.

Irrespective of the success of such efforts, should Christians advocate the unilateral abandonment of nuclear weapons? There is a very important distinction between the use of weapons and the threat to use them. As destructive as nuclear weapons are, there is neither a Biblical nor a prudential reason to abandon their possession–and a concomitant apparent willingness to use them–as long as other nations possess them and are also apparently willing to use them. The unilateral abandonment of nuclear weapons would reduce the threat to Soviet citizens, for instance, but it would multiply not only the danger to the American people but also, possibly, the likelihood of war. While the U.S. foreign policy record, including an imperialistic war against Spain in the nineteenth century, dubious intervention in Vietnam in the 1960s, and persistent support for Third World autocrats, leaves much to be desired, it pales in comparison with the brutal performances of both the Soviet Union and China. These are, after all, nations that have unhesitatingly murdered millions of their own people to achieve different political and ideological goals. A foreign policy based on trust with such states would be suicidal, something the gospel does not mandate.

However, should we use nuclear weapons if deterrence fails? Retaliation against military and industrial targets would be justified. And if the initial nuclear exchange was limited, a further deterrent purpose might be served by a restricted retaliatory strike. But destroying Soviet cities simply in response to the loss of American lives would probably serve no valid purpose. (Huge population losses might foment internal upheaval in the U.S.S.R.; a nuclear strike would also weaken the Soviets' war making capabilities. But these are weak rationales upon which to justify killing millions of people.) Of course, there would be at least one serious practical problem with trying to implement this sort of "nuclear bluff"–keeping the strategy secret. For if it was known to be U.S. policy, then our possession of the weapons would have no deterrent value.

Despite the fact that there will always be war, believers are obligated to be the peacemakers whom Christ said would be blessed. Part of that peacemaking is working to resolve conflicts and reduce arms stocks. But another aspect is evidencing a willingness to defend one's self, family, and community, and with nuclear weapons, if necessary.

## PROTECTIONISM

There is no specific Bible verse on trade policy. The ancient Israelites obviously had contact with surrounding nations, but there were apparently no barriers to voluntary economic exchange among the different peoples.

The only general Biblical principle that applies to the issue is that government is not to be a tool of injustice and oppression, especially against the poor. And protectionism, which raises consumer prices by limiting imports, is a policy that benefits a very narrow constituency, such as auto company shareholders and employees, while harming the general public (as well as foreign workers). Christians should view any use of government to promote the financial interest of a minority at the expense of the overall polity with suspicion.

However, the issue is not primarily a theological one. Are limits on foreign trade good policy? The answer is an unambiguous no.

The issue of foreign trade and American industry became a very hot political issue in 1987 and 1988. Yet the arguments advanced by supporters of higher tariffs and tighter quotas were generally faulty. Though the trade deficit was large, that figure merely represents an aggregation of private commercial transactions; it has no intrinsic value. In contrast, underlying economic factors remained healthy. Between 1982 and 1987 the economy created twelve million new jobs. Despite fears that low-paying employment has come to dominate the economy, the vast majority of new jobs continued to be middle and high wage–93 percent of them during the first half of the 1980s. Moreover, the share of the economy dedicated to manufacturing has remained generally stable for decades, including years with large trade deficits.

Nor does protectionism save jobs. Instead, it preserves a few jobs at the expense of many others. (Which is why the practice may very well be both unjust and oppressive in a Biblical sense.) First, workers in import-related industries are fired as their goods are barred in the U.S.: the auto import industry alone employs 165,000 people. Second, export workers lose their jobs as trade constricts. Third, other domestic workers are hurt because consumers' resources are sucked into protected industries. That is, American consumers who spend $1,500 more on a U.S. auto because of import quotas have $1,500 less to spend on other products. Hence, while the car producers gain, other domestic industries shrink.

Finally, trade barriers are hideously expensive, costing consumers an estimated $65 billion annually. The poor are particularly vulnerable: the Multi-Fibre Arrangement, which limits textile imports, is estimated to cost a family of four an average of $600 in higher clothing costs. Import barriers on shoes, because they have encouraged foreign firms to shift from basic footwear to fancier shoes, have pushed up the prices of cheaper models the most.

There is no doubt that some communities and some workers suffer when foreign goods displace American products in the marketplace. But protectionism is a grossly inefficient means of helping. For instance, quotas cost consumers $110,000 a year to preserve one steel job and $95,000 to save one auto job. It would be far better for the government to provide transitional assistance to help those workers move into new jobs. Thus, while Christians should work to alleviate the human cost of economic change, they should find the least costly way to do so.

## TAXES

With persistent deficits–$1.258 trillion worth between 1980
and 1987–many politicians, particularly on the left, advocate
sharply higher taxes. Some Christians would make the issue a
matter of Biblical morality. The Presidential Biblical Scorecard,
for instance, includes opposition to a tax increase as part of its
litmus test. In fact, Pat Robertson only received a 95 percent
score because he supported a hike in the levy on cigarettes.[46]

It is true that we should be wary of giving government
excessive authority to seize people's incomes. The Israelites
complained to the Jewish leader Nehemiah that they had to
mortgage their property and borrow money to pay royal taxes;
Samuel warned the people that a king would take a tenth of
their flocks and crops. Yet in 1987 the federal government
alone consumed 22.8 percent of the Gross National Product.

Nevertheless, the issue of higher taxes is a prudential
rather than a Scriptural issue. Though the expansive state that
now seizes so much of our wealth to transfer to influential
interest groups is not acting in a Biblical fashion, God does not
proscribe his people from passing one or another tax hikes.[47] A
good justification for doing so should be required, however.

In terms of the composition of federal finances, lower
taxes are not the cause of the deficit. In fact, between 1980 and
1987 annual federal spending rose from $590.9 billion to
$1.004 trillion, a 70 percent increase. Revenues, despite the
Reagan tax cut, grew from $517.1 billion a year to $854.1 billion,
a 65 percent jump. Thus, the overall budget problem is not inadequate revenue, but spending that has continued to race forward.[48] Christians may disagree over how much money the
federal government should spend and what programs it should
support; they may also argue about whether it is worse to accept
persistent deficits or to impose a tax increase. But they should
not be misled by the common assumption that the Reagan
administration has really cut either outlays or revenues.

## A CHRISTIAN POLITICAL PERSPECTIVE

The foregoing by no means represents *the* Christian political
agenda, or even a Christian political agenda. The Bible tells us
what life was like in ancient Israel, and thereby speaks to a
number of issues. But many of the Old Testament laws were
tied to the Jews' status as God's chosen people. Moreover,
there are many subjects on which God has given us far more

general principles than specific policies; relating His broad standards to the complex topics that come before us requires not only a commitment to the Lordship of Christ, but also knowledge, thoughtfulness, and simple prudence. And in applying such human attributes, Christians will continue to disagree over the judgments they reach.

Nevertheless, since believers start from common premises, their differences should consequently be smaller. There is a Biblical way of looking at issues. A Christian's perspective on abortion must be guided by the value that God obviously places on the life of the unborn. America's support for a foreign government must be consistent with Biblical standards of justice. And programs for the needy should be structured in a way to preserve recipients' dignity while preparing them for independence. Justice, righteousness, peace, and protection of all people, especially the poor, should be the watchwords of Christian involvement in politics.

# Conclusion: Christian Activism in the Public Square

*A*merica is nominally a religious country–96 percent of its people claim to believe in God and 74 percent say that Jesus is the Son of God. However, for many people religion is more a social affectation than a living reality: the United States is neither especially spiritual nor Christian. Slightly more than half of Americans say that religion is "very important" in their lives, yet only four out of ten people attend religious services in a typical week. Just 38 percent of Americans believe the Bible represents the Word of God; 30 percent consider themselves to be spiritually reborn.[1] And there is an active, secular elite concentrated in academia and the media whose influence is growing.

Thus, Christians today live in a very different country from the one founded two centuries ago. As the nation has changed, so has the relationship between religion and the state. Early American political leaders generally embraced the Christian faith; most public officials today uphold a doctrineless civil religion. At best, the latter concept is a harmless fiction that helps unify an increasingly pluralistic society. Even then it does little more than perform a symbolic role, however, for it lacks "the power to establish justice or to deal with national arrogance, selfishness, pride, and folly," write historians Robert Linder and Richard Pierard.[2] At worst, civil religion becomes an implicit, idolatrous deification of the state and its leaders, a denigration of the transcendent God of the Bible.

This crumbling of America's historic Christian consensus makes it all the more critical for believers to introduce Biblical values into the political arena. For there is no such thing as moral neutrality. If godly values–a commitment to justice, righteousness, individual freedom and dignity, and the welfare of the poor, for instance–do not predominate, then some other ethic will. The vacuum may be filled by totalitarianism, such as communism and Nazism, with the satanic state destroying lives and promoting injustice. Or the result may be the more tolerant materialism that dominates the West today, a sort of consumerist ethic where life largely revolves around consumption and the political process is viewed by many as merely another way to get more money or goods than one's neighbors do.

We are blessed, no doubt, to live in the U.S. rather than, say, the Soviet Union, but that does not make the bipartisan welfare state any less a failure. Its politics, for instance, largely lacks a genuine sense of public spiritedness. Government has become a battleground of interest groups, seeking to satisfy their members' unending greed and envy; crises in the schools, which don't teach, and the ghettoes, where life has degenerated into a permanent cycle of crime, poverty, and dependency, evoke unending debate and promises, but no solutions.

Today's envious society has proved to be particularly harsh in its treatment of the needy and those with little political influence. The wealthy can hire lawyers to arrange tax breaks; large corporations can engage lobbyists to seek subsidies and other special privileges. Labor unions can back politicians who will enact laws to protect their positions. And social welfare activists can use rhetoric about "social justice" to mask a degrading system in which they, rather than the poor people they supposedly serve, control the future of the needy. But the truly disadvantaged can only retreat further into communities that are collapsing.

Our problems involve not merely the process, but values. Evidence of a pervasive moral breakdown surrounds us. Teenage chastity is rare; the spectre of AIDS, not Judeo-Christian moral teaching, has slowed the sexual revolution. Employees steal from employers, kids rip hood ornaments off of cars to make jewelry, and motorists loot money bags dropped from a passing armored car. Even nonreligious political activists and congressmen now decry the lack of values-instruction of the young, but scores of public officials, Democrat and Republican alike, routinely violate basic ethical norms.

Finally, as the state has expanded, individuals have abandoned many of their responsibilities to other human beings. Controlling pollution is no longer seen as a matter of proper stewardship of God's resources, but legal restrictions by the Environmental Protection Agency. A safe factory floor is determined not by an employer's Biblical responsibilities to his workers, but by the Occupational Safety and Health Administration. The homeless are not seen as a problem for us personally, but for the city, the county, or the federal government—anyone else. Even many churches seem to put more effort into lobbying government than developing their own programs to meet basic social needs.

Not only is the status quo a failure, but there is no answer among the secular ideologies that now dominate political discourse. The promised Communist utopia is being radically revised even in its birthplace, the Soviet Union. Liberalism has aided and abetted the rise of the transfer society, in which envy has become perhaps the most important determinant of government action. Populism, which gained prominence in the presidential campaigns of several Democrats in 1988, incorporates an even more unvarnished appeal to resentment rather than justice. Conservatism as represented by President Reagan has proved to be only slightly less self-centered an ideology, protecting businessmen's profits rather than the welfare of Democratic interest groups. And classical liberalism, while promoting individual dignity, embodies a spiritual sterility that makes it an incomplete political perspective for a Christian.

In short, it is not enough for a believer to be a conservative or a liberal or a libertarian. He needs to be a Christian conservative, liberal, or libertarian. That is, he must evaluate issues from a Biblical perspective before he considers the ideological and prudential arguments which now dominate the political process. In a few cases, such as abortion, Scripture may prove to be decisive; more often than not, however, a Christian must apply reason within revelation, evaluating the issue on its practical merits. His final policy preference may be no different as a result, but a Christian must never forget that his political activities, no less than any other aspect of his life, are to be subject to the Lordship of Christ. We are to be obedient citizens, but our primary responsibility is to submit ourselves to God.

The most important means of promoting Biblical values in government is not political action. For if we act as "the salt of the earth" in our dealings with our neighbors, coworkers, and anyone else we come into contact with in our everyday lives, we will be witnessing to the gospel in the most powerful way possible. Even the way Christians treat each other is an implicit witness to the world: "All men will know that you are my disciples if you love one another," said Jesus (John 13:35).

In fact, Christians should pay particularly close attention to our behavior because the personal witness of those who claim to follow Jesus has such a profound impact, either positive or negative, on those to whom the Gospel is preached. If there are really forty-eight million evangelical Christians, a commonly-cited figure, then why is the moral fiber of the nation so badly torn? A group representing more than one-fifth of the entire population is a large amount of salt. That much seasoning, used properly, should flavor every part of society. In combating declining moral values, Christians need to first look to their personal interaction with those around them.

The church also has a prophetic role: to present the unvarnished gospel and to challenge people, both in and out of public life, who do not live up to godly standards. The prophets of the Old Testament, such as Jeremiah, did not run for office; instead, they confronted corrupt ruling establishments that had violated their responsibilities. What we need today is religious leaders speaking more to fundamental spiritual and moral issues—our society's ethic of envy, declining public morals, and lack of personal responsibility for the poor—and less to specific pieces of legislation. Anyone can become a policy expert, but only Christians can call America to account to Biblical standards.

Moreover, believers, acting individually as well as through their churches and Christian social organizations, can simultaneously help meet basic human needs and promote godly values in society. Roughly half of all charitable giving is religious-based; many of the most important private shelters and soup kitchens in major cities are run by Christian organizations.

Such social activism does not, of course, obviate the need for believers to be politically active; ignoring the public arena will allow non-Christian values to triumph in that sphere. However, believers should have no illusion that their political involvement will transform the nation spiritually. In 1986 pastor and activist Jamie Buckingham supported the presidential candidacy of Pat Robertson because he believed that Robertson's "candidacy and his election would draw favorable attention to a God of the supernatural, and could very well be the catalyst to return the life of God to a church which, in many areas, is drawing its last breath."[3] Yet far from revitalizing the church, Robertson's candidacy split the evangelical movement; rather than serving as a clarion call for turning back to God, the campaign embarrassed the cause of Christian political activism.[4]

In short, just as government is not a redemptive institution, the political candidacy of even a dedicated Christian will not regenerate the Body of Christ or the civil polity. Service in government has as its main purpose justly administering the civil laws over believer and nonbeliever alike. A Christian president might provide an important moral role model, but he would still be king rather than priest or prophet.

Nevertheless, a dedication to the spiritual should not cause Christians to shun politics. Indeed, given the enormous power of government—virtually no human endeavor, however private, is now beyond the state's reach—abdication of one's political responsibilities would prove to be both dangerous and irresponsible. If nothing else, Christians must be prepared to defend their religious freedom from government encroachment. Restrictions on private schools, liability suits involving church discipline, bans on Bible clubs meeting in public schools, and legal attacks on Christian legislators all should be firmly resisted.

Believers should not, however, view politics in the opposite way, as a tool to forcibly evangelize. The purpose of Christian political activism should not be to seize control of government to promote Christianity. Jesus did not come to establish yet another interest group dedicated to using the state to get its way. Instead, God ordained the civil state to ensure justice in a sinful world, a commitment to fairness that encompassed unrighteous as well as righteous, aliens as well as Israelites, and weeds as well as wheat.

In fact, there may have been no greater disaster for the cause of the gospel, in contrast to the material interests of the clerical class, than the marriage of church and state which first occurred under Constantine. Christ, not the Roman Empire, was the true bridegroom of the church; its adulterous affair destroyed the church's independence and position of moral leadership. In the face of organized repression and a paganistic culture, Christianity spread throughout the entire Roman Empire. But once the church became the official state religion, it degenerated spiritually, even instigating mass injustice.

What was to have been a transcendent message of spiritual liberation became an adjunct to the Roman policy of political repression. The many attempts at clericocracy during medieval times fared even worse.

True, few believers today advocate a total Christian society in which the government would impose Biblical norms on nonbelievers. But some religious right activists have been careless in word and deed, exacerbating the fears of non-Christians of an onrushing ecclesiocratic state. For instance, one liberal critic of Falwell claimed that the Southern Baptist minister intended "to make America Christian and politically right-wing conservative. To force Christianity into every school and stifle any and all other religious and non-religious beliefs, activities and persuasions."[5]

Unfortunately, polls show that many other Americans feel the same way about Falwell, even though the charges are false. In fact, the Moral Majority tried to involve conservative Jews and Catholics as well as Protestant fundamentalists and respected the separate roles of church and state, pushing a political platform that was scarcely more theological than that advanced by any of a number of other conservative groups.[6] But some of the Moral Majority's rhetoric was not so reasonable. In one direct mail letter, for instance, Jerry Falwell, then the organization's head, denounced "amoral liberals" who were "trying to corrupt our nation from its commitment to freedom, democracy, traditional morality, and the free enterprise system." He solicited contributions so that he could "go into the halls of Congress and fight for laws that will protect the grand old flag."[7]

Of course, the secular political establishment has exhibited an enormous amount of hypocrisy in its reaction to the religious right. When liberal Protestant denominations protested the Vietnam War and segregation and lobbied Congress on everything from budget cuts to foreign aid, their involvement was considered to be only right. Civil rights activist Joseph Rauh, for one, called the sight of Episcopal priests outside a congressional committee room as "the most beautiful sight I had ever seen."[8] Similarly, when black churches across America collected cash for Jesse Jackson's presidential campaigns in both 1984 and 1988, their action was viewed as completely natural. "The church was and still remains the primary organizing headquarters for the black community's participation in politics," explains Representative William Gray (D-Pennsylvania), himself an ordained minister.[9]

Yet when Falwell mobilized fundamentalists politically, the reaction of mainstream public officials and the media was hostile, even apoplectic at times. Ideology undoubtedly was the primary reason, though culture and class status probably played a role as well. The liberal Protestant churches, for instance, tend to represent America's upper crust. Many fundamentalists, in contrast, are less well-heeled and well-educated. Moreover, they truly believe in a living, transcendent God who is relevant to today, something that frightens the nation's largely secularized elite, which believes in few ultimate truths.

Nevertheless, Christian political activists have an obligation–especially in the face of such an unfair double standard–to demonstrate that they are promoting society-wide justice, not just their personal theological perspectives. Instead of pressing for organized Christian prayer in public schools, for instance, believers should support a truly open atmosphere in which religion can be discussed and beliefs shared. Christians should lobby not to ban textbooks that promote "secular humanism," but to ensure the use of educational materials that promote no specific faith or ideology, secular humanism or other, and which honestly portray the role of religion and all other factors in American history and society. Rather than trying to get civil government to pay for the ubiquitous Christmas creche, believers should request equal access to public lands and buildings while offering to foot the bill themselves. In all of these cases the bottom line result is similar, but the goal perceived by the public is dramatically different. The emphasis is on believers working to ensure justice and fairness for all in the public square, rather than on Christians seizing control of the state apparatus to get theirs.

Most issues do not directly involve the organized church, of course. But Christians have no less a duty to be involved in these areas. For government was established by God to achieve certain godly ends. And Christians should work to see that it fulfills its proper role.

The state's mandatory duty is to regulate improper actions by sinful men. One aspect of that role is protecting life and property from violence, theft, and fraud. In doing so, government is obligated to operate justly, treating all citizens fairly and preventing oppression of the weak by the strong. Public officials are to create a stable social framework within which Christians can, in Paul's words, "live peaceful and quiet lives in all godliness and holiness" (1 Timothy 2:2). Finally, the state may have some role in helping the poor and needy, though the primary responsibility in this regard is placed on individuals and the church.

The Bible also establishes clear limits on government's purview. The state cannot restrict the worship of God. Nor may public officials promote idolatry by treating themselves as if they were divine. Moreover, the overall authority of government is also to be limited, for just as coercion is required in some cases to restrict the harm that may be committed by fallen man, the state's coercive power must be restricted to protect the governed from harm by the equally sinful rulers.

In between the mandatory and the prohibited lies a large area where government policy is discretionary, often more a matter of prudence than theology. Though the Bible gives us relatively clear guidance on a few issues, such as abortion, and more general principles to apply in areas such as welfare, it provides us with neither a holy political ideology nor a detailed godly legislative agenda. We must apply reason within revelation, honestly interpreting verses and studying their exegesis; believers must also consider the unique roles of other godly institutions, particularly the family and the church. Finally, Christians should make the same common-sensical judgments that everyone else should–but often does not–make, judging whether a proposal would achieve its purported goal in a cost-effective manner. Christians have a unique moral framework to apply to every policy discussion, but they cannot derive every answer directly from Scripture.

The need for Christian political involvement has never been greater. Dozens of nations around the world are at war; Third World underdevelopment is pervasive, and millions will starve to death this year. Our own government is often the cause of gross injustice at home and abroad. A black underclass sinks further into an enervating cycle of poverty, crime, and dependency. The problems are easy to see, but the solutions seem ever more remote as ambitious politicians play to the voters' envy and greed in their endless search for votes.

Yet popular acceptance of the role of religion, at least of evangelical Christianity, in the political process may have peaked. In 1987 Jerry Falwell backed out of politics entirely. A year later Pat Robertson's presidential candidacy crashed and burned. After his dramatic second-place showing in Iowa polls showed that half of all Republicans, let alone Democrats, would not vote for him under any circumstances, a negative rating virtually unprecedented for any politician. And with a new administration destined to take office on January 21, 1989, the religious right seems unlikely to retain the prominence that it achieved during Ronald Reagan's administration.

Where in politics, then, do Christians go from here?

First, believers need to continue promoting political involvement—but as an outgrowth of Christian responsibility, rather than loyalty to a particular candidate. The one major success of Robertson's candidacy was to bring large numbers of evangelicals into the political process. These people need to be encouraged to remain active, whether simply as voters or as caucus-goers, party officials, and candidates, in order to help shape both the moral tone of political discourse and specific policies in the future. They have a responsibility beyond sitting back, waiting for a potential Robertson presidential bid in 1992; they need to work to promote a just civil order today and next week.

Second, Christians need to clarify the role of religion in politics. It is critical that believers understand and make clear to others that we are involved in politics for basically the same reason as non-Christians—to make a more just and prosperous America. Believers need to explain that while we cannot leave our faith at home, for it animates our concern for our country and its people, we are not attempting to use the state to enforce church doctrines.

Indeed, Christians should never forget that personal salvation will come through the efforts of the Holy Spirit, not Uncle Sam. (The belief in the redemptive role of government by adherents of the statist ideologies that now percolate throughout the political system is essentially theological, though of the humanist variety.) Thus, Christians should press for a public square in which Biblical values are treated with respect and incorporated into the common moral values that will ultimately govern believers and nonbelievers alike in today's secularized society.

Third, Christians need to work with nonbelievers, not to try to exclude them from the political process. Religious activist Tim LaHaye has expressed his desire to see the time when "the real American people will regain their country and culture." In his view, "no humanist is qualified to hold any governmental office in America–United States senator, congressman, cabinet member, State Department employee, or any other position that requires him to think in the best interest of America."[10] Pat Robertson said essentially the same thing on "The 700 Club" before he ran for office.

There is nothing wrong, and much that is right, with Christians supporting Christians for public office. After all, there is no reason that we should have to choose between Martin Luther's proverbial smart Turk and dumb Christian, since there are plenty of bright Christians qualified to run for office. But the state is a civil rather than a ecclesiastical institution. It must govern nonbelievers as well as Christians. Attempting to "Christianize" public institutions is at the very least impractical; if politics begins to split down religious lines, it will be the evangelical minority that will find itself isolated and excluded. Moreover, setting a theological litmus test for public office is fundamentally unfair, an affront to Biblical justice. Jesus instructed His followers to leave the separation of the weeds and wheat up to the Father; attempting to deny nonbelievers influence over the institution that regulates their lives and confiscates their incomes ostentatiously violates this Biblical injunction.

Fourth, as discussed earlier in this chapter, Christians must frame their goals in terms of justice for all rather than privilege for a Christian few. Godly love is inclusive; we are to love our enemies as well as our friends. So too should Christian politics be dedicated to the welfare of all people. That is, political activism should result from believers' devotion to the good of all of God's creatures, not to some narrowly conceived self-interest.

Fifth, believers should show an appreciation of the so-called seamless garment woven by the gospel.[11] Christians may differ over the specific aspects of such a philosophy–a consistent pro-life philosophy doesn't necessarily mean supporting every federal training program or unilateral nuclear disarmament. But we need to take our faith, which applies to the whole person, and fashion an overarching political philosophy. Christians who actively campaign against abortion need to demonstrate a concern, in both word and deed, for the plight of pregnant teens. Supporters of aid to anti-Communist insurgencies need to recognize the evil of right-wing autocrats. Believers committed to activist government support for the poor need to also campaign against programs that enrich influential interest groups at the expense of the poor and middle class. And so on.

Sixth, Christians must be prepared to act as the conscience of the polity. Many voters, whether they be Democrats or Republicans, end up voting their wallet. Are they employed? Are wages up? Is the politician promising to bring home some pork to the district?

However, godly government is to be a force for justice and righteousness, not a financial cornucopia for the electoral victors. In the same way that both John the Baptist and Jesus challenged both the masses and a corrupt political/ecclesiastical ruling establishment, Christians today need to infuse the political dialogue with a debate over fundamental moral values. The average politician is mainly interested in reelection, and the average voter is primarily concerned about his paycheck; if believers won't call this nation to account for its moral failings, who will? The institutionalization of envy and materialism, mistreatment of the poor, mass killing of the unborn, and acquiescence in the face of widespread domestic and foreign injustice—God will judge the nation for its actions in such matters. Christians need to focus attention on these issues.

Lastly, believers who take an active role in politics must exhibit the fruit of the Spirit detailed by Paul in his epistles. Some politicians, many of whom claim to be Christians, friendly to the religious right and the evangelical left, for instance, have shown little of God's love, instead exhibiting self-righteousness, callousness, and extreme partisanship. Yet someone claiming to be a disciple of Christ, who is concerned about his neighbor and who cares for the unfortunate, should demonstrate "love, joy, peace, patience, kindness, goodness, faithfulness, gentleness and self control" (Galations 5:22, 23). Politics is often a rough and dirty game, but if Christians really have been transformed by the Holy Spirit, we need to act differently. In all that we do we are personal witnesses for Christ, especially where we seek to put ourselves on display before the local community or nation through political involvement. Believers in politics must faithfully put God before personal ambition, electoral success, and any other goal.

Such an approach is still not likely to yield a Christian

majority in Congress. However, our goal should not be to, willy-nilly, thrust believers into office, but rather to elect people who will govern wisely and justly. Thomas Jefferson, a deist, served ably as President because his political philosophy, though not specifically Christian, was consistent with Biblical principles. Believers should support candidates because we believe they would do the best job, not because they are "one of us."

And even were believers to take over many more positions of political authority, we should have no illusions about bringing about the immediate onset of the Kingdom of Heaven. Christians, too, are vulnerable to the temptations of power: throughout history clerics who possessed secular authority have exhibited no lack of brutality and venality. Moreover, on many specific policies a Christian consensus will never be likely. Evangelical Senators Mark Hatfield (R-Oregon) and William Armstrong (R-Colorado), for example, worship the same God and follow the same Bible, but vote quite differently.

Nor would a common Christian political agenda, even if one were achievable, result in a national spiritual revival. For as important as is the political realm, its impact on men's hearts is quite limited. Some religious activists, on the left as well as the right, have treated the defeat of their political partisans as a spiritual loss, but the God of the Bible is not limited by the results of last week's congressional vote or last year's election. A government that respects Biblical values might help promote a social climate more conducive to Christian evangelism. But the gospel probably spread more rapidly when it was treated as a pariah cult by the Roman authorities than when the church was backed by state power. We must place our faith in Jesus, not the President, as high priest.

Instead, our political goals should be more modest. One is simply to interject God's moral imperatives into current political discourse. Christians should try to force public officials who are caught up in parochial politics to think about the more general public welfare. In short, believers should be dedicated to making people confront fundamental Biblical values in their political activities as well as all other aspects of their lives.

Christian political activism should also be dedicated to changing the tone of today's policy debate. Issues ranging from Central America to budget cuts generate rancor and partisanship; motives are impugned, wisdom is questioned, and minds are closed. So long as so much money and power is at stake in Washington's policy battles, politics will never be a pristine exercise in civics textbook self-government. But increased political participation by believers willing to hold public officials accountable could help cause interest groups as well as politicians to look beyond their immediate advantage.

Moreover, political involvement should be seen as but one part of a long-term educational effort to transform social values that usually transcend the political arena. Respect for life, concern for the poor, and rejection of materialism are all aspects of the gospel that need to be inculcated into people's whole lives. Americans' commitment to these and other values have steadily deteriorated in recent decades; a reversal is not likely to occur overnight, even if Christians gain increased political influence. But we should measure success in lives transformed, not in legislation passed.

Finally, Christians should work for legislative gains without becoming preoccupied about our win/loss record. Today's political process is fundamentally corrupt; the values that animate many public institutions and officials are not Biblical. And it will not be easy for Christians to turn the system around. Failures may nevertheless promote the educational process; small gains may provide the cornerstone for later victories. In any case, Christians should never forget that lobbying is secondary to evangelizing. The mind of "the enemies of the cross of Christ" are "on earthly things," wrote Paul. "But our citizenship is in heaven" (Philippians 3:19, 20).

The naked public square, as Richard John Neuhaus has warned, is indeed a dangerous place. For if godly values do not reign in the political arena, then ungodly ones will. And the ultimate result of a moral vacuum has too often been the satanic state, the totalitarian regime which tries to remake man in its own image.

Thus, Christians have an obligation to apply their faith to civic affairs. They shouldn't mistake government for the church, nor ecclesiastical rules for civil laws. But they should insist that the state live up to its Biblical role as a just and righteous institution ordained by God, a bulwark against repression and a defender of the poor.

Where the issues are prudential rather than moral, believers should exercise the wisdom that God has given them to choose the policy that makes the most practical sense. The Bible does not tell us whether the latest transportation bond issue is justi- fied; instead, the Lord gave us minds to make that judgment.

Most important of all, though, Christians should never forget that the political realm is secondary. "My kingdom is not of this world," Jesus told Pilate. "If it were, my servants would fight to prevent my arrest by the Jews. But now my kingdom is from another place" (John 18:36). The state, like every other worldly institution, will pass away; God's Kingdom, in contrast, is eternal.

Religion and politics not only can be but should be related. Christians not only can be but should be active in public affairs. However, we must remember that our ultimate alle- giance is to God and our corresponding priority is to promote the gospel. "Each one should be careful how he builds," wrote Paul. "For no one can lay any foundation other than the one already laid, which is Jesus Christ" (1 Corinthians 3:10, 11). We need to build on this foundation in all that we do, including politics.

# NOTES

*INTRODUCTION*

1 Charles Colson, *Kingdoms in Conflict* (New York and Grand Rapids: William Morrow and Zondervan, 1987), p. 288.

*CHAPTER ONE A Christian Political Perspective*

1 Richard John Neuhaus, *The Naked Public Square* (Grand Rapids: Eerdmans, 1986, 2nd ed.), p. 8.
2. *Ibid.*, p. 152.
3. Argues Rabbi Joshua Haberman, president of the Foundation for Jewish Studies: "The Bible gave our nation its moral vision. And today, America's Bible Belt is our safety belt, the enduring guarantee of our fundamental rights and freedoms." Joshua Haberman, "The Bible Belt Is America's Safety Belt," *Policy Review*, Fall 1987, p. 44. The relationship of different ideologies to Biblical principles is discussed in greater detail in Chapter Three.
4. Herman Hattaway and Lloyd Hunter, "The War Inside the Church," *Civil War Times*, January 1988, p. 29.
5. Paul Johnson, *A History of Christianity* (New York: Atheneum, 1976), pp. 437, 438.
6. Quoted in *ibid*, p. 438.
7. Quoted in A. James Reichley, "The Evangelical and Fundamentalist Revolt," in Richard John Neuhaus and Michael Cromartie, eds, *Piety and Politics: Evangelicals and Fundamentalists Confront the World* (Washington, D.C.: Ethics and Public Policy Center, 1987), p. 83. (Falwell's statement–an uncomfortable bit of hyperbole when it was first uttered during the 1980 election campaign–is now far more disturbing, given the revelations of the First Lady's reliance on an astrologer, apparently with Ronald Reagan's acquiescence, to determine his schedule throughout his two terms as President. See Donald Regan, *For the Record: From Wall Street to Washington* (San Diego, CA: Harcourt Brace Jovanovich, 1988), pp. 3, 28, 68, 70, 300, 359.)
8. "Leaders of the Christian Right Announce Their Next Step," *Christianity Today*, December 13, 1985, p. 65.
9. *United Methodist Newscope*, November 21, 1980.

10. Cited by Neuhaus, p. 41.
11. "Liberation Priest Praises Soviets," *Washington Times*, August 14, 1987, p. D-5.
12. "Kemp Says School Boards Have Right to Deny Homosexuals," *San Diego Union*, December 22, 1987, p. A-23.
13. Robertson ended his active campaigning in April 1988, after gaining only a handful of delegates. However, he vowed to run again in 1992: "Out of what seems to be defeat we are laying the foundation for a great victory for this nation. It may not be in 1988 ... but I am not going to quit.... That is his plan for me and for this nation," said Robertson. "Robertson Hears Call to Run Again in '92," *Washington Times*, April 4, 1988, p. A-2.
14. Quoted in Sidney Blumenthal, "The Religious Right and Republicans," in Neuhaus and Cromartie, p. 271.
15. Jeremiah O'Leary, "Reagan Declares That Faith Has Key Role in Political Life," *Washington Times*, August 24, 1984.
16. Charles Colson, *Kingdoms in Conflict* (New York and Grand Rapids: William Morrow and Zondervan, 1987), p. 46.
17. Dick Polman, "Falwell Tunes in to New Era of Accountability," *San Diego Union*, December 20, 1987, p. D-7.
18. Which should not be surprising in a pluralistic society where the majority of people are not seriously committed to following God, whatever their formal church ties. For this reason Christians should be more sensitive to the need for accommodation with and tolerance of nonbelievers where symbolic issues and government outlays are involved. Christians have a right to worship God and to apply our Biblically derived moral standards to matters of public concern. In contrast, we have no similar right to force non-Christians to pay for a Christmas creche. And prayer in public schools is another dubious cause: nondenominational prayer led by an unbelieving teacher entails a public ritual calculated more to offend unbelievers than to glorify God.
19. *New York Times*, March 6, 1984.
20. Steve Schmidt, "Atheists Threaten to Sue Over Park Nativity Scene," *San Diego Union*, December 22, 1987, p. B-1.
21. Nat Hentoff, "Religion on School Property," *Washington Post*, November 1, 1984, p. A-25.
22. Paul Vitz, *Censorship: Evidence of Bias in Our Children's Textbooks* (Ann Arbor: Servant Books, 1986), p. 15.
23. Lawrence Feinberg, "Court Backs Equal Benefits for Georgetown University Homosexual Groups," *Washington Post*, November 21, 1987, p. A-10.
24. "Leaders of the Christian Right Announce Their Next Step," *Christianity Today*, December 13, 1985, p. 65.
25. William McManus, "Getting Our House in Order: Economic Justice and the Church," in Dennis Corrado and James Hinchey, eds, *Shepherds Speak: American Bishops Confront the Social and Moral Issues That Challenge Christians Today* (New York: Crossroad, 1986), p. 67.
26. Quoted in Stanley Hauerwas, *A Community of Character* (Notre Dame, IN: 1981), p. 79.
27. James Skillen, "Public Justice and True Tolerance," in Neuhaus and

Cromartie, p. 167.
28. Marjorie Hyer, "Bishops Urge Catholics to Vote on Moral Basis," *Washington Post*, October 17, 1987, p. D-12.
29. *Daily Christian Advocate*, May 7, 1952.
30. Henry Hyde, *For Every Idle Silence* (Ann Arbor, MI: Servant Books, 1985), pp. 12, 13.
31. Neuhaus, p. 30.

CHAPTER TWO *The Failure of the Bipartisan Welfare State*

1. Lou Cannon, "'Let's Bring Them to Their Feet with Our Closing Act,' Reagan Tells Aides," *Washington Post*, January 29, 1988, p. A-14.
2. Jerry Herbert, ed., *America, Christian or Secular?: Readings in American Christian History and Civil Religion* (Portland, OR: Multnomah, 1984), p. 83.
3. A detailed listing of the pork and poison in the December 1987 budget legislation is provided by Doug Bandow, "The Dirty Secrets of the 1987 Continuing Resolution," *Heritage Foundation Backgrounder*, No. 630, February 10, 1988.
4. Beneficiaries obviously pay taxes directly and through their employers, but current retirees are receiving between three and five times what they paid in. With the rapid rise in taxes in recent years, today's workers will receive a far lower–even negative, in some cases–return on their forced contributions. For a review of the problems facing the program, see Doug Bandow, "Sun City for Social Security," *The American Spectator*, October 1985, p. 17.
5. Doug Bandow, "America's Permanent Dependent Class," *Policy Review*, Spring 1987, p. 73.
6. Cited by Richard Cornuelle, *Healing America* (New York: G. P. Putnam's Sons, 1983), p. 30.
7. President's Council on Private Sector Initiatives, *Unshackling the People: Overcoming Barriers to Community Self-Help and to Other Private Sector Initiatives*, October 6, 1986, p. 4.
8. James Bovard, "Busy Doing Nothing: The Story of Government Job Creation," *Policy Review*, Spring 1983, pp. 93-97.
9. President's Council on Private1 Sector Initiatives, p. 3.
10. Michael Balzano, *Federalizing Meals-on-Wheels: Private Sector Loss or Gain?* (Washington, D.C.: American Enterprise Institute, 1979).
11. Martha Willman, "Legal Stew Keeps Food From Needy," *Los Angeles Times*, January 14, 1987, p. I-38.
12. S. David Young, *The Rule of Experts* (Washington, D.C.: Cato Institute, 1987), p. 1.
13. Doug Bandow, "The Trucking War," *Libertarian Review*, February 1980, p. 16.
14. Joint Economic Committee, *Youth and Minority Unemployment* (Washington, D.C.: Government Printing Office, 1977), p. 7.
15. An illuminating account of the moral baseness of Woodrow Wilson's campaign to involve the U.S. in World War I is provided by Walter Karp, *The Politics of War* (New York: Harper & Row, 1979).
16. America's support for Marcos, for instance, is reviewed by Raymond Bonner, *Waltzing with a Dictator* (New York: Times Books, 1987).

CHAPTER THREE *The Need for a New Political Paradigm*

1. Paul Johnson, *Modern Times* (New York: Harper & Row, 1983), p. 729.
2. An egregious example of Castro's mendacity combined with a cleric's naivete' is Frei Betto, *Fidel and Religion: Castro Talks on Revolution and Religion with Frei Betto* (New York: Simon and Schuster, 1987).
3. Quoted in Philip Taubman, "Classless Soviet Far Off, Paper Says," *New York Times,* January 27, 1986, p. A-4.
4. Quoted in Mikhail Bernstam, "The Collapse of the Soviet Welfare State," *National Review,* November 6, 1987, p. 41. See also Steven Plaut's "Worker's Paradise?," *Commentary,* February 1981, p. 82. Nor are other Eastern bloc countries exempt from the same malady. Romania's economy is in shambles, with strict rationing of food, energy, and other goods. Poland regularly suffers from a catastrophic shortfall of medicine and other health care products. Reports hematologist Dr. Zofia Kuratowska, who works in Warsaw's main cancer hospital, "You can say, in general, that about 60 percent of the drugs we need are not here.... I mean antibiotics, cardiac drugs, cancer drugs, anesthesia." Quoted in Charles Powers, "Medical Shortages Cause Polish Health Care Crisis," *Los Angeles Times,* February 5, 1988, pp. I-34, 35.
5. Robert Ericksen, *Theologians Under Hitler* (New Haven: Yale University Press, 1985), p. 1.
6. Paul Althaus, *Kirche und Staat Nach Lutherische Lehre* (Leipzig: 1935), p. 29.
7. Paul Johnson, *A History of Christianity* (New York: Atheneum, 1976), p. 492.
8. Mimeographed flyer entitled "What is Creativity All About?""
9. Classical liberalism developed in Europe throughout the seventeenth, eighteenth, and nineteenth centuries. It was a complex movement that borrowed from the Enlightenment, the American and French revolutions, and the rise of the middle class in industrial societies. In general classical liberalism "emphasized reason instead of tradition, contract rather than status, the present and the future instead of the past, the value and rights of the individual instead of that of existing power-holders, whose claims based on the superiority of cast or creed it challenged. Basically liberalism has been an attitude in defence of the individual man and citizen in defiance of the arbitrary acts of government." E. K. Bramsted and K. J. Melhuish, eds, *Western Liberalism: A History in Documents from Locke to Croce* (London: Longman, 1978), p. xvii. In practice this philosophical school was instrumental in developing the constitutional system involving limited government power, civil rights, and property ownership that characterizes most Western nations.
10. For instance, see Murray Rothbard, *For a New Liberty: The Libertarian Manifesto,* rev. ed., (New York: Collier Books, 1978), pp. 45-69.
11. Biblically speaking, the individual is, of course, required to be motivated by more than self-interest, even 'enlightened self-interest.' He ... must serve his neighbors' interests as well as his own, and he must

not do so out of 'selfishness and empty conceit' (Philippians 2:3, 4)." Thomas Atwood, "Ethics of Political Economy: The Biblical Perspective" (unpublished thesis, 1986), p. 21.

12. Lay Catholic theologian Michael Novak argues that "Democratic capitalism suffers from the underdevelopment of guidance for a spiritual life appropriate to its highly developed political and economic life." *The Spirit of Democratic Capitalism* (New York: Simon & Schuster, 1982), p. 140.

13. Milton Friedman, *Capitalism and Freedom* (Chicago: University of Chicago Press, 1962), p. 12.

14. Brian Griffiths, *The Creation of Wealth: A Christian's Case for Capitalism* (Downers Grove, IL: InterVarsity Press, 1984). Theonomist R. J. Rushdoony criticizes political liberalism as a "logical development of theological liberalism, in that both involve a transfer of sovereignty from God to man; both rest on a concept of the independence of time from eternity, implicitly or explicitly." *Politics of Guilt and Pity* (Fairfax, VA: Thoburn Press, 1978), p. 313.

15. In Rushdoony's view, "The conservatives, being usually less advanced and less systematic, represent the statist evil in milder form: their position is still not theologically founded, except in a minority of cases." *Christianity and the State* (Vallecito, CA: Ross House Books, 1986), p. 19.

16. The Institute for *Cultural Conservatism, Cultural Conservatism: Toward A New National Agenda* (Washington, D.C.: Free Congress Research and Educational Foundation, 1987), p. 8.

CHAPTER FOUR *Biblical Principles: the Role of Government*

1. acques Ellul makes a creative argument that Christ is referring to a rebellious angel rather than God. However, this interpretation does not square with Paul's discourse in Romans. Jacques Ellul, *The Subversion of Christianity* (Grand Rapids: Eerdmans, 1986), p. 115.

2. Why does God command obedience to such imperfect human structures? Part of the answer is undoubtedly that God uses the civil authorities to fulfill His historical plan. For instance, the Lord declared through the prophet Jeremiah to Judah's King Jehoiachin, "I will hand you over to those who seek your life, those you fear–to Nebuchadnezzar king of Babylon and the Babylonians" (Jeremiah 22:25). Another reason reflects the fact that man's spiritual relationship to God overshadows his political association with his neighbors. Thus, Christians should not damage their witness by unnecessarily resisting civil authority, which would "offend" nonbelievers–the reason Jesus gave for paying the temple tax (Matthew 17:27). God does not legitimize the activities of government today as much as declare that His purposes simply transcend its claims: he tolerates rather than exalts secular rulers. For a Christian anarchist's attack on civil disobedience on these grounds, see Vernard Eller, *Christian Anarchy* (Grand Rapids: Eerdmans, 1987), pp. 195-210.

3. Eller argues that a Christian's response to government cannot be contextual, that is, based on the rightness of its conduct at the time. Eller, pp. 42-43. However, Paul clearly states that government "is

God's servant to do you good" (Romans 13:4). If rulers act otherwise, they are flouting the purpose for which their kingdoms were created, calling in question a Christian's duty to obey. Writes James Skillen, "We are not enjoined to obey evil commands of [fallen] powers. Rather, we are subject to the Lord in all things and are subject to government God's command in order to fulfill His justice. Likewise, governments are also subject to [this] norm ..., and insofar as they do not serve the Lord in rendering justice, they are not his obedient servants." "The Bible, Politics, and Democracy: What Does Biblical Obedience Entail for American Political Thought?," in Richard John Neuhaus, ed., *The Bible, Politics, and Democracy* (Grand Rapids: William B. Eerdmans, 1987), p. 72.

4. Obviously not just any policy disagreement can warrant defiance. Fundamental moral principles–such as a clear violation of God's commandments–should be at stake. Moreover, resistance seems more justifiable if alternative, godly authorities are available to follow. For instance, God raised up Jehu to destroy the house of Ahab (2 Kings 9). Similarly, the Lord used Gideon to free the Israelites from Midian and Jephthah to defeat the Ammonites (Judges 6, 11). God order the Israelites in Judah under Rehoboam not to try to suppress the rebellion of the ten tribes of Israel (2 Chronicles 11:4). And the Lord prepared David for the kingship even while Saul reigned. In the same way the American revolutionaries arguably constituted a substitute for the leadership of the British Crown. A thoughtful attempt to set forth some Biblical standards on this issue is John Jefferson Davis, *Evangelical Ethics: Issues Facing the Church Today* (Phillipsburg, NJ: Presbyterian and Reformed Publishing Co., 1985), pp. 208-226.

5. In Mosaic Israel all positions of leadership were held by believers, though as the Jewish nation fell away from God its government became more secularized. Queen Esther lobbied King Xerxes to save the Jewish people after he decreed their destruction. Daniel, shadrach, Meshach, and Abednego all served in teh Babylonian court. Christ made no effort to get Zacchaeus to abandon his position as a tax collector or convince Nicodemus and Joseph of Arimathea to leave the Sanhedrin. Moreover, the Christian faith reached members of the civil government in Rome ("Caesar's household," mentioned in Philippians 4:22) and Corinth (Erastus, that city's "director of public works," cited in Romans 16:23). In neither case case were the new believers apparently directed to quit their jobs.

6. This helps provide a guide on how a Christian President should act in the scenario posed by Charles Colson, where Jewish extremists plan to blow up the Dome of the Rock. *Kingdoms in Conflict* (New York and Grand Rapids: William Morrow and Zondervan, 1987), pp. 9-40. Though such an action might be seen by some believers as a precursor to Christ's return, the President's Scriptural duty is to carry out the civil responsibilities of his office, not to try to advance Biblical prophecy. He must, however, apply Scriptural principles to help determine what his public obligations are–to promote justice, for instance–and how they can best be fulfilled, in contrast to, say, President John F. Kennedy's pledge to act "without regard to outside

religious pressure or dictate." Quoted in Colson, p. 284. If an office-holder's theological and civil duties conflicted irreconcilably, he should resign, as Pat Robertson pledged to do in such a circumstance. "The Gospel According to Robertson," *U.S. News & World Report*, February 22, 1988, p. 21.

7. Rousas John Rushdoony, *Politics of Guilt and Pity* (Fairfax, VA: Thoburn Press, 1978), p. 338.

8. Robert Mounce, *The Book of Revelation* (Grand Rapids: Eerdmans, 1977), p. 251.

9. Rushdoony, *Politics of Guilt and Pity* p. 30. Similarly, Thomas Atwood argues that "modern man seems to care more about his material security than he does about his biblical right (and duty) to self government under God." "Ethics of Political Economy: The Biblical Perspective" (unpublished thesis, 1986), p. 58. This is one of most important flaws in liberation theology, for it is essentially a political analysis dressed up in the rhetoric of the gospel. But instead of providing spiritual freedom, the revolutionary state offers a competing claim of (political) transcendence. See Eller, pp. 41, 42.

10. John Calvin, *Institutes* II, Book II, Chapter VII, p. x.

11. In fact, in his covenant with Noah God decreed that "from each man, too, I will demand an accounting for the life of his fellow man. Whoever sheds the blood of man, by man shall his blood be shed" (Genesis 9:5, 6).

12. Abraham bought a burial site from the Hittites. The Lord divided the Promised Land between the different tribes and set forth rules to govern the personal inheritance of the property. Paul and Peter engaged in the businesses of tent-making and fishing, respectively. Christ told parables involving the purchase of goods and investment of money. And the letter to the Hebrews observes that the readers "joyfully accept the confiscation of your property," a procedure obviously used to punish Christians who otherwise had a legal right to their goods (Hebrews 10:34).

    Moreover, while Ananias and his wife Sapphira died for attempting to defraud God, Peter stated that "didn't it /the land/ belong to you before it was sold? And after it was sold, wasn't the money at your disposal?" (Acts 5:4). Similarly, Christ respected the right of both the wealthy young ruler and the tax collector Zacchaeus to dispose of their money (they exercised their legally-guaranteed rights in quite different ways, of course).

13. These two concepts are obviously related. Rushdoony, for one, argues that they are the same. Rousas John Rushdoony, *Christianity and the State* (Vallecito, CA: Ross House Books, 1986), pp. 37, 38.

14. The distinction between universal and particular justice is explained in Ronald Nash, "The Two Faces of Evangelical Social Concern," in Richard John Neuhaus and Michael Cromartie, eds, *Piety and Politics: Evangelicals and Fundamentalists Confront the World* (Washington, D.C.: Ethics and Public Policy Center, 1987), pp. 134-137.

15. Stephen Monsma argues that "the suffocating of freedom and opportunities—that is, an unjust order—can arise from societal attitudes, traditions, and structures as well as from unjust laws. Justice is not

merely a negative concept–not only the absence of certain restrictions on our activities–but a positive concept: the existence of actual opportunities that allow us to make morally responsible choices." Stephen Monsma, "The Moral Limits of Government," in Neuhaus and Cromartie, p. 221. However, as superficially appealing as this definition may be, one must distinguish between policies which may seem desirable because they advance the interests of one or more groups, and justice, which guarantees a fair process. The Bible appears to focus on the latter concept.

16. Rushdoony, *Politics of Guilt and Pity*, p. 339. Similary, Atwood argues that "God births individuals into unique individual endowments of abilities and material wealth, in accordance with His laws and with His will and pleasure." Thus, "each person is individually responsible to God for his actions and, one day, will give account of these actions to God." p. 23.

17. "The message of the Jubilee is not God's model share-the-wealth plan a la Huey Long or Jesse Jackson, but rather is this: 'You have squandered the inheritance I gave you in Eden, but I have returned it to you in the Year of the Lord.' " Bill Anderson, "Jubilee and Economics," *World*, April 4, 1988, p. 13. At most, the Jubilee Year can be treated as a restraint on a monopoly in Israel's most important economic resource. See Atwood, p. 42.

18. This sort of economic fairness is, however, an important aspect of *personal* justice and fairness. "Do not take advantage of a widow or an orphan," God instructed the Israelites (Exodus 22:22). Mosaic law set forth rules governing other economic duties to one's neighbors as well, an issue covered later in this chapter. But the Bible appears to leave responsibility for maintaining brotherly economic relations to individuals, not give it to the state.

19. Inflation is another, more subtle, form of economic oppression practiced by interests–debtors and government officials, for instance–that benefit from a depreciating currency. See Herbert Schlossberg, *Idols for Destruction: Christian Faith and Its Confrontation with America Society* (New York: Thomas Nelson Publishers, 1983), pp. 91-102.

20. Saint Augustine, *The City Of God* (New York: The Modern Library, 1950), pp. 112, 113.

21. Monsma, p. 225.

22. For example, they were to allot a special tithe to "the aliens, the fatherless and the widows" (Deuteronomy 14:29). People were not to charge interest on loans or sell at a profit food to the needy (Leviticus 25:37; Exodus 22:25). The Israelites were to leave crops at the edges of their fields as well as the gleanings for the poor; they were not to retrieve sheaves of grain that had been overlooked in the harvest (Leviticus 19:9-10; Deuteronomy 24:19). People were also instructed to allow the needy to gather food from their fields and vineyards every seventh year (Exodus 23:11). Moreover, the poor's prescribed offering to God was less–doves or pigeons instead of lambs (Leviticus 5:7).

23. Individuals obviously have a responsibility to care for their neighbors irrespective of the government's activities. The Good Samaritan did not trundle his charge off to a local welfare agency, but paid the

innkeeper himself. And it is impossible to imagine someone standing before Christ justifying his failure to help the hungry, thirsty, naked, and sick because of his electoral support for a public dole (Matthew 25:31-46).

24. Two of the Hebrew words for the poor, *ani* and *anaw*, mean "wrongfully impoverished or dispossessed." Gerhard Kittel and Gerhard Freidrich, eds, *Theological Dictionary of the New Testament*, Vol. 6 (Grand Rapids: Eerdmans, 1964), p. 888.

25. It is critical, of course, that believers, whatever their financial states, not place their trust in material goods, as did the young man who walked away from Jesus. "You cannot serve both God and Money," said Christ (Luke 16:13). Indeed, He instructed His followers to "Be on your guard against all kinds of greed; a man's life does not consist in the abundance of his possessions" (Luke 12:15). Similarly, Christ directed His listeners to store up treasures in Heaven rather than on earth (Matthew 6:19). Doing so requires believers to fulfill their duties of stewardship, which includes assisting the needy. See Atwood, p. 15.

The bad fruit that can grow out of a lust for material riches is evident throughout the Bible. And the end result is disaster: "People who want to get rich fall into temptation and a trap and into many foolish and harmful desires that plunge men into ruin and destruction. For the love of money is a root of all kinds of evil," wrote Paul (1 Timothy 6:9, 10).

26. For example, the final document released from a 1979 Conference of Latin American Bishops in Puebla, Mexico, had a section entitled "A Preferential Option for the Poor." In essence, the bishops argued that the church is to be biased towards the materially poor in both its evangelistic and political roles. See, e.g., Gustavo Gutierrez, "Liberation and the Poor: The Puebla Perspective," *in Third World Liberation Theologies: A Reader*, ed. Deane William Ferm (Maryknoll, NY: Orbis Books, 1986), p. 25.

27. Scholars disagree over whether interest was proscribed for all loans, or just personal credit.

28. Writes Kenneth Myers: "Israel had an obligation to be a convenantally righteous nation, to meet standards that God did not establish for, say, Egypt. Israel was a holy nation as no nation before or since could claim to be. Its national identity was a mechanism of God's redemptive work in a unique way. In every aspect of its national life as ordered by God Israel was anticipating the character of the people of God upon the consummation of redemptive history. Its obedience or disobedience in civil matters had consequences more like the apostasy of a church than the tyranny of a modern nation. The tyranny of Egypt was certainly an offense to God, but it was not compounded by the breaking of the covenant. Egypt's oppression of the poor was a civil sin of a state never in peculiar relation to God. Israel's oppression of the poor was a civil sin *and* a mockery of God's electing love and grace." "Biblical Obedience and Political Thought: Some Reflections on Theological Method," in Neuhaus, p. 24.

29. Difficult cases—"whether bloodshed, lawsuits or assaults"—also could be brought to a place chosen by God for the priests to decide (Deuteronomy 17:8-10). The fact that such a practice is impossible

today does not mean that the civil authorities should give up trying to punish crimes like murder; instead, the courts will simply be unable to resolve cases where the available evidence is not determinative. For this reason the rule that a "reasonable doubt" is enough to acquit a criminal defendant seems appropriate.

30. In contrast, as discussed earlier, one can argue that some public assistance to the needy may help avert God's judgment on a nation even if many of the people are not personally generous. The difference between corporate enforcement of personal moral norms, such as Sodom's sexual practices, and of broader social responsibilities, such as Judah's support for the needy and maintenance of justice, is that the former primarily concerns man's relationship to God, while the latter also involves man's duty to his fellowman. Since the government has been ordained to regulate man's interpersonal relations, it has a better claim to help ensure the fulfillment of neighborly responsibilities than personal obedience to God. Nevertheless, Atwood argues persuasively that the state is only intended to respond to sinful "commissions," or overt acts, and not "omissions," such as a failure to fulfill one's stewardship duties. See Atwood, pp. 38, 35.

31. Rushdoony, *Politics of Guilt and Pity*, pp. 179-9.

32. Similarly, Peter wrote, "be sympathetic, love as brothers, be compassionate and humble. Do not repay evil with evil or insult with insult, but with blessing" (1 Peter 3:8, 9). And Christ instructed His listeners: "Do not resist an evil person. If someone strikes you on the right cheek, turn to him the other also. And if someone wants to sue you and take your tunic, let him have your cloak as well. If someone forces you to go one mile, go with him two miles" (Matthew 5:39-41).

Above all else Christians are to love—and not just God and their friends. "Love your enemies, do good to those who hate you, bless those who curse you, pray for those who mistreat you," said Jesus in the Sermon on the Mount (Luke 6:27, 28). Even good works do not overcome a lack of love. Wrote Paul to the Corinthian church, "If I give all I possess to the poor and surrender my body to the flames, but have not love, I gain nothing" (1 Corinthians 13:3).

33. Dutch theologian H. M. Kuitert, for one, argues that Christ's instructions in the Sermon on the Mount cannot be followed in a political context. *Everything Is Politics But Politics Is Not Everything* (Grand Rapids: William B. Eermans, 1986), pp. 100-11.

34. In fact, Vernard Eller has suggested a useful distinction between political and spiritual justice. The civil authorities are in no position to offer spiritual grace; instead, they are to maintain a just secular order, in which all people are treated impartially and fairly. And that means punishing the guilty. In contrast, God, through Christ's crucifixion, has provided for the remission of sins, a form of theological justice that transcends anything in the world. As Christians we are to love and forgive as we try to apply God's values to the world around us, but we are not authorized to displace the system of political justice that serves unbeliever and believer alike. Only when the kingdom is fulfilled will that system, too, pass away. Eller, p. 256.

35. Richard John Neuhaus, *The Naked Public Square*, 2nd ed. (Grand Rapids: Eerdmans, 1986), p. 11.

CHAPTER FIVE *Biblical Principles: The Transcendence of the Spiritual*

1. Peter Leithart, "Cynicism and Cosmetic Reform," *Chalcedon Report*, February 1988, No. 271, p. 3.
2. The united church-state is often described, in common parlance, as a "theocracy." But the Greek word theokratia only means "the rule of God," which all Christians should desire; theocracy does not necessarily imply any particular form of government or civil enforcement of religious doctrines. "Ecclesiocracy" and "clericocracy," in contrast, refer to rule by the clergy, an arrangement which Christians as well as unbelievers have reason to fear.
3. In fact, who but God could judge men's hearts? "Many will say to me on that day, 'Lord, Lord, did we not prophesy in your name, and in your name drive out demons and perform many miracles?,'" Jesus warned His listeners, but "Then I will tell them plainly, 'I never knew you. Away from me, you evildoers'" (Matthew 7:22, 23). Obviously, sinful men operating through imperfect human institutions cannot make this sort of assessment. After all, God told the prophet Samuel that "The Lord does not look at the things man looks at. Man looks at the outward appearance, but the Lord looks at the heart" (1 Samuel 16:7).
4. Ironically, persecution during medieval times often was motivated by believers' recognition that the spiritual superseded the political. R. J. Rushdoony makes the interesting point that the reason a liberal society like our own is particularly shocked over religious intolerance is because it considers religion to be a personal, even frivolous matter: "What people really object to nowadays in the death of Servetus is that a man should be executed for so trivial a thing as religion—heretical religion, of course, but still religion, a thing peripheral to life and this world." *Rushdoony, Politics of Guilt and Pity*, p. 266. That totalitarian societies often punish political heresy with death is similarly condemned, but does not seem so curious to the same people. This does not represent a defense of religious persecution, of course, but it helps explain why the phenomenon occurred.
5. Quoted in Richard John Neuhaus, *The Naked Public Square*, 2nd ed. (Grand Rapids: Eerdmans, 1986), p. 8.
6. Interestingly, Rushdoony contends that the Inquisition was used to build state power at the expense of the church's influence. *Christianity and the State*, pp. 136-138.
7. Paul Johnson, *A History of Christianity* (New York: Atheneum, 1987), p. 305. Of course, the religious struggles during this period were often intertwined with politics, such as the Habsburg family's bid for European dominance. See, e.g., Paul Kennedy, *The Rise and Fall of the Great Powers* (New York: Random House, 1987), pp. 31-41. Moreover, blame for the horrific conflicts was not equally shared—the unending violence resulted largely from the Catholic Church's reliance on state power to extirpate any threat to its spiritually dead ecclesiastical structure. But the Reformers also proved all too willing to use secular influence for their own advantage, rather than seeking to create a just social order for all people, which is the Biblical ideal.

8. In fact, persecution seems most incompatible with the Calvinist doctrine of predistination, since it holds that God has chosen the elect–and government action cannot, therefore, affect who is saved and who is not. In any case, an important test of obedience for believers it to set aside one's own preferences and to submit to God's will. This must include a genuine humility in attempting to ascertain what God's will is and a consequent caution in advancing what one perceives to be God's Kingdom. The need for circumspection is greatest where the issue involves coercing one's neighbors. A mistaken zeal in one's personal life usually will not greatly affect the lives of others; in contrast, the impact of such an attitude magnified by the power of government can be both far-reaching and catastrophic.

9. Neuhaus, p. 122.

10. Another example is the Catholic doctrine of transubstantiation, that is, that the bread and wine change into the body and blood of Jesus during the Eucharist, has been similarly contested. Luther advocated an alternative tenet called consubstantiation. But the Calvinists rejected the doctrine in its entirety–and a s a result were considered little better than Anabaptists by Lutherans.

11. Ibid., p. 115.

12. Quoted in Johnson, p. 87.

13. James Skillen, "Public Justice and True Tolerance," in Richard John Neuhaus and Michael Cromartie, eds, *Piety and Politics: Evangelicals and Fundamentallists Confront the World* (Washington, D.C.: Ethics and Public Policy Center, 1987), pp. 164, 165.

14. Vernard Eller, *Christian Anarchy* (Grand Rapids: Eerdmans, 1987), p. 23. And how true his observation proved to be. "Some aspects of the development of Christianity in the Roman World from the time of Constantine onwards are none too pleasant," writes theologian and historian F. F. Bruce in his usual understated tone: "the evident patronage extended to Christianity by the ruling power made Christianity popular in an undesirable sense. Christian leaders were tempted to exploit the influential favour they enjoyed, even when it meant subordinating the cause of justice to the apparent interest of their religion. On the other hand, they were inclined to allow the secular power too much control in church affairs, even if it was by way of gratitude for the imperial good will. Where church leaders were able to exercise political as well as spiritual authority, they did not enjoy any marked immunity from the universally corrupting tendency of power." *The Spreading Flame* (Grand Rapids: Eerdmans, 1958), p. 293.

15. Johnson, p. 77.

16. Jacques Ellul, *The Subversion of Christianity* (Grand Rapids: Eerdmans, 1986), p. 38.

17. Alistair Kee, *Constantine Versus Christ* (London: SCM, 1982), p. 154.

18. In 904, for instance, Sergius III murdered his two rivals; after his death his former lover, who came from one of Italy's most influential families, and her husband killed the new pope, eventually making her son (whose father was Sergius III) the Vicar of Christ. Later popes imprisoned, starved, and poisoned each other or their competitors,

all the while claiming to be God's anointed on earth. At different times secular rulers like Otto III and Henry III intervened to choose the ruler of the Holy See. Henry IV of Germany marched on Rome to depose Gregory VII, who had excommunicated Henry and encouraged rebellion against that monarch. Henry installed Clement III in Rome, and Gregory died in exile. Urban II eventually expelled Clement from Rome, but Henry V invaded Italy to force Urban's successor, Paschal II, to abandon the traditional fuedal privileges of bishops. Centuries later Pope Boniface VIII unsuccessfully battled Philip IV of France. Boniface allied himself with Germany's Emperor Albert, who had usurped the throne, and prepared to excommunicate Philip; French forces kidnapped Boniface. After the deaths of Boniface and his short-lived successor, Benedict XI, who was rumored to have been poisoned, opposing parties contended for the papacy, leading to the victory of the Francophiles in Clement V. Clement reigned for nine years but never visited Rome, residing instead in Avignon, France; twenty-three of twenty-four of his new cardinals were French, and several were his relatives. It was decades before the papal court returned to Rome, but political intrigue, murder, corruption, nepotism, andhedonism continued, on and on.

19. Justo Gonzalez, *The Story of Christianity*, Vol. 1 (San Francisco: Harper & Row, 1984), p. 373.
20. Johnson, p. 484.
21. Ibid., p. 480.
22. A. James Reichley, *Religion in American Public Life* (Washington, D.C.: Brookings, 1985), pp. 278, 279.
23. Dean Kelley, *Why Conservative Churches Are Growing: A Study in Sociology of Religion* (New York: Harper & Row, 1977), pp. ix, x, 134-135. H. M. Kuitert worries that politicization "is the ruin of the Christian church" for the church "is forced to be untrue to itself. As a church it knows no other power than faith and it can fight only with the sword of the Spirit. If it brings its spiritual power into worldly power-play, then it irrevocably becomes a political subject, as we have seen, a party in politics, or a political party–and then it is no longer the church." Kuitert, p. 146.
24. "Leaders of the Christian Right Announce Their Next Step," *Christianity Today*, December 13, 1985, p. 65.
25. Quoted in Sidney Blumenthal, "The Religious Right and Republicans," in Neuhaus and Cromartie, p. 283.
26. Eller, p. 23.
27. Neuhaus, p. 141.
28. Ellul, p. 133.
29. "Leaders of the Christian Right Announce Their Next Step."
30. Writes Kuitert, "theology is not the usual means or instrument for liberation from social misery and political oppression. If we want a strategy for rebellion and opposition to oppression, we must go somewhere other than theology." P. 74.
31. Charles Colson, *Kingdoms in Conflict* (New York and Grand Rapids: William Morrow and Zondervan, 1987), p. 236.

CHAPTER SIX *Church and Government: The Historical Experience*

1. Allen Hertzke, Representing God in Washington: *The Role of Religious Lobbies in the American Polity* (Knoxville, TN: University of Tennessee Press, 1988), p. 124. Of note is the fact that more frequent church attendance correlates with a greater commitment to protecting the life of the unborn.
2. Charles Villa-Vicencio, *Between Christ and Caesar* (Grand Rapids: Eerdmans, 1986), pp. 3, 4.
3. Paul Johnson, *A History of Christianity* (New York: Atheneum, 1987), p. 48.
4. Eusebius, *The History of the Church from Christ to Constantine* (New York: Dorset Press, 1965), p. 402.
5. Villa-Vicencio, p. 6.
6. Johnson, p. 69.
7. Reprinted in Villa-Vicencio, p. 16.
8. Johnson, p. 130.
9. *Ibid.*, p. 115.
10. Villa-Vicencio, pp. 36, 37.
11. Johnson, pp. 174, 175.
12. *Ibid.*, p. 196.
13. Ernest Henderson, *Select Historical Documents of the Middle Ages* (New York: Biblo & Tannen, 1965), p. 463.
14. Quoted in Johnson, p. 393.
15. The church's stance made the American heirarchy particularly uncomfortable, since the government was formally separated from all churches and the "civil religion" that dominated public life was essentially Protestant. There had even been fears that "Americanism" would be included as a form of modernist heresy in Pope Pius' 1907 *Lamentabili* decree.
16. Quoted in Villa-Vincencio, p. 117.
17. *Ibid.*, pp. 118, 119.
18. He wrote: Civil "government is distinct from that spiritual and inward Kingdom of Christ, so we must know that they are not at variance. For spiritual government, indeed, is already initiating in us upon earth certain beginnings of the Heavenly Kingdom, and in this moral and fleeting life affords a certain forecast of an immortal and incorruptible blessedness. Yet civil government has as its appointed end, so long as we live among men, to cherish and protect the outward worship of God, to defend sound doctrine of piety and the position of the church ...." Calvin, *Institutes of the Christian Religion:* 2 (Philadelphia: Westminister Press, 1960), p. 1487.
19. The traditional view is that Calvin supported the execution of Servetus, while advocating a less horrific form of execution than burning. Kenneth Latourette, *A History of Christianity* (New York: Harper & Row, 1953), p. 759. However, some scholars believe that the Geneva authorities decided to execute Servetus over Calvin's opposition.
20. Villa-Vicencio, p. 51.
21. In fact, he wrote that Christians did not need a civil government: If all the world were composed of real Christians, that is, true believ-

ers, there would be no need for or benefits from prince, king, lord, sword, or law. They would serve no purpose, since Christians have in their heart the Holy Spirit, who both teaches and makes them do injustice to no one." But since the number of believers were few, and even many of them did not truly follow Christian precepts, "God has provided for them a different government beyond the Christian estate and kingdom of God." *Ibid.*, pp. 49, 50.

22. Martin Luther, Interpretation of Psalm 101, quoted in H. G. Haile, *Luther: An Experience in Biography* (Princeton, NJ: Princeton University Press, 1980), p. 101. Notably, Luther disavowed, at the beginning of his ministry, at least, the right of the state to punish heretics, for, he wrote, "Christ's government does not extend over all men; rather, Christians are always a minority in the midst of non-Christians." Quoted in Villa-Vicencio, p. 50. Luther viewed an individual's spiritual relationship with God as being no less important than did Calvin, but the German Reformer did not believe the state of that relationship to be the responsibility of the civil authorities. However, as the papacy's attempt to crush the Reformation intensified, he increasingly relied on the secular German princes for support and dropped his tolerant attitude towards Anabaptists and other detested sects; by 1531 he was advocating that "Protestant extremists" be executed by the government.

23. Quoted in Villa-Vicencio, p. 62.
24. *Ibid*, pp. 74, 75.
25. John Eidsmoe, *Christianity and the Constitution: The Faith of the Founding Fathers* (Grand Rapids: Baker Book House, 1987), p. 33.
26. Quoted in Villa-Vicencio, p. 77.
27. *Ibid.*, p. 79.
28. Timothy Smith, *Revivalism and Reform in Mid-Nineteenth Century America* (Nashville, TN: Abingdon, 1957), p. 60. In fact, it was a group of Baptists to whom Thomas Jefferson penned the letter containing his famous reference to "a wall of separation between church and state." Baptists have proved extremely skeptical of any sort of cooperative relationship between the two institutions because of the rough handling accorded their denomination by government throughout history. Writes British Congregationalist Cecil Northcott, "The richer and more fruitful source of religious liberty lies in the witness of the Baptist churches whose devotion to this idea, through the years of persecution in Protestant Europe, makes their place a foremost one in the history of liberty." *Religious Liberty* (New York: Macmillan, 1949), p. 28.
29. Fiotis Litsas, *A Companion to the Greek Orthodox Church* (New York: Greek Orthodox Archdiocese of North and South America, 1984), p. 226.
30. Villa-Vicencio, p. 182.
31. Vernard Eller argues that Desiderius Erasmus, who lived from 1466 to 1536, "can be understood as the first proponent of twentieth-century America's Social Gospel." *Christian Anarchy* (Grand Rapids: Eerdmans, 1987), p. 38. Erasmus was a Catholic who sympathized with some aspects of the Reformation and opposed religious persecution. He tried to heal the Catholic/Protestant schism, and his moder-

ate course had a wide following throughout Europe. He was a pacifist and was skeptical of worldly power. Erasmus has also been termed a "Christian humanist," a school of thought that emphasized the value of secular pursuits and study even for believers. He also authored *The Education of a Christian Prince,* in which he called on the government to promote peace and social justice.

32. Stephen Colwell, *New Themes for the Protestant Clergy* (Philadelphia: 1851), p. 244.
33. James Davison Hunter, "The Evangelical Worldview Since 1890," in Richard John Neuhaus and Michael Cromartie, eds, *Piety and Politics: Evangelicals and Fundamentalists Confront the World* (Washington, D.C.: Ethics and Public Policy Center, 1987), pp. 27, 28.
34. Phillip Berryman, *Liberation Theology* (New York: Pantheon Books, 1987), p. 4.
35. Quoted in Deane Ferm, ed., *Third World Liberation Theologies: A Reader* (Maryknoll, NY: Orbis, 1986), p. 17.
36. Quoted in Harold Lindsell, The New Paganism: Understanding American Culture and the Role of the Church (San Francisco: Harper and Row, 1987), p. 244.
37. Villa-Vicencio, p. 146. Similar liberation themes have arisen within other ethnic groups, such as the Hispanic community. Andres Guerrero, director of the Hispanic Ministries Program in the Catholic Diocese of Saginaw, Michigan, argues that "the Chicano experience is one of oppression" and that the church has a duty to help liberate Hispanics from the strictures of white society. In his view, "Chicano theology ought to align itself with the theologies of liberation from Latin Amerca, Africa, Asia, and North American movements–Black, feminist, Asian, and Native American theologies." *A Chicano Theology* (Maryknoll, NY: Orbis, 1987), p. 159.
38. *Ibid.*, pp. 160, 158.
39. Villa-Vicencio, p. 198.

CHAPTER SEVEN *Applying Biblical Principles*

1. Vernard Eller, *Christian Anarchy* (Grand Rapids: Eerdmans, 1987), p. 191.
2. Richard John Neuhaus, *The Naked Public Square,* 2nd ed. (Grand Rapids: Eerdmans, 1986), p. 28.
3. Writes Hendrik Van Riessen: "No particular bearer of authority on earth is the highest power from which other forms of authority are deduced and derived.... The social relationships exist together on a basis of equality; the one not subordinate to the authority and control of the other. Subjection to authority exists only within a relationoship. Societal relationships properly stand in a coordinate relation to each other, not in a preferred or subordinate position.... The state is not above but coordinate to other forms of society. Why? Because every sphere ought to obey its own laws; each after its own kind, and according to its own created structure." *The Society of the Future* (Philadelphia: The Presbyterian and Reformed Publishing Co., 1965), pp. 71, 73. This system is what James Skillen calls "structural pluralism." "The Bible, Politics, and Democracy: What Does Biblical

Obedience Entail for American Political Thought?," Richard John Neuhaus, ed., *The Bible, Politics, and Democracy* (Grand Rapids: William B. Eerdmans, 1987), p. 65.

4. Rousas J. Rushdoony, *Politics of Guilt and Pity* (Fairfax, VA: Thoburn Press, 1978), p. 144.

5. Andrew Kirk, *The Good News of the Kingdom Coming* (Downers Grove, IL: InterVarsity Press, 1983), p. 120.

6. The church must also reprove believers for violating God's law, whether or not it is punished by government. Paul told the Corinthian believers not to associate with Christians involved in sin. "What business is it of mine to judge those outside the church? Are you not to judge those inside?" he asked. "Expel the wicked man from among you" (1 Corinthians 5:12, 13).

7. Quoted in Paul Johnson, *Modern Times* (New York: Harper & Row, 1983), p. 209.

8. Ronald Sider, "An Evangelical Theology of Liberation," in Richard John Neuhaus and Michael Cromartie, eds, *Peity and Politics: Evangelicals and Fundamentalists Confront the World* (Washington, D.C.: Ethics and Public Policy Center, 1987), p. 157.

9. William McManus, "Getting Our House in Order: Economic Justice Within the Church," in Dennis Corrado and James Hinchey, eds, *Shepherds Speak: American Bishops Confront the Social and Moral Issues That Challenge Christians Today* (New York: Crossroad, 1986), pp. 62-73.

10. Orestes Brownson, *The Works of Orestes A. Brownson*, Vol. XIX, collected and arranged by Henry Brownson (New York: AMS Press, Inc., 1966), p. 442.

11. *Pierce v. Society of Sisters* (1925), reprinted in Paul Brest, *Processes of Constitutional Decisionmaking: Cases and Materials* (Boston: Little, Brown and Co., 1975), p. 756.

12. Even then Christians should not ignore political issues involving education. Believers need to be ever vigilant to oppose state interference with home and private schooling. Moreover, all individuals, Christian or not, have a duty to ensure that the government does not use the public schools as a means of indoctrinating the vast majority of students who attend state institutions. The Soviet Union, for instance, uses its control of education to advance both atheism and communism; many American public schools promote much milder forms of humanism and collectivism.

13. Eller, p. 187.

14. Often the problem was more local than denominational. In 1947 the Southern Baptist Convention declared itself for nondiscrimination, but many individual congregations were rather less enthused about the prospect of integration.

15. An example of a passionate Christian relentlessly pressing for Biblical justice and righteousness through the political system is William Wilberforce's campaign against the British slave trade, a story recounted in Charles Colson, Kingdoms in Conflict (New York and Grand Rapids: William Morrow and Zondervan, 1987), pp. 95-108. Where a believer is entitled to use civil disobedience, and even violence, to advance political ends is a complicated issue that lies

beyond the scope of this book.

16. Eller, p. 246.

17. Argues fundamentalist Edward Dobson, "Man's inherent quest for power and domination, his propensity for evil and destruction, demand a system of governance that is predicated upon higher laws and limited government that respets the rights and freedoms of all." "The Bible, Politics, and Democracy," in Neuhaus, p. 14.

18. A. James Reichley, *Religion in American Public Life* (Washington, D.C.: The Brookings Institution, 1985), p. 53.

19. See John Eidsmoe, *Christianity and the Constitution: The Faith of the Founding Fathers* (Grand Rapids: Baker Book House, 1987), pp. 77-342. A more skeptical view is provided by David Gill, "Faith of the Founding Fathers?," in Jerry Herbert, ed., *America, Christian or Secular?* (Portland, OR: Multnomah Press, 1984), pp. 131-146.

20. The exact nature of America's Christian heritage has been much disputed. See, for instance, Herbert. The initial colonies represented diverse but often intolerant sects. For example, the 1641 Massachusetts Body of Liberties, the commonwealth's legal code, provided for the death penalty for blasphemy, witchcraft, and the worship of other gods. State churches persisted even after ratification of the national Constitution; Massachusetts did not disestablish the Congregationalist Church until 1833 and imprisoned an anti-Christian polemicist for blasphemy as late as 1838.

Moreover, the First Amendment did not erect the "wall of separation" that Jefferson wrote of. Its prohibition against the "establishment of religion" did not even apply to the states until this century, when the Supreme Court ruled that the Fourteenth Amendment "incorporated" the clause. And the nation's founders would have been amazed at the way their handiwork was eventually twisted to, for instance, void tuition tax credits. See Daniel Dreisbach's detailed review of the Supreme Court's long legacy of misinterpretation. *Real Threat and Mere Shadow: Religious Liberty and the First Amendment* (Westchester, IL: Crossway Books, 1987).

Nevertheless, despite the early Americans' continuing commitment to matters spiritual, the original Puritan ideal of a total Christian society enforced in part by civil authority had been effectively abandoned by the 1700's. Observes historian Paul Johnson: "In America as a whole, religion continued to be the dynamic of society and history. The difference was that Christianity now became a voluntary movement, or series of movements, rather than a compulsory framework." Paul Johnson: *A History of Christianity* (New York: Atheneum, 1987), p. 424.

21. Quoted in Reichley, p. 105.

22. Eidsmoe, p. 51. For a general look at the impact of Christianity on the nation's formation, see Benjamin Hart, *Faith and Freedom: The Christian Roots of American Liberty* (Dallas: Lewis & Stanley, 1988).

23. Eidsmoe, pp. 363-364. See also Robert Bellah, "Religion and the Legitimization of the American Republic," in Herbert, pp. 74, 75. The Constitution, in Article I, Section 8, Clause 10, also refers to "offences against the Law of Nations," which, Eidsmoe argues, flows from the same concept.

24. For a thorough discussion of how the Supreme Court has backed away from enforcing the Constitution's protection for economic freedom, see Bernard Siegan, *Economic Liberties and the Constitution* (Chicago: University of Chicago Press, 1980); Bernard Siegan, *The Supreme Court's Constitution: An Inquiry Into Judicial Review and Its Impact on Society* (New Brunswick, NJ: Transaction Books, 1987) pp. 41-88.

25. Jefferson's phrase "the pursuit of happiness" was not an exhaltation of hedonism. Instead, writes historian Forrest McDonald, "It entailed love of country and rigorous attention to the duty of making oneself as virtuous, moral, and useful a member of society as possible." Forrest McDonald, *Alexander Hamilton: A Biography* (New York: W. W. Norton Co., 1979), p. 56.

26. Federal action may directly supplant private initiatives, like the Meals-On-Wheels program, discussed in chapter 2, or indirectly relieve people of their feeling of responsibility for the poor. Moreover, high tax rates leave individuals far less income to donate to charity–in a sense seizing for government welfare programs what they would otherwise have devoted to private philanthropic organizations.

27. Kenneth Myers makes the nice distinction between major and minor premises: "If the major premise of my argument is drawn from Scripture (e.g., God hates injustice), but the minor premise is based on empirical analysis (e.g., capitalism is unjust), I cannot assert that the conclusion (e.g., God hates capitalism) is simply the teaching of the Word of God. I *can* say that God hates injustice and that, in my judgment, capitalism is unjust. But the truth of the minor premise is not determined either by the truth of the major premise or by the validity of the argument. Continually repeating the major premise with prophetic fervor will not demonstrate the truth of the minor premise. Only sustained examination of the facts and argumentation from them can do that." "Biblical Obedience and Political Thought: Some Reflections on Theological Method," in Neuhaus, p. 23. 28. Eller, p. 189.

29. For instance, the publication cites Acts 19:25, which quotes a pagan artisan attacking Paul for preaching the gospel, which had led to a reduction in orders for silver idols of the goddess Artemis: "He called them together, along with the workmen in related trades, and said: 'Men, you know we receive a good income from this business.'" Dave Balsiger, *Presidential Biblical Scorecard*, Spring 1988, p. 12. The relationship of this verse to the issue of comparable worth is, at best, obscure.

30. As was discussed in chapter 4, the Old Testament economic regulations, such as the Jubilee Year, related primarily to the Israelites' status as the chosen people and the fact that God had directly given them their land after the Exodus as part of His covenant with them.

31. Abusive reliance on the death penalty was evident in the South earlier this century, when blacks were often convicted of such crimes as rape on questionable evidence and then executed; blacks were also far more likely to be sentenced to death than whites for the same crime, a problem that persists to some degree today, and not just in

the South. See, e.g., "Death Penalty Opponents Weigh Change in Strategy," *Sojourners*, June 1988, p. 12. A different perversion of the state's power to kill is China's promiscuous use of capital punishment, with periodic mass executions. Exacting the ultimate penalty for a wide variety of crimes–small-scale theft was once punishable by death in Great Britain–cheapens the value of life, which is sacred in God's eyes.

*CHAPTER EIGHT* Applying Biblical Principles: Some Examples

1. Madeleine L'Engle, "What May I expect From My Church?," in Stanley Atkins and Theodore McConnell, eds., *Churches on the Wrong Road* (Chicago: Regnery, 1986), p. 260. Similarly, writes Dutch theologian H. M. Kuitert, "a theologian does not need to be the group ideologist of a society or of one part of it. If he or she wants to avoid that, then it is evident that in and with theology he or she is making a protest against society. Because this protest is meant to change society, even where it does not announce this aim, it is a form of political theology." *Everything Is Politics But Politics Is Not Everything* (Grand Rapids: William B. Eerdmans, 1986), pp. 63, 64.

2. For most of us this is obviously "easier said than done." We are all imperfect humans, and our philosophical outlook is likely to color our theological interpretations. This writer, no less than anyone else, would like to believe that not only is he right, but that God backs his position.

3. Charles Colson, *Kingdoms in Conflict* (New York and Grand Rapids: William Morrow and Zondervan, 1987), p. 290.

4. As discussed in chapter 4, these three themes seem to dominate Scriptural references to the role of government. Other goals–say, historical preservation, may be valid, but they should be consistent with the basic three.

5. Allen Hertzke, *Representing God in Washington: The Role of Religious Lobbies in the American Polity* (Knoxville, TN: University of Tennessee Press, 1988), pp. 124-126. Interestingly, a number of the mainline denominations have begun backing away from their pro-abortion stances. In April 1988 the American Baptist Churches, which have traditionally been far more liberal than the Southern Baptist Convention, announced that they were reevaluating their position on the issue. "The great proliferation of abortion has made us stop and look at what's happening here," said Gloria Marshall, head of the denomination's abortion task force. George Cornell, "Baptist Church Reversing Abortion Stand," *Escondido Times-Advocate*, April 8, 1988, p. A-8.

6. The rhetorical labels have themselves become part of the controversy: pro-life and pro-choice being viewed positively, anti-abortion and pro-abortion being used negatively. Intellectual combatants have often used unborn child and fetus in the same way, but I will use these two terms interchangeably.

7. The issue is whether verse 22 refers to a miscarriage or a premature live birth. John Jefferson Davis, *Abortion and the Christian* (Phillipsburg, NJ: Presbyterian and Reformed Publishing Co., 1984), pp. 49-52.

8. A detailed analysis of Scripture is provided by Davis, *ibid.*, pp. 35-62. See also Paul Fowler, *Abortion: Toward an Evangelical Consensus* (Portland, OR: Multnomah, 1987), pp. 95-157.

9. Davis, pp. 41, 42.

10. In a book that caused a storm of controversy in evangelical circles, D. Gareth Jones wrote that the unborn "may be one of us, but they have yet to manifest the characteristics we expect of personhood and of beings made in the image and likeness of God." *Brave New People*, 2nd ed. (Grand Rapids: Eerdmans, 1985), p. 161. The problem with this argument is that it is not rooted in Scripture. Nowhere does God speak of "personhood"; instead, He treats the unborn as valued life, apparently no different than the rest of us. For a sharp attack on Jones' argument see Fowler, pp. 85-90.

11. Despite the claims of abortion supporters, relatively few fatalities or injuries would likely result from violations of a legal ban on abortion because most illegal abortions would be performed by doctors. See, e.g., Ian Gentles, "Good News for the Fetus," *Policy Review*, Spring 1987, p. 50.

12. Perhaps the strongest argument is that to force a mother to give birth despite the risk of death would be to essentially require her to commit suicide, which is inconsistent with Biblical principles.

13. See Jerry Adler and Lisa Drew, "Waking Sleeping Souls," *Newsweek*, March 28, 1988, p. 70.

14. There are aspects to these activities, such as engaging in sex in a public place or knowingly spreading an infectious disease, that may warrant some form of government regulation. But punishment for consensual, private conduct, though sinful, should be left to God. (In fact, even under Mosaic law sodomy had to be "established by the testimony of two or three witnesses," in which case the act would probably have been performed in public (Deuteronomy 19:15).)

15. The issue of a pregnant rape victim, however rare the occurrence, is far more difficult, since the mother-to-be lacks any responsibility for the baby. In this case, involving two innocent parties, I personally do not believe that it would be right for the state to intervene to prevent an abortion. But that is a prudential rather than a Biblical judgment, since, in my view, Scripture does not provide a categorical answer. Obviously many Christians will disagree with this conclusion.

16. Thomas Klasen, *A Pro-Life Manifesto* (Westchester, IL: Crossway, 1988), p. 15.

17. Aside from the substantive issue of abortion, the Supreme Court decision in *Roe v. Wade*, which struck down restrictive state laws, was flawed on legal grounds–it was not so much bad constitutional law as simply not constitutional law. See, for example, Dennis Horan, et.al., eds., *Abortion and the Constitution* (Washington, D.C.: Georgetown University Press, 1987).

18. Stanley Grenz, "What is Sex For?," *Christianity Today*, June 12, 1987, p. 23.

19. A serious problem may arise, however, if a hospital fertilizes more than one egg and disposes of the extra ones; in that case in vitro fertilization has led to one or more de facto abortions.

20. John Jefferson Davis detailed many of the potential pitfalls of these

practices even before the Baby M case. *Evangelical Ethics: Issues Facing the Church Today* (Phillipsburg, NJ: Presbyterian and Reformed Publishing Co., 1985), pp. 62-78.

21. In fact, adultery and other sexual practices are still formally prohibited in many states. In 1987 the New Hampshire legislature refused to repeal its statute criminalizing adultery, even though the law is no longer enforced. Alberta Cook, "Adultery Statute Survives Debate in New Hampshire," *National Law Journal,* April 20, 1988, p. 14.

22. An increasing number of observers are recognizing the fact that current policies not only are a failure, but are having destructive side effects. See, for example, *Why We Are Losing the Great Drug War* (New York: Macmillan, 1987); Ronald Hamowy, ed., *Dealing with Drugs* (Lexington, MA: Lexington Books, 1987); Steve Wisotsky, *Breaking the Impasse in the War on Drugs* (New York: Greenwood Press, 1986).

23. For those interested in more educational horror stories, see Chester Finn, Jr., "The Social Studies Debacle," *The American Spectator,* May 1988, p. 35; Russell Kirk, "Real Educational Reform," *National Review,* February 8, 1980, p. 161; "Sputnik Revisited?," *The Washington Post,* April 16, 1988, p. A-24.

24. In the wake of Congress' override in early 1988 of President Reagan's veto of the so-called Civil Rights Restoration Act, which greatly expanded regulation of recipients of federal funds, private schools that accepted vouchers could find themselves subject to additional state controls. Tax credits, in contrast, do not suffer from this disadvantage, since the money never technically flows through the government.

25. This issue is not just a mythic hobgoblin in the minds of a few fundamentalists. New Age philosophies are now widely utilized in Colorado schools. Fergus Bordewich, "Colorado's Thriving Cults," *The New York Times Magazine,* May 1, 1988, p. 42.

26. Because of the shared religious vision of most early Americans, Christianity was not barred from the early public schools. But long ago we lost that unifying spiritual commitment.

27. See Martin Morse Wooster, "Reagan's Smutstompers," *Reason,* April 1986, p. 26. Given the state's penchant for trying to supplant God and provide its own form of salvation, Christians should be wary of supporting laws that attempt to regulate men's consciences instead of their actions. People who commit sex crimes should be punished whether or not they view pornography; only clear and convincing evidence that obscene materials actually cause aggression could justify a government prohibition.

28. The official poverty rate, based on an estimate tied to food costs, is an arbitrary concept, excluding, for instance, the impact of noncash benefits like food stamps, which, if counted, would have cut the number of people below the poverty line from 33.1 million to 21.9 million in 1985. Nevertheless, no better measure has yet been developed and it is the most commonly cited standard.

29. Robert England, "Giving a Wealth of Goodwill," *Insight,* December 21, 1987, p. 10. Commitment to God clearly correlates with charitable giving. Those who regularly attend religious services donate an average of 3.1 percent of their incomes, while non-churchgoers give just .2 percent.

30. Robert Woodson, *Private Sector Alternatives to the Welfare State: A New Agenda for Black Americans* (Dallas: National Center for Policy Analysis, 1987).

31. Other conditions could also be attached to welfare payments to promote parental responsibility. For instance, Judy Kirsten, who directs a program for pregnant students at San Diego's Garfield High School, says: "The welfare system is destroying children. Liberals should accept some responsibility here. I would like the laws tightened so that you don't get welfare unless your kid is attending school and getting good prenatal care." Quoted in Richard Louv, "The Myths of Teen-Age Pregnancy," Copley News Service, March 23, 1988.

32. A thoughtful book dealing with some of these issues is Stuart Butler and Anna Kondratus, *Out of the Poverty Trap* (New York: Free Press, 1987). As mentioned earlier in the context of education vouchers, the attractiveness of this approach has been reduced by the "Civil Rights Restoration Act" and the consequent prospect of additional federal regulations tied to the grants.

CHAPTER NINE *Applying Biblical Principles: More Examples*

1. James Skillen and Theodore Malloch, *Justice for the Land: Land for the Caring* (Washington, D.C.: Association for Public Justice), pp. 7-9.

2. Pierre Crosson, "The Issues," in John Baden, ed., *The Vanishing Farmland Crisis* (Lawrence, KS and Bozeman, MT: University Press of Kansas and Political Economy Research Center, 1984), p. 8.

3. Hunger is widespread throughout the Third World, of course, but that is a problem of poverty and deteriorating economies, not inadequate farmland.

4. National Conference of Catholic Bishops, *Economic Justice for All* (Washington, D.C.: U.S. Catholic Conference, 1986), pp. 113-115.

5. For instance, the 1985 Farm Bill provided for a $1.1 billion program to pay dairy farmers–who had collected $14 billion in subsidies over the previous half dozen years–to go out of business. The "termination" checks ranged up to $10 million; 144 farmers collected more than $1 million each. The abuses of the agricultural subsidy system are legion. Doug Bandow, "America's Permanent Dependent Class," *Policy Review,* Spring 1987, p. 73. That such unjust transfers persist year after year may be attributable to what German economist Wilhelm Ropke called "the habit of regarding the state as a kind of fourth dimension, without stopping to think that its till has to be filled by the taxpayers as a whole." *A Human Economy: The Social Framework of the Free Market* (Chicago: Henry Regnery Co., 1960), p. 165.

6. Collectivizing agriculture by allowing farmers to vote to cut production would hike consumer costs by an estimated $20 billion annually, eliminate farm exports, and depress rural employment in farm support industries by some 130,000. Bandow, p. 75.

7. A disturbing account of Nicaraguan repression is provided by Ronald Radosh in "Nicaragua Revisited," *New Republic,* August 3, 1987, pp. 20-22. Conditions eased somewhat during talks over the Arias peace plan, but the fundamental machinery of repression remains in place.

And whether the modest liberalization will survive the planned disbandment of the contras is an open question.

8. Another goal is aiding democratic forces in other countries, in essence promoting justice in areas outside of our nation's control. While Christians can rightly support such efforts through their own and organized church activities, it is not clear that foreign intervention unrelated to America's security is a proper function for the government.

9. The Somoza regime, in contrast to the Sandinistas, placed essentially no restrictions on the church's evangelistic activities. Ron Lee, "Ministry Amid Adversity," *Christianity Today*, February 6, 1987, p. 32.

10. Observes foreign policy analyst Alan Tonelson: "The United States cannot turn Central America's banana republics into free, successful societies. But it can ward off the only security threat conceivable from the region. Washington should forget about the contras and the Arias plan and lay down the law to Moscow, Managua and other adversaries regarding acceptable and unacceptable foreign policy behavior in Central America. America's threats could be enforced with threats of military action–including the unilateral use of air and sea power, which would avoid another unwinnable jungle war." "Our Real Latin Stakes," *New York Times*, February 4, 1988, p. A-27. See also Ted Galen Carpenter, "Back to the Monroe Doctrine," *Wall Street Journal*, May 4, 1988, p. 22.

11. Such a buildup is probably unrealistic, given Nicaragua's economic problems, and the Sandinistas genuinely fear an American military invasion–so far this century the U.S. has intervened five times in Nicaragua. Moreover, one journalist who has covered Nicaragua believes that the Ortega regime's plans, which stress reserves rather than active forces, "probably have more to do with domestic politics inside Nicaragua than with military adventures outside the country." William Drozdiak, "Sandinistas: How Big a Threat?," *Washington Post*, January 31, 1988, p. D-5. Nevertheless, the proposal reflects the militarism that is so characteristic of Marxist-Leninist systems.

12. *The Presidential Biblical Scorecard* lists sixteen passages as pertaining to the issue, but few are even remotely relevant to whether wages should be set through the interplay of market forces or by government dictates. David Balsiger, *Presidential Biblical Scorecard*, Spring 1988, p. 12.

13. Richard Burr, "Are Comparable Worth Systems Truly Comparable?," Center for the Study of American Business, Washington University (St. Louis), July 1986, Study no. 75. A good overall review of the issue is provided by Robert Rector, "The Pseudo-Science of Comparable Worth: Phrenology for Modern Times," The Heritage Foundation, February 29, 1988, Backgrounder no. 635.

14. Office of the Assistant Secretary of Defense (Public Affairs), "Military Manpower Recruiting and Reenlistment Results for the Active Component–End of Fiscal Year (FY) 1987," News Release, p.1.

15. See, e.g., David Armor, statement before the Subcommittee on Manpower and Personnel, Senate Committee on Armed Services, March 24, 1987; Doug Bandow, "The Case Against Conscription,"

*Journal of Contemporary Studies*, Fall 1982, p. 43; Doug Bandow, "Mercenary Morality," *New Republic*, October 19, 1987, p. 20.

16. Andrew Kirk, *The Good News of the Kingdom Coming* (Downers Grove, IL: InterVarsity Press, 1983), pp. 30, 29, 44-46.

17. Paul Heyne, "Christianity and 'the Economy,'" *This World*, Winter 1988 (20), p. 36.

18. There is a wide range of systems between laissez-faire and total government control; the present welfare state remains essentially capitalistic because of widespread private property ownership and people's largely unconstrained right to produce, buy, and sell goods and services in the marketplace.

19. Raymond Gastil, ed., *Freedom in the World: Political Rights and Civil Liberties*, 1987-88 (Westport, CT: Greenwood Press, 1988), pp. 74, 75.

20. Kirk, p. 30.

21. See Peter Berger, *The Capitalist Revolution* (New York: Basic Books, 1986), pp. 140-171.

22. For a penetrating analysis of the Latin American economy and liberation theology, see Michael Novak, *Will It Liberate?* (Mahwah, NJ: Paulist Press, 1987). Another valuable analysis of the issue is Ronald Nash, ed., *Liberation Theology* (Milford, MI: Mott Media, 1984).

23. Socialist moralism, writes Wilhelm Ropke, "asks too much of ordinary people and expects them constantly to deny their own interests. The first result is that the powerful motive forces of self-interest are lost to society. Secondly, the purposes of this 'higher' economic morality can be made to prevail only by doing something eminently immoral, namely, by compelling people–by force or cunning and deception–to act against their own nature." Ropke, p. 120.

24. The economy has grown dramatically between 1929 and 1986; during that period labor's share of the combined total of wages plus profits has risen from 81.6 percent to 94.2 percent. William Peterson, "Putting an End to Adversarial Unionism," *New York Times*, July 26, 1987, p. F-2. In contrast, a 1986 Joint Economic Committee study found that weak economic growth contributed more than family dissolution to the rise in poverty between 1979 and 1985. Spencer Rich, "Poverty Rise Laid to Weak Economy," *Washington Post*, December 22, 1986, p. A-4.

25. Kirk, p. 26.

26. Of course, a just social fabric is most effectively based on Judeo-Christian values. Observes Ropke, "Economic life naturally does not go on in a moral vaccum. It is constantly in danger of straying from the ethical middle level unless it is buttressed by strong moral supports. These must simply be there and, what is more, must constantly be impregnated against rot. Otherwise our free economic system and, with it, any free state and society must ultimately collapse." Ropke, p. 124. Similarly, Thomas Atwood contends that "A moral, evangelical church and a moral, stewardly public are absolutely required in order to actively hold the free markets responsible." Thomas Atwood, "Ethics of Political Economy: The Biblical Perspective" (unpublished thesis, 1986), p. 65.

Three recent books that discuss the relationship between

Christianity and economics in greater detail are Brian Griffiths, *The Creation of Wealth: A Christian's Case for Capitalism* (Downers Grove, IL: InterVarsity Press, 1984); Ronald Nash, *Poverty and Wealth: The Christian Debate Over Capitalism* (Westchester, IL: Crossway, 1986); Franky Schaeffer, ed., *Is Capitalism Christian?* (Westchester, IL: Crossway, 1985).

27. For a more detailed discussion of this issue, see Doug Bandow, ed., *Protecting the Environment: A Free Market* Strategy (Washington, D.C.: The Heritage Foundation, 1987).

28. Robert Crandall, *Controlling Industrial Pollution: The Economics and Politics of Clean Air* (Washington, D.C.: The Brookings Institution, 1983), pp. 44-51.

29. Jim Wallis, "The Powerful and the Powerless," in Richard John Neuhaus and Michael Cromartie, eds., *Piety and Politics: Evangelicals and Fundamentalists Confront the World* (Washington, D.C.: Ethics and Public Policy Center, 1987), p. 192.

30. For a comprehensive review of foreign aid policy, see Doug Bandow, ed., *U.S. Aid to the Developing World: A Free Market Agenda* (Washington, D.C.: The Heritage Foundation, 1985).

31. Cited in P. T. Bauer, *Reality and Rhetoric: Studies in the Economics of Development* (Cambridge, MA: Harvard University Press, 1984), pp. 86, 87.

32. See Doug Bandow, "Foreign Aid Prescriptions," *American Spectator*, September 1986, p. 21.

33. Kirk, p. 82.

34. It is also extremely difficult to equalize incomes over time for two reasons. First, some people are more productive and skilled than others, and will do better financially as a result. See Atwood, pp. 46, 47. Second, government programs are usually skewed to benefit the influential rather than the needy. Despite massive federal transfer programs, the distribution of income in America has remained essentially constant since 1947. Walter Williams, "Income Equality Mirage," *The Washington Times*, February 16, 1988, p. D-3.

35. The Pentagon's estimates are actually higher than those of private analysts. See Melvyn Krauss, *How NATO Weakens the West* (New York: Simon and Schuster, 1986), p. 29.

36. Doug Bandow, "Korea: The Case for Disengagement," The Cato Institute, December 8, 1988, Policy Analysis, No. 96, pp. 5-6.

37. NATO has come under serious attack by a number of analysts in recent years, including David Calleo, *Beyond American Hegemony* (New York: Basic Books, 1987); Krauss; and Earl Ravenal, *NATO: The Tides of Discontent* (Berkeley, CA: University of California at Berkeley, 1985).

38. Bandow, "Korea."

39. Ruth Leger Sivard, *World Military and Social Expenditures: 1987-88* (Washington, D.C.: World Priorities, 1987), p. 31. Of course, mass slaughter is not limited to armed conflicts: countries like the USSR and China have killed millions of their own people through executions, imprisonment, and starvation. But it is war that led to the success of the Soviet revolution and the imposition of communism on Eastern Europe.

40. A strained interpretation yields one possible reference. In describing the work of the different apostles, Paul observed that "The man who plants and the man who waters have one purpose, and each will be rewarded according to his own labor" (1 Corinthians 3:8). Paul is referring to spiritual work and pay, but one could argue that the principle of tying labor to reward applies elsewhere. However, a verse like this probably should not be stretched so far.
41. Among the studies worth reviewing include Thomas Sowell, *Minimum Wage Escalation* (Stanford, CA: Hoover Institution, 1977); Finis Welch, *Minimum Wages: Issues and Evidence* (Washington, D.C.: American Enterprise Institute, 1978); Walter Williams, *Youth and Minority Unemployment*, Joint Economic Committee, U.S. Congress, July 6, 1977.
42. A recent comprehensive look at the Catholic Church's position is George Weigel's *Tranquillitas Ordinis: The Present Failure and Future Promise of American Catholic Thought on War and Peace* (New York: Oxford University Press, 1987).
43. An excellent book that deals with this subject in more detail is Keith Payn and Karl Payne, *A Just Defense: Weapons and Our Conscience* (Portland, OR: Multnomah, 1987). A nonreligious look at the morality of nuclear weapons is provided by James Child, *Nuclear War: The Moral Dimension* (New Brunswick, NJ: Transaction Books, 1986).
44. Vernon Grounds, ed., *Nuclear Arms: Two Views on World Peace* (Waco, TX: Word Books, 1987).
45. Jim Wallis, *Waging Peace* (San Francisco: Harper & Row, 1982), p. 12.
46. Balsiger, p. 20.
47. A tax increase passed specifically to finance an immoral activity–say the invasion of Canada or the enrichment of the Fortune 500–would arguably be invalid on grounds other than tax policy, though money is fungible.
48. In fact, while the 1981 Reagan tax-rate cuts reduced projected revenues between 1981 and 1989 by $1.488 trillion, revenues increased during the same period by $1.529 trillion due to inflation-induced bracket creep, before indexing took effect; Social Security tax hikes originally enacted in 1977; and five subsequent tax hikes. As a result, the Reagan administration's legacy to the American people has actually been a $41 billion tax increase. Karen Riley, "Congress Giveth Then Taketh Away," *Insight*, February 15, 1988, p. 20.

*CHAPTER TEN* Conclusion: Christian Activism in the Public Square

1. "Three Other Perspectives," *World*, February 22, 1988, pp. 5, 6.
2. Richard Pierard and Robert Linder, *Civil Religion and the Presidency* (Grand Rapids: Zondervan, 1988), p. 293.
3. "Should Pat Robertson Run for President?", *Christianity Today*, September 5, 1986, p. 54.
4. Morton Kondracke, "Immoral Robertson," *New Republic*, March 21, 1988, p. 13.
5. Arthur Frederick Ide, *Tomorrow's Tyrants* (Dallas: Monument Press, 1985), p. 235.
6. See, e.g., Edward Dobson, "The Bible, Politics, and Democracy," in

Richard John Neuhaus, ed., *The Bible, Politics, and Democracy* (Grand Rapids: William B. Eerdmans, 1987), pp. 4-8.

7. "Is Our Grand Old Flag Going Down the Drain?," undated letter, Jerry Falwell.

8. Quoted in James Adams, *The Growing Church Lobby in Washington* (Grand Rapids: Willaim B. Eerdmans, 1970), p. 10.

9. Lynda Wright, "Politics and the Pulpit," *Newsweek*, February 15, 1988, p. 28.

10. Tim LaHaye, *The Battle for the Mind* (Old Tappan, NJ: Revell, 1980), p. 78.

11. The term has become a code-word for leftist political action, but the overall Christian community should reclaim the phrase, since it accurately describes the import of Christ's teaching.

# SCRIPTURE INDEX

# INDEX